Issues in Reli

The Interpretation of John

Issues in Religion and Theology

SERIES EDITORS

Titles in the series include:

Issues in Religion and Theology 9

The Interpretation of John

Edited with an Introduction by

JOHN ASHTON

FORTRESS PRESS
Philadelphia | SPCK
London

First published in Great Britain 1986
SPCK
Holy Trinity Church
Marylebone Road
London NW1 4DU

First published in the USA 1986
Fortress Press
2900 Queen Lane
Philadelphia
Pennsylvania 19129

Library of Congress Cataloging in Publication Data
Main entry under title:

The Interpretation of John.

   (Issues in religion and theology; 9)
   Bibliography: p.
   Includes index.
   1. Bible. N.T. John—Criticism, interpretation,
etc.—Addresses, essays, lectures. I. Ashton, John,
1931– . II. Series.
BS2615.2.I57 1986   226′.506   85–45536
ISBN 0–8006–1774–6

British Library Cataloguing in Publication Data

The Interpretation of John.—
(Issues in religion and theology, 9)
   1. Bible. N.T. John—Commentaries
   I. Ashton, John   II. Series
   226′.506   BS2615.3

   ISBN 0–281–04213–6

Filmset by Northumberland Press Ltd, Gateshead
Printed in Great Britain by Richard Clay (The Chaucer Press) Ltd, Bungay, Suffolk

Contents

Acknowledgements

Rudolf Bultmann, "The History of Religions Background of the Prologue to the Gospel of John", was first published in *Eucharisterion: Festschrift für H. Gunkel* II (Göttingen: Vandenhoeck & Ruprecht, 1923) 3–26, and is translated by permission of the publisher. Copyright © the estate of R. Bultmann 1923, 1976.

Paul Lamarche, "The Prologue of John", is translated by permission of the author from *RSR* 52 (1964) 497–537. Copyright © P. Lamarche 1964.

Ignace de la Potterie, "The Truth in Saint John", is translated by permission of the author from *RivB* 11 (1963) 3–24, and reprinted by permission of the publisher, Paideia Editrice. Copyright © I. de la Potterie 1963.

Peder Borgen, "God's Agent in the Fourth Gospel", is reprinted by permission from J. Neusner (ed.), *Religions in Antiquity* (Leiden: E. J. Brill, 1968) 137–48. Copyright © P. Borgen 1968.

Günther Bornkamm, "Towards the Interpretation of John's Gospel", was first published in *EvT* 28 (1968) 8–28, and reprinted in *Studien zum Neuen Testament* (Munich: Kaiser Verlag, 1985). It has been translated by permission of the author. Copyright © Kaiser Verlag 1968, 1985.

J. Louis Martyn, "Source Criticism and Religionsgeschichte in the Fourth Gospel", is reprinted by permission from D. G. Miller (ed.), *Jesus and Man's Hope* (Pittsburgh: Pittsburgh Theological Seminary, 1970) I, 247–73. Copyright © Pittsburgh Theological Seminary 1970.

Nils Alstrup Dahl, "The Johannine Church and History", is reprinted by permission from W. Klassen and G. F. Snyder (ed.), *Current Issues in New Testament Interpretation* (New York: Harper & Row and London: SCM Press, 1962) 124–42. Copyright © W. Klassen and G. F. Snyder 1962.

Wayne A. Meeks, "The Man from Heaven in Johannine Sectarianism", is reprinted by permission from *JBL* 91 (1972) 44–72. Copyright © W. A. Meeks 1972.

The Contributors

JOHN ASHTON is University Lecturer in New Testament at the University of Oxford and Fellow of Wolfson College.

RUDOLF BULTMANN (1884–1976) was Professor at Marburg from 1921 until his retirement in 1951. His classic Meyer commentary on John (1941) was published in English in 1971.

PAUL LAMARCHE is Professor of Sacred Scripture at the Faculté de Théologie, Philosophie et Sciences Humaines, Centre-Sèvres, Paris.

IGNACE DE LA POTTERIE is Professor of New Testament at the Pontifical Biblical Institute in Rome. He has written extensively on the Fourth Gospel, most notably *La Vérité dans Saint Jean* (1977).

PEDER BORGEN is Professor of New Testament at the University of Trondheim, Norway. Since his monograph *Bread from Heaven* (1965) he has written several articles on John's Gospel, now collected in *Logos was the True Light* (1983).

GÜNTHER BORNKAMM was Professor of New Testament at Heidelberg from 1949 until his retirement in 1971. His *Jesus of Nazareth* (1960) and *Paul* (1971) are widely read in many languages.

J. LOUIS MARTYN is Edward Robinson Professor of Biblical Theology at Union Theological Seminary, New York. His *History and Theology in the Fourth Gospel* appeared in 1968 (revised 1979) and some of his essays on John have been reprinted in *The Gospel of John in Christian History* (1979).

NILS ALSTRUP DAHL is Emeritus Professor of New Testament at Yale University and Divinity School. Since his early monograph on the People of God (*Das Volk Gottes*, 1941) he has written many outstanding articles, some of which have been reprinted in this series.

WAYNE A. MEEKS is Professor of Religious Studies at Yale University. His monograph *The Prophet-King* appeared in 1967 and *The First Urban Christians* in 1983.

Series Foreword

The Issues in Religion and Theology series intends to encompass a variety of topics within the general disciplines of religious and theological studies. Subjects are drawn from any of the component fields, such as biblical studies, systematic theology, ethics, history of Christian thought, and history of religion.

The series aims to address these issues by collecting and reproducing key studies, all previously published, which have contributed significantly to our present understandings. In each case, the volume editor introduces the discussion with an original essay which describes the subject and its treatment in religious and theological studies. To this editor has fallen the responsibility of selecting items for inclusion. Together the essays are intended to present a balanced overview of the problem and various approaches to it. Each piece is important in the current debate, and any older publication included normally stands as a classical or seminal work which is still worth careful study. Readers unfamiliar with the issue should find that these discussions provide a good entrée, while more advanced students will appreciate having studies by some of the best specialists on the subject gathered together in one volume.

The editor has, of course, faced certain constraints: analyses too lengthy or too technical could not be included, except perhaps in excerpt form; the bibliography is not exhaustive; and the volumes in this series are being kept to a reasonable, uniform length. On the other hand, the editor is able to overcome the real problem of in-accessibility. Much of the best literature on a subject is often not readily available to readers, whether because it was first published in journals or books not widely circulated or because it was originally written in a language not read by all who would benefit from it. By bringing these and other studies together in this series, we hope to contribute to the general understanding of these key topics.

The series editors and the publishers wish to express their gratitude to the authors and their original publishers whose works are reprinted or translated here, often with corrections from living authors. We are also conscious of our debt to members of the editorial advisory board, who have been prepared to spare much time and thought for the project.

DOUGLAS A. KNIGHT   ROBERT MORGAN

Abbreviations

ATR	*Anglican Theological Review*
Bib	*Biblica*
BZ	*Biblische Zeitschrift*
BZNW	Beihefte zur *ZNW*
CBQ	*Catholic Biblical Quarterly*
C.H.	Corpus Hermeticum
EvQ	*Evangelical Quarterly*
EvT	*Evangelische Theologie*
ExpTim	*Expository Times*
GCS	Die Griechischen Christlichen Schriftsteller der ersten drei Jahrhunderte
HeyJ	*Heythrop Journal*
HTR	*Harvard Theological Review*
Int	*Interpretation*
JBL	*Journal of Biblical Literature*
JSNT	*Journal for the Study of the New Testament*
JTS	*Journal of Theological Studies*
NT	*Novum Testamentum*
NTS	*New Testament Studies*
NTT	*Norsk Teologisch Tidsskrift*
OLZ	*Orientalische Literaturzeitung*
PG	*J.-P. Migne, Patrologia Graeca*
PL	*J.-P. Migne, Patrologia Latina*
RB	*Revue Biblique*
RGG	*Religion in Geschichte und Gegenwart*
RHPR	*Revue d'histoire et de philosophie religieuses*
RivB	*Rivista Biblica*
RSPT	*Revue des sciences philosophiques et théologiques*
RSR	*Recherches de science religieuse*
SBL	Society of Biblical Literature
Str-B	H. L. Strack and P. Billerbeck, *Kommentar zum NT aus Talmud und Midrasch*
TDNT	G. Kittel and G. Friedrich (ed.), *Theological Dictionary of the New Testament*
TLZ	*Theologische Literaturzeitung*
TRu	*Theologische Rundschau*
TU	Texte und Untersuchungen
USQR	*Union Seminary Quarterly Review*
ZNW	*Zeitschrift für die neutestamentliche Wissenschaft*
ZTK	*Zeitschrift für Theologie und Kirche.*

Introduction
The Problem of John

JOHN ASHTON

The Johannine Problem is not single but several, with many changing faces. Of course on one level this Gospel is relatively *unproblematic*, when compared, say, with the extraordinary complexities of the Synoptic Gospels, which cannot be studied adequately in isolation from one another. Whether or not John (if one may use this traditional name without prejudging the issue of authorship) had direct knowledge of Matthew, Mark or Luke, he certainly did not build on them as extensively as Matthew and Luke, according to the most widely held view of the matter, built on Mark.[1] Moreover the conceptual world of the Fourth Evangelist, as well as the language in which he enshrines it, is so beautifully harmonious and consistent that even the notorious David Friedrich Strauss, no respecter of traditional beliefs, could speak of this Gospel as a "seamless garment", free from the stitches and sutures that disfigure the other three. Much later Wilhelm Bousset expressed the more cautious opinion that the Gospel was the product of a single school, a view which may be said to have prevailed until the present day. One modern scholar, R. A. Culpepper (1975), has attempted to give a closer definition to the concept of "school" by comparing the Johannine community with the great centres of learning like the Stoa or the Academy that had been founded in Greece some centuries earlier. So if there are still problems about the Fourth Gospel, what are they, and how do the scholarly articles reproduced in this book attempt to tackle them?

Academic studies of this Gospel, despite their astonishing range and diversity, may all be conveniently grouped under three broad headings, the first two of which roughly correspond to the two great riddles highlighted by Rudolf Bultmann in his classic, seminal but still untranslated article of 1925[2], and held steadily in view in every one of the numerous studies he was to publish in the years to come. The first of these, "the riddle of where John's Gospel stands in relation

1

to the development of early Christianity", I sum up under the heading, *History*; the second, "what is the central insight (*Anschauung*) of the Gospel, its basic idea (*Grundkonzeption*)?", I reduce to *Theology*. It will soon become apparent that these categories, like the third, *Composition*, cover a wide variety of approaches. But first a necessary disclaimer. In what follows there is no attempt to give a comprehensive survey of Johannine scholarship. This task has in any case been competently performed by Robert Kysar in two lengthy studies (1975 and 1985 – see Bibliography: Surveys). (Those who also have access to the German periodical *Theologische Rundschau* will not need to be reminded that for them there is even less need of yet another exhaustive examination of recent scholarship.) My purpose is more modest: it is simply to state and explain *the kinds of question* that have been addressed to the text in the last half-century or so and to indicate how the selected articles fit into this suggested pattern of research – to locate them on the map.

1 *History*

(a) *Origins*

"The origin of the Johannine writings is, from the stand-point of a history of literature and dogma, the most marvellous enigma (*das wundervollste Räthsel*) which the early history of Christianity presents." So formulated as early as 1886 by Adolf von Harnack in his huge *History of Dogma* (vol. I, ET 1894, 96f.), this enigma has yet to receive a satisfactory solution. The first of the essays printed in this collection is one of two major articles (the other has already been mentioned), in which Bultmann adumbrated the answer that was to receive definitive shape in his great commentary. What he eventually came to see as the key to the solution was what he called a "revelation-discourse source", gnostic in origin, which the evangelist had taken over and adapted to his Christian purposes, demythologizing it as he went along. Bultmann was not the first to propose a gnostic source for the Gospel (as long ago as 1788 J. D. Michaelis had suggested that the term *Logos* had been borrowed from the Gnostics), nor was he the first to integrate such a theory into a major commentary (see the second edition of Walter Bauer's *Johannesevangelium*, published in 1925), but no one before or since has employed the theory so effectively to illuminate the dark corners of the Gospel. Unfortunately, all but a tiny handful of exegetes have rejected Bultmann's source theory as unproved and improbable, and since it was the keystone of his commentary his grand interpretation has collapsed with it.

This is not to say that only a few people now accept the theory of the Gospel's gnostic origins. In fact this is probably still the most widespread view among German exegetes, as well as many others. Some, notably Ernst Käsemann, hold that the evangelist himself was virtually a gnostic, a position represented in its most extreme form by the work of Luise Schottroff (1970). Others, such as Rudolf Schnackenburg, hold more moderate views, admitting the thesis of gnostic influences but refusing to consign the Gospel itself to any docetic dustbin. Thus Günther Bornkamm, whose lengthy review of Käsemann's *Testament of Jesus* is itself a noteworthy contribution to Johannine studies, wholeheartedly accepts Käsemann's own un-critical but more tentative acceptance of the hypothesis of a gnostic background.[3] Wayne Meeks, in his careful and thorough study, *The Prophet-King* (1967), refers to the argument that Bultmann had put forward forty years earlier: the presence in the Gospel of a typically gnostic schema, that of the descent/ascent of a heavenly messenger, which "has been and remains the strongest support for the hypothesis that the Johannine Christology is connected with gnostic mythology" (*The Prophet-King*, 297). Since the publication of Meeks' book, however, both Charles E. Talbert (1976) and Peder Borgen (1977) have produced evidence showing that this schema, a particularly crucial one in the Fourth Gospel, was found in this period throughout the Mediterranean basin (Talbert) and especially in the Jewish tradition (Borgen). Such gnostic influences as are discernible upon the Gospel may have reached the evangelist through Jewish channels. The discovery at Nag Hammadi, in 1945, of a large body of Coptic texts has convinced many scholars, among them the cautious R. McLachlan Wilson (1982), that there did exist, perhaps very early indeed, a kind of gnosis independent of Christianity. Simone Pétrement has recently (1984) put up a strong defence of the contrary view.

Further support for the theory that the origins of the Gospel are to be sought in Judaism (though partially perhaps in a Judaism already tainted by gnosticism) may be found in Alan F. Segal's impressively well-researched study, *Two Powers in Heaven* (1977), where he is able to show that the idea of a second power in heaven, rivalling that of the one true God, was felt as a threat quite early in the common era among "orthodox" rabbinical circles.

It should perhaps be added that the suggestion that the Gospel's origins were fundamentally Jewish is not at all new. It was defended, maybe a trifle untidily,[4] by Adolf Schlatter in a book that received little attention even in the German-speaking world: *Die Sprache und Heimat des vierten Evangelisten* (1902); and in 1916, writing presumably in ignorance of Schlatter's work, the English scholar G. A. Box remarked that "it would not be difficult to derive from this literature (Jewish midrash) a good deal of illustrative material which would form a remarkably suggestive Jewish background for the Fourth Gospel. The Johannine Gospel is indeed Jewish through and through, and it is much to be desired that a commentary on it, written from this point of view, could be produced" (24f.). This desideratum was partly met by the idiosyncratic and truncated commentary of Hugo Odeberg, published in 1929, a syncretistic work if ever there was one, drawing indiscriminately upon a vast range of literature, including the Hermetica and the Mandaean writings as well as such intertestamental material as was then available, plus all the riches of rabbinical Judaism. This work, like the more one-sided commentary of Schlatter (1930), is something of a magpie's nest; but there are glittering insights tucked away in the stuff and fluff, and Odeberg's robust independence ensures that his is among the most interesting and valuable of modern commentaries.

Since the publication of Bultmann's *Das Johannesevangelium* in 1941 the commentaries have been piling up steadily. Most of these are respectable, some are outstanding. But none has attempted more than a desultory tinkering with Bultmann's "first riddle", and such light as they shed upon it is at best fitful and indirect. Most of the real work has been done in articles and monographs.

One scholar who has never lost sight of the Bultmannian problematic is Wayne Meeks. In his book, *The Prophet-King* (1967), however, rather than attempting a comprehensive answer to the riddle, he concentrates on a single theme, the Moses typology of the Gospel, in an effort to delineate its possible origins. But although this study is in many respects a model of the kind of research required if agreement is ever to be reached on this issue, it remains nevertheless quite inconclusive, partly perhaps because Meeks' chosen area of research is too far from the centre of the evangelist's elaborate christological web, partly because he felt, no doubt rightly, that the state of scholarship at the time did not allow him to offer more than a guided tour of the various possibilities.

On the face of it, Siegfried Schulz's enquiry (1957) into the motif of the Son of Man might seem more likely to take us into the heart of John's Christology. But his treatment of this theme, after a painstaking methodological introduction, is perfunctory and unsatisfactory, and the actual results of his research, after he has chased the gnostic hare up a few blind alleys, are meagre and disappointing. Much more impressive, indeed one of the most exciting studies of the Gospel to have appeared in the last decade, is Jan-A. Bühner's *Der Gesandte und sein Weg im vierten Evangelium* (1977). In examining the notion of divine emissary (rightly singled out by Bultmann as *the* central motif of the Gospel, its *Grundkonzeption*), Bühner is at the same time deliberately tackling Bultmann's first great riddle. For Bühner the Johannine problem is a matter of "giving the Johannine community its proper place in the history of early Christianity, of locating its literature in the genesis of the New Testament as a whole, and finally of identifying the origin of its christological schema – the journey (*Weg*) of the Son of God who is sent into the world and then returns to his heavenly home" (*Gesandte*, 1). With this Bühner moves directly to the centre of the Johannine Christology. And if he occasionally appears to lose direction, with the result that his book tends to meander somewhat, he nevertheless succeeds admirably in his main aim and in doing so sheds much incidental light on such logia as the "I am" sayings, which may seem at first sight to have little to do with the theme of mission.

An alternative solution, concentrating much more upon the wisdom motif of the Prologue (on which see Bultmann's article below) is offered in an informative article by James D. G. Dunn (1983). But the connection between the Prologue and the remainder of the Gospel is much looser than Dunn maintains: his is at best a partial answer to the problem.

(b) Situation

It is worth pointing out that in formulating his own version of the Johannine problem, which is not after all notably different from that of Bultmann, Bühner uses the expression "Johannine community", a term familiar enough nowadays to pass unregarded, but which nevertheless conceals a major shift of emphasis, a radical change of direction in Johannine research. Much of the credit for this must go to J. Louis Martyn, whose *History and Theology in the Fourth Gospel* first appeared in 1968. It is probably the most important monograph on the Gospel since Bultmann's commentary. This is how he outlines his project: "Our first task ... is to say something as specific as possible about the actual circumstances in which John wrote his Gospel. How are we to picture daily life in John's church? May one sense even in its exalted cadences the voice of a Christian theologian who writes *in response to contemporary events and issues* which concern, or should concern, all members of the Christian community in which he lives?" (xviii). On the preceding page Martyn had cited Harnack's classic statement of the problem, but whereas Harnack was concerned with the origins of the *Gospel*, Martyn is much more interested in the situation of the *evangelist* and the audience he was addressing. This was a question which Bultmann, for all his acumen and assiduity, had left untouched. Why? Because he was convinced that the Gospel was designed to give a Christian answer to the timeless questions of the purpose and nature of human existence; for him the situation of those to whom the message was first proclaimed was of no particular significance.

Martyn's central insight was that the evangelist works constantly on two levels of presentation. The first of these, which Martyn calls *einmalig*, is the story level, the level on which we can read the Gospel as a straightforward account of the words and works of the earthly Jesus. But the main aim of the evangelist was to address the issues of his own day. He does this primarily by projecting back into the life and times of Jesus a description of the conflict of the Christian group with the authorities of the synagogue ("the Jews"). Chapter nine, for instance, the story of the healing of the man born blind, Martyn sees as an account of how the Jews reacted when a member of the synagogue, at the instigation of a leading Christian prophet, defected to the Christian group. He does not think that the evangelist was, as he puts it, "analytically conscious" of the two-level drama; but he believes that such an analysis is necessary if a modern reader is to appreciate exactly what is going on.

Martyn argued strongly that the expulsion of the Johannine group from the synagogue was a direct result of the insertion of a new clause, cursing heretics, into the synagogue prayer commonly known as the Eighteen Benedictions. There is rabbinic evidence that just such a clause, the *Birkath-ha-Minim*, was added to the Twelfth Benediction at the request of Gamaliel II at Yavneh (Jamnia), some time, then, between 80 and 115 A.D. (Martyn himself favours a date around 85 A.D.) It may be that in insisting on a direct causal link between the two events Martyn is stretching the evidence somewhat.[5] Nevertheless it should be stressed that the essence of his interpretation remains unaffected by any doubts of this kind, since it depends primarily upon a careful analysis of passages in the Gospel unambiguously alluding to excommunication from the synagogue (John 9:22; 12:42; 16:2). It remains very likely that there was a direct link between Yavneh and the turbulent relationship between Jews and Christians in the region where the Gospel was conceived and composed. The exact nature of this link, however, remains uncertain, because neither the Gospel itself nor the *Birkath-ha-Minim* can be dated with any precision. It is quite possible, for instance, as both Barnabas Lindars (1981, "Persecution") and William Horbury (1982) suggest, that the Jamnian ordinance simply reinforced the earlier, more drastic measures attested in John.

Martyn followed up his book with a number of brilliant articles, one of which is reproduced below.[6] In these he has attempted to probe more deeply into the history of the community. Then in 1979 came the second revised edition of *History and Theology*. Meanwhile there had been a fruitful interchange between him and Raymond Brown, who had been stimulated by Martyn's work to tackle similar questions and to explore further the hypothesis that there were a number of different groups and factions within the early Christian Church and the Johannine community in particular.[7] This vein of research may not be totally exhausted.

2 *Theology*

(a) Central ideas

Bultmann's answer to his second great riddle, that concerning the basic idea of the Gospel, its *Grundkonzeption*, was that it is to be found "in the constantly repeated proposition that Jesus is the emissary of God (e.g. 17:3, 23, 25), who through his words and deeds brings revelation. He performs the works given him by the Father, he speaks what he has heard from the Father or what he has seen in his presence. The man who believes is saved; he who does not is lost. But there lies the riddle. What precisely does the Jesus of John's Gospel reveal? One thing only, though put in different ways: *that* he has been sent as Revealer" (1925, 102, *Exegetica* 57).

Apart from the concluding sentence no one is likely to quarrel with this answer. For Bultmann, of course, the concept of a divine emissary is derived from gnostic mythology and must be discarded if one is to arrive at the heart of the evangelist's message, which consists, according to him, of *ein blosses Dass*, a bare and unadorned "that". Here is where the article of Peder Borgen reproduced below offers genuine illumination. There is no need, when investigating the theology of Jesus' role as the agent or special representative of God, to turn to Mandaism or other gnostic systems for the source of the evangelist's idea – it is to be found ready to hand in the Jewish tradition. In fact Borgen's article could equally well have been placed under the rubric of history and origins, since although primarily intended as a contribution to exegesis, i.e. the understanding of the *text*, it also sheds considerable light on the question of the source of the evangelist's central ideas.

One reason for including Lamarche's article on the Prologue is to illustrate the extraordinary range of interpretations this most enigmatic text is still able to elicit. Perhaps Lamarche is over-hasty in adopting as one of his guidelines (*critères*) the relationship of the Prologue to the thought-world (*mentalité*) of the NT. And one may be generally suspicious of chiastic patterns especially when so many alternatives are available,[8] all argued with the same vehemence and conviction. But in his actual exegesis Lamarche is both original and profound.[9] There is some irony in the fact that in reaching for really cogent arguments he, like de la Potterie, has to step well outside the scriptural text.

It may appear from the opening of de la Potterie's article that he is motivated partly by a desire to scotch the Bultmannian snake. But he is first and foremost an exegete and his massive thesis, *La Vérité dans Saint Jean* (1977), from whose earlier sketches this article is distilled, is a striking example of the results that can be achieved by combining a sweeping knowledge of the background with a microscopic scrutiny of the text.

(b) *The Bultmannian problematic*

Of the essays assembled here none has a greater theological urgency than that by Günther Bornkamm, as he attempts to grapple with Ernst Käsemann's *Testament of Jesus*. But Käsemann's own work needs to be seen in the context of his lifelong engagement with the thought of his teacher, Bultmann.

Only glimpses of Bultmann's challenging version of Johannine Christology can be found in the early article on the Prologue printed here. He reserved a detailed exegesis for his commentary. The key to his understanding comes in his discussion of the crucial verse 14, adopted, he believed, from the gnostic source. He placed all the emphasis upon the first half of the verse: "And the Word was made flesh...". One might be forgiven for supposing that for Bultmann the naked "that" of the incarnation is predicated of a shadowy wraith of a man, with little or no individual substance and thinnish blood in his veins. But, Bultmann insisted, a man nonetheless. This was precisely where Käsemann, in his important and influential article on the Prologue (1957 ET 1969), took issue with him, adroitly turning the tables by shifting the weight of the exegesis onto the second half of the verse in question: "...and we have seen his glory". For Käsemann what courses in the veins of the Johannine Christ is not blood at all, but ichor. He was quick to point out that the immediate impression given by this "stranger from heaven", as de Jonge calls him, was of a "God striding over the earth", not an authentically human figure but one invested with all the appurtenances of divinity, and possessing a clear awareness of both his origin and his end. Not an ordinary man, then, subject to the bewilderment and uncertainty that is the lot of human kind, but a being beyond our ken, radiating from the outset that aura of divinity which the Gospel calls his glory.

How far Käsemann is justified in his criticism of Bultmann, or

Bornkamm in his criticism of Käsemann's docetic version of Johannine Christology, must be left to the reader to judge. To be as fair as possible to Käsemann I have appended some notes summarizing the answers he gave to Bornkamm in the third (1971) German edition of *Jesu Letzter Wille* (*The Testament of Jesus*).

(c) Other themes

Of the numerous other Johannine themes that are not represented directly in this collection three deserve especial mention: the Son of Man, the Paraclete and eschatology.

Both the provenance of the Son of Man passages and their significance within the general context of Johannine theology continue to be hotly debated. Schulz (1957) followed Bultmann in opting for a gnostic origin. Schnackenburg denies this and appeals instead to Christian tradition, though he admits the possibility that "for the descent and ascent of his Christ John drew on Gnostic notions" (1965, 541). Here is the nub of the difficulty, for although John is clearly indebted to the synoptic tradition in, for example, the triple prediction of the passion (3:14; 8:24; 12:32–4) his Son of Man, unlike that of the Synoptists, both descends and ascends, and furthermore seems to have descended first (3:13).

Schnackenburg asserted that "apart from the Son of Man logia themselves, there seem to be no grounds for assuming that the concept of the Son of Man has greatly influenced the Fourth Gospel" (1965, 534), whereas a recent writer, W. R. G. Loader (1984), though following Schnackenburg in taking the thirteen occurrences of the term as "a cluster", places them right at the heart of the evangelist's theology.

According to C. H. Dodd, "for John the Son of Man is the *alēthinos anthrōpos*, the real or archetypal Man, or the Platonic Idea of Man" (1953, 244); and in the only monograph devoted exclusively to this topic, F. J. Moloney reaches the remarkable conclusion that "there is a concentration on the human figure of Jesus in the use of the 'Son of Man'. It is a title which is entirely dependent upon the incarnation" (1976, 213). For J. L. Martyn, "the titles Son of Man and Son of God have become interchangeable for John" (1968, 193); while for Lindars the Son of Man in John is simply "the agent of the revelation which is disclosed on the cross" (1983, 155) and he discounts all more portentous readings based on the idea of the Son of Man as a heavenly apocalyptic figure.

Amidst all this disagreement, the observations of Wayne Meeks, in the article reproduced below, deserve great respect. If the discussion is to be further advanced it is likely to be along the lines proposed by Borgen (1977) and Christopher Rowland, in his suggestively-titled article, "John 1:51, Jewish Apocalyptic and Targumic Traditions" (1984).

The name "Paraclete", like "Son of Man", remains imperspicuous and the origin of the title even more so; but the *role* of the Paraclete is very much clearer, as a number of books and articles testify, among them the essay of de la Potterie in the present collection. George Johnston's thoroughly-researched study (1970) gives a good survey of earlier work and contains a number of interesting but speculative proposals; for instance the thesis that behind the figure of the Paraclete is to be detected an attack upon the excessive prominence given in certain Christian circles to the angel Michael. Along with a number of other works published about the same time, Johnston's book is well summarized and reviewed by Kysar (1975). Nothing written since has superseded the piece appended by Raymond Brown to volume II of his commentary, which draws upon the OT and intertestamental literature to illustrate the "tandem relationship" between Jesus and the Paraclete that is such an important element in the evangelist's own conception of the nature of the gospel genre.

In talking of the Fourth Gospel, the term "eschatology" is commonly used to cover the key ideas of judgement, (eternal) life and, more problematically, resurrection. Since it has a built-in reference to the eschaton, the end, the word might seem highly inappropriate to cover the evangelist's conception of the immediate availability of life in the present experience of the believer. On the other hand the expression "realized eschatology" that is used to get round this objection is no more paradoxical than the Gospel's own "eternal life" (*aiōnios zōē*), employed metaphorically to suggest the anticipation on earth of the life of the world or age (*aiōn*) to come.

Only a handful of scholars (Beasley-Murray, 1946; van Hartingsveld, 1962) refuse to recognize that "eternal life" in this sense completely overshadows the traces of futuristic eschatology that are still evidently present in the Gospel (John 5:28f.; 6:39, 40, 44, 54; 11:24f.; 12:25). But the tension between the two groups of sayings is variously explained. Some solve the problem by denying that the futuristic sayings are the work of the evangelist. Bultmann, as we shall see, assigned them to an "ecclesiastical redactor"; others (Boismard, 1961; Richter, 1977) think they belong to the pre-history of the gospel text. Most scholars, however, attempt some kind of reconciliation. Dodd, for instance, sees them as a concession to the popular belief in the general resurrection, "a truth of less importance than the fact that the believer already enjoys eternal life" (1953, 148), but one equally dependent upon the life-giving power of Christ. Barrett (1947/48) sees the apparent contradiction as a particularly striking example of the tension between the "already" and the "not yet" that pervades the whole of the NT. Much later (1972) he integrated this view into a comprehensive theory of John's "dialectical theology". Finally, David Aune, in a most interesting study, concludes that "the Jesus of the Fourth Gospel is depicted as the dispenser of eschatological life and judgment because that is the primary way in which he was experienced within a cultic setting by the community" (1972, 135). For Aune the presence of two opposing eschatologies constitutes only a small part of the problem posed by John's radically new theology of eternal life.

The contrast between these two ways of resolving the seemingly contradictory views found side by side within the Fourth Gospel – elimination on the one hand, reconciliation on the other – is one very important example of a wider opposition between those whose immediate response to theological or textual inconsistencies is to reach for their scissors and those who prefer to paper over the cracks...

3 *Composition*

(a) *Diachronic*

The term "diachronic" was used by Ferdinand de Saussure in his famous *Cours de linguistique générale* (1913, 117–40) to refer to the approach of linguistic theorists chiefly interested in the *history* of languages. The alternative approach is "synchronic": the study of the interlocking relationships that go to make up a language at a particular point in time, ignoring the problem of how it reached that state in the first place. The two approaches, then, though quite distinct, are not mutually exclusive. In the study of individual texts, however, although the partizans of the synchronic method can certainly acknowledge the possibility that the text had a pre-history, they cannot take this into account in practice. Consequently they tend to emphasize both the extreme difficulty of getting back behind the received text and the nugatory nature of anything likely to be learned by doing so.

Bultmann had organized his commentary on the basis of an extremely elaborate theory of the Gospel's composition. His source theory, already complex enough, only partially accounted for the Gospel's awkwardnesses and inconsistencies. The signs source, the revelation-discourse source and the passion-and-Easter narrative source were simply the materials with which the evangelist worked. After him an "ecclesiastical redactor" (the German word *kirchlich* makes him sound much more "churchy") was wheeled in to explain those features of the book that failed to live up to Bultmann's own pure and powerful conception of the evangelist's theology. On almost any hypothesis[10] most of the final chapter appears as an afterthought, whether or not it is held to be composed by the original author. To the secondary editor responsible, as he saw it, for the "appendix" of chap. 21 Bultmann also and especially attributed the occasional intrusions of a superfluous sacramentalism and an old-fashioned futuristic eschatology which in his eyes spoiled the total effect.

But this was not all. What of those awkward transitions, "aporias" as they are sometimes called, most notoriously the conclusion of chap. 14, where, after a brisk "rise up, let us be off", Jesus carries on talking for a further three chapters? Bultmann would have preferred to explain these as the result of editorial decisions on the part of the evangelist himself, snipping away at the documents he had before him and then reassembling them as best he could. Finding himself unable to do so, he eventually resorted to a version of the old "displacement" theory, a particular favourite of British scholarship, according to which the pages of the Gospel were somehow scattered and then put together in the wrong order. (This theory has some staunch defenders even today.)[11] The purpose of Bultmann's own highly ingenious rearrangement (most helpfully analysed and lucidly set out by D. Moody Smith (1965)), was simply to restore the text as nearly as possible to the condition it was in when it left the evangelist's desk.

Of the various elements that go to make up Bultmann's intricate reconstruction of "the Gospel of John", few have attracted much support. One of his key ideas, however, borrowed, like the ecclesiastical redactor, from Alexander Faure (1922) was that the evangelist had among his sources a collection of miracle stories, commonly known nowadays as the "signs source" or, in Robert T. Fortna's up-dated version of the theory (1970), the signs *gospel*. Many scholars continue to be sceptical about the possibility of successfully reconstructing any document that does not already bear the distinctive stamp of the Johannine style. Among those who do accept the hypothesis of the signs source there are two distinct ways of viewing it. Bultmann himself regarded it as a source *tout court*, but others have seen it as a *Grundschrift*, a sort of basic document upon or around which the Gospel as we know it was eventually constructed. The proposal of a *Grundschrift* was not new either. Julius Wellhausen had strongly upheld it in his short commentary of 1908. But the term itself (not used by Bultmann) suggests the possibility that the Gospel grew by gradual accretion; it coheres nicely with Raymond Brown's idea (1966) that the Gospel underwent a series of different editions. Spotting this, J. L. Martyn (1977) has used a combination of the two hypotheses to buttress his independent version of the history of the Johannine community.

One may reject the idea of a signs source whilst accepting that of a number of different editions. This is Barnabas Lindars' view of the matter. Deeply suspicious of any detailed reconstruction of an alleged original source, he nevertheless argues that what we have today is a "revised and considerably expanded" version of the original Gospel (1971, 60).

Though they disagree in certain important respects, Brown, Martyn and Lindars concur in their *general* explanation of how the Gospel reached its present form. As one might expect, there is no shortage of more radical proposals, some of which depend upon the improbable assumption that the evangelist thoroughly disapproved of the whole tenor of the source he was using and devoted a lot of time and energy to putting it right.[12] A similar assumption was also one of the main weaknesses of Bultmann's theory.

Unlikely though it is that any consensus will be reached on a detailed solution to the problem of how the Gospel was composed, I believe it to be established beyond reasonable doubt that both the Johannine community and its book had a *history*. But this does not mean that it is possible to reconstruct this history with any certainty, or indeed with any plausibility. Among those scholars who have raised quizzical eyebrows at the efforts, first of Bultmann and subsequently of Martyn and his pupil Robert Fortna (1970), to distinguish between source and redaction, three deserve special mention: C. H. Dodd, C. K. Barrett and M. de Jonge. Dodd's classic study (1953) is built on the principle of integral interpretation; Barrett has frequently defended John, with skill and tenacity, against the charge of inconsistency (1982, *passim*); whilst de Jonge prefaces his excellent collection of essays on the Johannine writings with a remark which many others would endorse: "the present author is very skeptical about the possibility of delineating the literary sources in the Fourth Gospel and does not share the optimism displayed by some of his colleagues when they try to distinguish between sources and redaction" (1977, viii). This is surely a warning to be taken to heart, especially when it is delivered by a scholar of de Jonge's learning and perspicacity. And even those preparing to embark on an expedition which he declines to join would be well advised to take on board some at least of the equipment he provides throughout his book.

(b) Synchronic

In its neat new modern dress the synchronic approach to Johannine studies is not represented in this collection. We have already seen that many scholars shy away from the delicate task of distinguishing the work of the evangelist from that of his redactor. Many of these would also subscribe to the principle of integral interpretation, convinced that it is the job of the exegete to make sense of the text as it stands and not to chop it around in the interests of a purely speculative consistency. Certainly there is much to be said for the canonical approach: this is the Gospel that was accepted by the Church as an authentic expression of its faith; this, and not some hypothetical restoration, scraped clean of futuristic eschatology and sacramentalism, is the document that has inspired Christian thinkers over the centuries. The proponents of such an approach are in any case quick to avail themselves of the resources derived from their own and others' historical research. The need for this is patent and admitted by all, if only in order to comprehend the words the evangelist uses: *alētheia* (truth) is a case in point.

Since there has long been in existence an abundance of commentaries, articles and monographs dedicated to the interpretation of the traditional text, printed in the traditional order, what, it may be asked, is so new about the new approach, unless it be the introduction of an extra bit of jargon, synchronic as opposed to diachronic? Jargon is indeed part of the answer; but broadly speaking, the difference appears to consist in a greater responsiveness to the minutiae of the surface text and a readiness to attach more importance to these than to the jumble of historical, textual, philological, religious and theological information that is the staple fare furnished in commentaries.

One of the first to apply the methods of what he calls "German textual linguistics" and "American discourse analysis" to the study of the Gospel was Birger Olsson (1974), though he restricted his enquiry to a single narrative episode (the marriage feast of Cana) and a single extended discourse (the Samaritan woman). This is how he outlines his project:

> My investigation is concerned with the message and the nature of the text and not with its situation, insofar as these two elements can be kept separate. *From an analysis of the constitutive elements in the text I shall try to determine its message and then describe its linguistic and literary form (text type).* Thus I join the ranks of the few scholars who hold that the Johannine problem must first of all be solved from an analysis of the "Darstellungscharakter" of the Gospel. My investigation is primarily *linguistic* in character, although the message of the extant text which I am trying to establish is that inherent in the historical situation of the text and not in a setting contemporary to us. (pp. 2–3)

Far from spurning the assistance of historical criticism, Olsson perhaps uses it too indiscriminately, particularly when he follows A. M. Serra (1971) in reading the Cana episode in function of what he calls "the Sinai-screen", which in practice is applied less as a screen than as an interpretative grid.

Though it would be wrong to dismiss Olsson's analytic technique out of hand, it would certainly benefit from some pruning. He does his method and his cause a disservice by making such heavy weather of textual data which in principle should be reasonably perspicuous to any alert and sensitive reader.

A comparable approach is taken by R. Alan Culpepper in *The Anatomy of the Fourth Gospel* (1983). Much of the interest of this book is to be found in its first, introductory chapter and in the second, headed "Narrator and Point of View". Culpepper illuminatingly exploits the distinction between author and narrator, and expounds the characteristics of the latter: omniscience, omnipresence and an occasional intrusiveness. (Olsson had already made some similar suggestions in a section of his book headed "The Remarks of the Narrator".)

In the remainder of his book Culpepper deals somewhat stodgily with plot, characters, implicit commentary (misunderstanding, irony, symbolism) and the implied reader. His exhaustive list of the evangelist's use of irony and misunderstanding is likely to be helpful to beginners.

In his final chapter, dealing with the Gospel's intended readership, Culpepper resumes the "window on the world" approach he had earlier renounced in favour of Murray Krieger's model of the text as "mirror" (an infelicitous simile, surely, except for readers whose only purpose in looking at the text is to see their own image staring back at them). He concludes that the implied reader "is not Jewish but . . . either a Christian or one familiar with Christianity". But this is to be lured into accepting the evangelist's own undoubtedly biased picture of those he calls "the Jews". One of the distinctions offered in the methodological introduction to this book is that between "narratee" and "implied reader". In what follows this distinction lies inert and unused, even where it might have been profitably applied to dispel a particularly unfortunate confusion. The very fact that Jesus ("*your* law", 8:17) and the disciples ("for fear of the Jews", 20:19) dissociate themselves so completely from "the Jews" of the Gospel shows that these are not to be identified in any straightforward way with the real Jews who inhabited the world of John's intended readership.

One may doubt whether "the Johannine problem" can be solved by literary analyses of the kind proposed by Olsson and Culpepper. But this is no reason to dismiss them as without value. They make a refreshing change from the verse-by-verse exegesis imposed by the commentary format, whose general effect is to dull the reader's natural attentiveness to the kind of literary data that engage the interest of formalists and structuralists. Has anyone, for instance, ever remarked upon the contrast between John 3 and 4 in terms of night/day, town/country, inside/outside, male/female? Of course, one might ask how significant these oppositions are when compared to the contrast between Pharisee and Samaritan picked up by all except the flimsiest of the commentaries. But to ask is not to answer and there must be room for studies of such questions. Especially welcome would be an examination of the pressures exerted by the thought of the evangelist upon a style that is distinctive to the point of monotony – provided only that it could be carried out with some economy and grace.

3 *Conclusion: history and exegesis*

To a theologian history without exegesis is empty; to a historian exegesis without history is blind. It should be apparent that unless backed up by reliable historical information of various sorts and from various sources no study of the Gospel can be of more than fleeting interest to the scholar. The very diversity of the Johannine problem authorizes a number of different approaches; it is only to be expected that concentration upon one or other of its aspects should put the rest temporarily out of focus. The various questions that can be put to the text prompt different methods of analysis and require different kinds of explanation, material, formal, causal, final. We can learn from Aristotle that these explanations, far from being mutually exclusive, complement and to some extent supplement one another. The trick is to keep all the balls in the air at once.

None of the articles in this collection is completely one-sided. All to a greater or less extent intermingle history and exegesis. But the most successful are those that transcend this opposition and are formally aware of the kind of interpenetration suggested by Martyn's title, *History and Theology*. In the essay included here, Nils Alstrup Dahl was writing, as he often did, ahead of his time. It is marked by a sort of rambling purposefulness and shows a sensitivity to the sheer complexity of the Johannine problem seldom evinced in more recent scholarship. But the crown of this collection, already a classic, must be the article of Wayne Meeks, dense but not opaque, learned but not ponderous. An important part of the answer to "the problem of John" lies in the "harmonic reinforcement" of social and doctrinal pressures within the community that he detects and so subtly analyses. Will there be other studies like it?

NOTES

1 The question whether John had any direct knowledge of the Synoptic Gospels continues to be hotly debated. Yet nothing very important hangs on it; and the evidence points in contrary directions (which is why there is so much disagreement). Nobody denies that John was acquainted with the synoptic tradition (or traditions) in the broad sense. The really intriguing question is what use he made of it (or them). Both Peder Borgen (1979) and Barnabas Lindars ("Discourse", 1981; "John", 1981) have examined how John may have adapted certain sayings of Jesus. Theirs is a fruitful approach because of the light it sheds on the evangelist's literary techniques and his theological concerns. D. Moody Smith (1985) 145–72, provides a balanced assessment of the earlier questions.

2 A useful summary of this key article is to be found in the opening chapter of Wayne Meeks' *The Prophet-King*.

3 For an exposition of the more moderate viewpoint see K.-W. Tröger (1976).

4 Cf. W. A. Meeks (1975), esp. 166, n. 15.

5 Later he modified his view: *History* (1979), 50–62.

6 The others are now conveniently gathered together in *The Gospel of John* (1979).

7 See Brown's articles (1977, 1978, 1979) and his book, *The Community of the Beloved Disciple* (1979).

8 Apart from the suggestions of Lund and Boismard mentioned by Lamarche himself (p. 43) see R. A. Culpepper (1981) and I. de la Potterie (1984).

9 I have attempted to marry the insights of Bultmann and Lamarche in an article entitled "The Transformation of Wisdom" (1986).

10 The most recent exception to this generalization is P. S. Minear (1983).

11 See A. Q. Morton and J. McLeman (1980).

12 See especially Langbrandtner (1977); Richter, *Studien* (1977).

1

The History of
Religions Background of the
Prologue to the Gospel of John*

RUDOLF BULTMANN

I

No understanding of the Johannine Prologue[1] can be achieved except
on the basis of a reliable answer to the question of the *unity of the
Gospel*. And the question whether the Prologue itself is a unity cannot,
of course, be answered conclusively without reference to the whole
Gospel. Even so I think one is entitled to treat the Prologue separately,
partly because the question of the unity of the whole must after all
begin from a study of individual passages and partly because in the
case of the Prologue the problem is, in my opinion, relatively simple.
The first question, as is generally acknowledged, is whether vv. 6–8
and 15 were included in the original version. Here I completely concur
with Wellhausen, who explains these verses as later insertions, and I
will not repeat his reasons here, which have not, in my view, been
refuted by the recent work of E. Meyer and H. Leisegang.[2] In excising
these verses I do not wish, for the present, to say anything about the
manner or purpose of their insertion, or to deny that the final redactor
was anxious to give the whole passage a consistent meaning. I will
simply add that in my view v. 17 too is a secondary insertion. This
verse is a rather pedantic exegetical observation in which (1) Jesus
Christ, not yet named, makes an appearance as sudden as it is
superfluous, and (2) the antithesis between grace and law (the only
occurrence of this concept in the Gospel) adds an alien, Pauline note
which contrasts with vv. 14 and 10.

---

* First published in *Eucharisterion: Festschrift für H. Gunkel II* (Göttingen, 1923)
3–26. Translated by John Ashton.

We are left therefore with the following text[3] to investigate:

1   In the beginning was the Word
and the Word was with God,
and the Word was God
2   He was in the beginning with God.
3   All things were made through him
and without him was made nothing [that was made].[4]
4   In him was life
and the life was the light of men.
5   The light shines in the darkness,
and the darkness has not overcome it.
9   (This) was the true light
that enlightens every man [coming into the world].[5]
10   He was in the world, and the world was made through him,
yet the world knew him not.
11   He came to his own home,
and his own people received him not.
12   But to all who received him
[who believed in his name]
he gave power to become children of God;
13   who were born not of blood nor of the will of the flesh nor of
the will of man
but of God.
14   And the Word was made flesh
and dwelt among us,
and we have beheld his glory, glory as of the only Son from the
Father,
full of grace and truth.
16   For from his fullness have we all received,
grace upon grace.
18   No one has ever seen God;
the only Son, who is in the bosom of the Father, he has made
him known.

The first exegetical problem is this: *Up to what point is the pre-existent Logos the subject of the passage, and at what point is he succeeded by the historical Jesus?* The commentators are divided. Spitta and Zahn refer even v. 4 to the incarnate Logos, the historical Jesus. According to B. Weiss the historical Jesus is presupposed, not indeed by v. 4, but by v. 5. According to Heitmüller, v. 9 portrays the entry of the Logos into the world and vv. 10 and 11 describe the distressing tragedy of Jesus' life. Holtzmann and Bauer give a rather more complex explanation along the same lines. Harnack, followed by Holtzmann and Bauer, illustrates the uncertainty of the matter when he says that the Prologue "has the human reality in view right from the outset (*sic*), but considers it *sub specie aeternitatis*". Similarly Loisy.

The first *clear* mention of the incarnation is in v. 14: "the Word was made flesh". This does not sound as if there had already been talk of the Incarnate One. A reader not conversant with the whole cannot quite understand v. 4 of the historical Jesus: so can this understanding be ascribed to the author? There would hardly be any temptation to find the Incarnate One in vv. 4f. were it not for the presence of the apparently clear statements in vv. 10f., whose parallelism with v. 5 then affects the understanding of vv. 4f. And can vv. 10f. refer to anything other than "the tragedy of Jesus' life"? Possibly, yes. In my view we should follow Zahn and others in asserting the strongly felt parallelism between v. 5 and vv. 10f. (even clearer once vv. 6–8 have been excised); on the other hand vv. 9–13 must be explained with reference to vv. 4f. – that is to say they must be taken of the pre-existent Logos.[6]

It is obvious, of course, that vv. 10f. could not but remind the Christian reader of the tragedy of Jesus' life, and consequently it is hard to imagine that the author did not intend this. But this difficulty disappears as soon as one sees that the Prologue *builds upon an earlier written source* (*Vorlage*) in which not just vv. 1–5 but also vv. 9–13 spoke of a pre-existent divine being. In fact it is impossible to understand how a Christian author could have invented the idea that the pre-existent Jesus entered the world which was his, only to be met with non-recognition by the world and his own people's refusal to receive him. On the other hand pre-Christian and non-Christian speculations of this sort are known to us; even their application to Jesus is not unique. That the Prologue in general has made use of pre-Christian ideas is widely acknowledged; it is commonly supposed that these were the Logos speculations of Alexandrian Judaism. How far this is correct will appear later. At any rate, anyone who is inclined to accept that the cosmological speculations of vv. 1–3(4) depend on some pre-Christian tradition has every reason for asking whether there is not also a similar dependence discernible in the salvation-historical speculations of vv. 5, 9–13.

II

Matt. 23:37 (=Luke 13:34) points us in the right direction. Like numerous other scholars I take this saying concerning Jerusalem to be a citation from Jewish wisdom-literature.[7] Wisdom is speaking: ... how often would I have gathered your children together ... and you would not. Divine wisdom laments that her pains on behalf of men (or rather of the Jews) and her plan to bring them revelation have been frustrated by human opposition. Here too there are speculations of a kind in the background, and these become evident as soon as one looks at the Jewish material in context.

For the moment I shall not be entering into the passages that treat the pre-existence of wisdom and her cosmic role: I can more or less take this aspect of *Jewish wisdom-speculation* for granted: it is well-known.[8]

The first and most important question concerns Jewish thinking about the role of wisdom as a pre-existent divine and cosmic figure in salvation-history.

We may start from Ben Sirach. In Sir. 24:1–11 wisdom, speaking of herself as a pre-existent, cosmic being, says that she had the peoples and nations for her own possession (v. 6).[9] She continues:

> Among all these I sought a resting-place (*anapausis*);
>   I sought in whose territory I might lodge (*aulizesthai*). (v. 7)

Up to this point the parallel with the Johannine Prologue is illuminating, but this is where it stops; for wisdom already occupies a dwelling-place on earth, namely in Israel:

> Then the one who created me assigned a place for (*katapauein*) my tent; and he said, "Make your dwelling (*kataskēnoun*) in Jacob, and in Israel receive your inheritance." (v. 8)

Here, however, the author is clearly latching onto an old tradition, and editing it in the spirit of a legally-oriented spirituality.[10] In chap. 24 he applies the old wisdom-speculation to the law, as is plain from v. 23:

> All this (i.e. what has been said about divine wisdom) is the book of the covenant of the Most High God, the law which Moses commanded us.[11]

In this reference to the law the old speculations have been modified. And if we are to suppose that the Johannine Prologue (and Matt. 23:37 = Luke 13:34) originally offered a perfect parallel to these, then one of two things would follow: *either* Ben Sirach has completely reversed the original statement (that wisdom found *no* dwelling-place on earth) *or* that the older wisdom speculation, like John 1:12, was referring to exceptional cases: in general wisdom is rejected, but a handful of people receive her. And this is what Ben Sirach will have seized on: the exceptions are actually to be found in Israel, who in this respect has a unique place among the peoples and nations. Whether She belongs to God alone (W. 8f.) but

A passage from Baruch (Bar. 3:9–44) confirms and extends the parallelism. Here too the subject is wisdom, whose cosmic role is alluded to in 3:29–36. Then, as in Sir. 24:23, it is said of her that:

> She is the book of the commandments of God
> and the law that endures for ever. (4:1)

Here too, then, the old wisdom-speculation is interpreted to refer to the law, and Israel is seen as possessing wisdom (3:37). But here there clearly emerges what we could only assume in the case of Ben Sirach: this speculation contained the idea that wisdom is rejected by men. In contradiction to a secondary addition (3:37), Israel is said to spurn wisdom (3:11–13); the princes of the nations, those who rule over the beasts of the earth, the merchants of Medan and Thema,[12] the giants, etc., did not know wisdom and perished for their folly.

But this is not all! The whole passage is a sermon preaching repentance, exhorting the acceptance of wisdom:

> Hear the commandments of life, O Israel;
> give ear and learn wisdom. (3:9)

> Turn, O Jacob, and take her;
> walk toward the shining of her light. (4:2)

Furthermore, we notice that in apparent contradiction to the tone of reproach that permeates the whole sermon, there is a strong emphasis upon the hiddenness of wisdom: no one finds the way to her; God alone has managed to find her (3:29–36). From this it follows that the communication of wisdom depends entirely upon revelation and consequently that the sermon resembles a self-revelation or self-presentation of wisdom, which is what lies behind Sir. 24:1–34 and is also to be encountered in other sources. Moreover the contradiction between the hiddenness of wisdom was not part of the original *meaning* of the passage, but is a consequence drawn from men's rejection of her. How correct this inference is will soon be apparent. But for the moment we must stick to the portrayal of the hiddenness of wisdom.

Bar. 3:29f. reads as follows:

> Who has gone up to heaven and taken her,
> and brought her down from the clouds?
> Who has gone over the sea, and found her,
> and will buy her for pure gold?

To this may be added Deut. 30:11–14, a late passage:

> For this commandment which I command you this day is not too hard for you, neither is it far off.
> It is not in heaven, that you should say,
> "Who will go up for us to heaven, and bring it to us, that we may hear it and do it?"
> Neither is it beyond the sea, that you should say,

"Who will go over the sea for us, and bring it to us, that we may
    hear it and do it?"
But the word is very near to you; it is in your mouth and in your heart,
    so that you can do it.

Here there is a vague notion of hidden wisdom as the counterpart
of the revealed law, and it is instructive for the history of this whole
tradition that Paul gives the idea a new twist by interpreting Deut.
30:11–14 of "the word of faith" (Rom. 10:6–8).[13]

Job 28 too speaks of the pre-existent and cosmic figure of hidden
wisdom. Here the underlying speculation does not emerge very clearly,
but we are certainly entitled to see these three passages from Ben
Sirach, Baruch and Deuteronomy as a later reading, or rather an
alternative version of an original wisdom-speculation. In Job there
is not yet any reference to the law.

Now we may ask whether there is good ground for the earlier
assumption that the idea of the hiddenness of wisdom is derived from
her rejection by mankind. And there is. *1 Enoch* 42:1–3 reads:

Wisdom found no place where she could dwell, and her dwelling was in
heaven. Wisdom went out to dwell among the sons of men, but did not
find a dwelling; wisdom returned to her place and took her seat in the
midst of angels. And iniquity came out from her chambers; those whom
she did not seek she found, and dwelt among them, like rain in the desert,
and like dew upon parched ground. (Knibb)

There is probably another allusion to the same theme in *1 Enoch*
84:3, where it is said of God:

No wisdom escapes you; it does not turn away from your throne, nor from
your presence. (Knibb)

This is also probably how 4 Ezra 5:9f. is to be understood, where
what the old wisdom speculation recounted of the first days is applied
to the troubles of the last days.

And wisdom shall withdraw into its chamber,
and it shall be sought by many but shall not be found,
and unrighteousness and unrestraint shall increase on earth.

The Syriac Apocalypse of Baruch also uses this tradition:

And many will say to others at that time,
Where has discretion hidden itself,
And where has wisdom fled for refuge? (48:36: Brockington)

But the most important passage is Prov. 1:20–32, which reflects
the whole myth. First comes wisdom's fruitless invitation:

> How long, O simple ones, will you love being simple?
> How long will scoffers delight in their scoffing
>   and fools hate knowledge? (v. 22)

Then comes the judgement (vv. 23b–27):

> I will make my words known to you.
> Because I have called and you refused to listen,
>   have stretched out my hand and no one has heeded,
> and you have ignored all my counsel
>   and would have none of my reproof,
> I also will laugh at your calamity;
>   I will mock when panic strikes you,
> when panic strikes you like a storm,
>   and your calamity comes like a whirlwind,
>   when distress and anguish come upon you.

In what follows, the ancient wisdom-myth is clearly recognizable: pre-existent wisdom, who assisted God at the creation, seeks a dwelling-place on earth among men; but she seeks in vain – her message is rejected. She comes to her own, but her own do not receive her. So she goes back to heaven and remains hidden. Now men do seek her, but she is no longer to be found: God alone knows the way.[14] Yet one piece is still missing. In Sir.24:1–11 the suggestion is made that the hiddenness of wisdom is not absolute, but that wisdom reveals herself to particular chosen souls; these, for Ben Sirach and Baruch are the Israelites. What we have here is obviously a later adaptation of the original idea, and this also emerges quite clearly in Wisdom 7. This is a depiction of the cosmic significance of wisdom in which ancient eastern speculation is clothed in the language of hellenistic, and especially Stoic philosophy (7:21–6). The passage continues:

> Though she is but one she can do all things,
>   and while remaining in herself she renews all things;
> in every generation she passes into holy souls
>   and makes them friends of God, and prophets;
> for God loves nothing so much as the man who lives with wisdom. (vv. 27–8)

So there are exceptions: in the *massa perditionis* there are some favoured souls to whom wisdom reveals herself, who accept her and as a consequence become friends of God and prophets. Sir. 6:20–2 and 15:7 may be understood as an echo of this idea, where it is asserted that wisdom is inaccessible to the majority, the foolish, and that only a few reach her. Above all we can now understand Wis. 7:14, where it is said of wisdom that:

there is an unfailing treasure for men;
those who use[15] it obtain friendship with God,
commended for the gifts that come from instruction.

Now we can understand Sir. 1:1–30 along the same lines, as a late wisdom poem with the old wisdom-speculation underlying it – though no doubt this sounds through only very softly here:

The root of wisdom – to whom has it been revealed?
Her clever devices – who knows them? (1:8)

She belongs to God alone (vv. 8f.) but

She dwells with all flesh according to his gift,
and he supplied her to those who love him (1:10)

She made among men an eternal foundation,
and among their descendants she will be trusted. (1:15)[16]

All this throws clear light on the *Prologue of John*, and it scarcely needs adding that in v. 12 the phrase "who believed in his name" is an exegetical gloss inserted by the redactor to give his source a Christian meaning. The followers of wisdom are called "children" and not "friends" of God or "prophets" as in the Book of Wisdom. This is like Luke 7:35 where Jesus and John the Baptist are represented as not belonging to this generation; they are "children of wisdom", those through whom wisdom is justified, i.e., shown to be just: "Yet wisdom is justified by (all) her children."[17]

III

Before going any further I propose to offer a brief survey of the cosmic role of pre-existent wisdom: this will help to give a fully-rounded view of the dependence of the Prologue of John upon wisdom-speculation.[18] Corresponding to the phrase, "in the beginning was the Word" (John: 1:1) is a description of wisdom as a pre-existent being, the first of God's creatures: "the Lord created me, the beginning (*archē*) of his ways" etc. (Prov. 8:22–6); "before time, from the beginning (*ap' archēs*) he created me" (Sir. 1:1–19; 24:3f., 9). Philo says of wisdom that she is "old enough to precede my birth and that of the entire universe" (*De virt.*, 62). Rabbinical exegesis actually finds wisdom in Gen. 1:1, by combining "in the beginning" (*bᵉrēʾšīt*) with Prov. 8:22, where wisdom is called *rēʾšīt darko*, "the beginning of his way". Similarly the Jerusalem targum renders Gen. 1:1 "in *wisdom* he created".[19] But the conception of wisdom as a creature must be a Jewish version of an older mythological idea portraying wisdom as an independent divine being. This is prominent wherever wisdom is described as God's companion, as in Prov. 8:30: "then I was beside him."[20]

So too:

> With thee is wisdom, who knows thy works
> and was present when thou didst make the world. (Wis. 9:9)

> She glorifies her noble birth by living with God,
> and the Lord of all loves her. (Wis. 8:3)

> Give me the wisdom that sits by thy throne. (Wis. 9:4)[21]

All this corresponds to "the Word was with God" of John 1:1f. In the Book of Wisdom, wisdom is also termed (in philosophical language) the breath, emanation and reflection of God (7:25f.); but Philo has an echo of the mythological concept in his reference to wisdom as the mother of the world, alongside God, who is the father (cf. *De ebriet.* 30, p. 361; *Leg. alleg.* II, 49, etc.), but at the same time as virginal (*De Cherub.* 48–50) or as God's virgin daughter (*De fuga et inv.* 50).

But as in John 1:3 this wisdom is also the creator of the world. Possibly, in Prov. 8:30 she is called "master-workman"; however this may be, she is said in Prov. 8:27–30 to be with God during the creation. According to Job 28:25–9 God searched wisdom out in creation. In Prov. 3:19 the mythology is toned down:

> The Lord by wisdom founded the earth;
> by understanding he established the heavens.

Similarly Wis. 9:1f.

> ...who hast made all things by thy word,
> and by thy wisdom hast formed man.

Wis. 8:4 is more strongly mythological:

> For she has been initiated into the knowledge of God,
> and is an associate in his works.

So too is Wis. 7:12:

> I rejoiced in them all, because wisdom leads them;
> but I did not know that she was their source (*genesis*)[22]

In Wis. 7:22, wisdom is called "the fashioner of all things", though it is true that immediately afterwards she is described in philosophical terms as a cosmic force, immanent in the world (7:22–8). Philo speaks of the wisdom "through whom the universe came into existence" (*De fuga et inv.* 109). And the conception of wisdom in *2 Enoch* is crudely mythological: in 30:8 it is recounted how wisdom creates man at God's behest;[23] and in 33:3f. God explains how "by my supreme

26

wisdom I have contrived it all – I created from the lowest foundation and up to the highest and out to their end" (F. I. Andersen).

IV

I believe it has been satisfactorily established that the Logos speculation of the Prologue of John derives from wisdom speculation present in Jewish sources. But now the question arises why a figure encountered in Jewish writings as *Wisdom* should be called *Logos* in the Prologue. The assumption that the evangelist made the change of his own accord is far from obvious. I think it probable that he intends his Prologue to correspond to the beginning of the sacred book of the Jews, but that Gen. 1 should have prompted him to substitute *Logos* for *Sophia*, wisdom, is highly unlikely – the more so because there is at best an indirect allusion to the "Word" in Gen. 1. In fact most scholars assume that he has borrowed the Logos concept from elsewhere. If it is correct that he has utilized a literary source, the most likely hypothesis is that the term was already present in this. No doubt this source stemmed directly not from pagan tradition but from hellenistic Judaism, on which the evangelist depends in other places as well.[24] We have therefore to ssume either that an idea of Logos analogous to that of wisdom had already been in existence for a long time or else that in this instance the Logos was substituted for the traditional wisdom figure. I believe the second suggestion to be the likelier of the two: which makes one think of *Alexandrian–Jewish speculation*; and in fact most scholars look to this for light upon the Johannine Logos. But a direct dependence on Philo can, I believe, be excluded. There is nothing *specifically* Philonic in the Prologue, even if the phrase "the Word was God" in v. 1 may somehow be traced to Philo's idea of the Logos as a "second God".[25] Of course Philo's Logos belongs to the same history of religions context; but it is a much more complicated affair. In any event there is certainly to be found in it a parallel to the Logos of the Prologue. No doubt too the Logos speculation of Alexandrian Judaism belongs to the context of the speculation of hellenistic Egypt, in whose adaptation of the old Egyptian theogony[26] the Logos plays a special role, one influenced by Stoic thinking, as a cosmic power. So one can readily understand that the Logos should have replaced the older wisdom figure in Alexandrian–Jewish circles. And if in the Prologue we find Logos instead of wisdom, this is scarcely surprising in view of the fact that in Philo also Logos and wisdom appear side by side. This will be discussed below.

V

It may now be possible to take a step further towards achieving some clarity on the question of the origin and nature of wisdom-speculation and so finally to assign the Prologue its place in its history of religions context.

In Wis. 7:2, it is said of wisdom that "in every generation she passes into holy souls". This sounds as if the revelation of wisdom is not casual or sporadic but relatively regular. It may indeed appear too bold to take the phrase *kata geneas* distributively. What comes next however ("she makes them friends of God, and prophets") clearly refers to particular individuals charged with the task of transmitting revelation; and other passages confirm that prophecy is explained by wisdom, and that it is wisdom who commissions the prophets, e.g. Sir. 24:32 (wisdom is speaking):

> I will again make instruction shine forth like the dawn,
> and I will make it shine afar;
> I will again pour out teaching like prophecy,
> and leave it to all future generations.

And this is where the wisdom saying in Matt. 23:34 belongs: "Therefore I send you prophets and wise men and scribes."[27]

Lastly we can now see the real meaning of Luke 7:35 (Matt. 11:19): the Baptist and Jesus are "children of wisdom" because they have been commissioned by wisdom as prophets. The idea is that wisdom not only tried to enlist mankind at the beginning of history, but that she continues to send messengers to proclaim her message to successive generations. This idea is basically what lies behind the constant repetition of the wisdom message, the calls to repentance and the recruiting campaigns, as in the collections of the sapiential poetry like Proverbs or Ben Sirach. [Bultmann continues this paragraph by illustrating, from art and literature, the long tradition of the special relationship between wisdom and prophecy.]

The idea of prophetic inspiration has almost vanished from the Prologue, where the light is focused exclusively on the single idea of the incarnation of the Logos. So those who, by way of exception, "did receive him" have become individuals with no particular role to play in the history of salvation; and even in the Jewish sources the function of wisdom's emissaries in the history of salvation has paled into insignificance. But originally the idea had much more solidity and importance. The omission in Matt. 23:29 of the introductory formula, "Therefore also the wisdom of God" (still present in Luke 11:49) has the effect of ascribing the words of wisdom to Jesus himself;

but there is a sure instinct at work here. When wisdom speaks, her emissary speaks too, and vice versa: the emissary's words are her words also. *Wisdom manifests and reveals herself in her emissary*; it is wisdom herself who preaches: "wisdom cries aloud in the street..." (Prov. 1:20); "Does not wisdom call..." (8:1); she addresses a warning to her sons (8:32ff.); "wisdom has built her house ... she has sent out her maids to call from the highest places in the town" (9:1–3); "wisdom exalts her sons..." (Sir. 4:11); she "will praise herself" (24:1).[28] In Sir. 24:32f. and especially Sir. 51:23f. the two subjects, wisdom and her emissaries, are interchangeable; here it is the teacher of wisdom who speaks;

> Draw near to me, you who are untaught,[29]
>   and lodge in my school.
> Why do you say[30] you are lacking in these things,
>   and why are your souls very thirsty?
> I opened my mouth and said,
>   Get these things for yourselves without money.
> Put your neck under the yoke,[31]
>   and let your souls receive instruction;
>   it is to be found close by.
> See with your eyes that I have laboured (*kopiān*) little
>   and found for myself much rest (*anapausis*). (vv. 23–7)[32]

What the teacher of wisdom says here of wisdom in the third person is paralleled by the more original form which is put into the mouth of Jesus in Matt. 11:28f.

> Come to me, all who labour (*kopiān*) and are heavy-laden,
>   and I will give you rest (*anapauein*).
> Take my yoke upon you, and learn from me;
>   for I am gentle and lowly in heart,
>   and you will find rest (*anapausis*) for your souls.

In *Odes Sol* 33 also the "perfect virgin", i.e. wisdom, appears and preaches:

> Turn, you sons of men,
> And you, their daughters, come...
> I will make you *wise* in the ways of truth...
> Hear me and be delivered. (Emerton)

So it is really wisdom herself who repeatedly comes out of hiding to descend on the earth, where she is embodied in her emissaries, the prophets. And Bar. 3:37, a remarkable verse, is not to be struck out as a Christian interpolation: rather it is a remnant of ancient wisdom-speculation reworked by the writer:

> Afterward she (wisdom) appeared on earth
>   and lived among men.[33]

29

[In the final paragraph of this section Bultmann argues that the same idea is found in a number of Manichean and Mandaean sources.]

VI

Of course the ultimate provenance of these ideas cannot be satisfactorily determined in this case simply on the grounds of literary priority. The researches of Bousset and Reitzenstein have, in my view, established that a much more ancient mythological speculation lies behind all the various statements and ideas we have been reviewing, though admittedly the origin of this wisdom speculation is not yet completely clear. But unquestionably the origin was not Jewish. The wisdom figure and its myth cannot have arisen in Israel. But here I want to tackle the question of origin only insofar as it arises directly out of the Prologue and the material we have just been looking at. For there is still some obscurity about the source used in John 1:1–13. When it is said that the Logos was the light of men (v. 4), this can hardly be taken to mean that he *intended* to be the light but failed because of human opposition; it must mean that the Logos *was in fact* the light of men. This is also clear from v. 9: "(This) was the true light, that enlightens every man.[34] This contradicts the dominant idea that mankind shuts itself off from God's revelation, which is effective in exceptional cases only. On the one hand the Logos is the immanent power of enlightenment that is active among mankind; on the other hand he succeeds in bringing revelation only to a few. This contradiction – *the Logos as an immanent cognitive power and as the bearer of revelation* – is not peculiar to this passage but permeates the whole of Jewish wisdom literature. That wisdom is both a hidden divine being and an active power affecting all human knowledge, craftsmanship and probity is presupposed throughout the wisdom literature, and is stated explicitly in Prov. 8:14ff. In Sir. 1 the tension is expressed quite clearly: "All wisdom comes from the Lord" (1:1); "the root of wisdom – to whom has it been revealed?" (1:6); "she dwells with *all* flesh according to his gift, and he supplied her *to those who love him*" (1:10).

Now there can be no doubt that the role of wisdom as an immanent cognitive force is extremely closely connected with her role as a cosmic power; this is also clear from what follows in John 1:1–4. The authority that has summoned everything into life and supports the existence of all creatures is at the same time the cognitive power that is active in all reasoning beings. It seems to me very questionable whether these two figures – the divine being as a cognitive and *creative* power on the one hand, and the divine being as the bearer of revelation on the other – properly belong together. It is more likely that they were joined together subsequently. In an enquiry into origins this question too demands attention. [In the remainder of this section Bultmann speculates further (though without reaching any conclusions) about the ultimate origin of the wisdom myth. He names Egypt, Babylon and Persia as possible sources.]

VII

There is still one question left concerning the Prologue. It should be clear by now that vv. 1–3 make use of a written source with the same content and chain of thought as is found in Jewish wisdom–speculation. It is moreover likely that the general outlook of the Prologue is that of Near Eastern theories concerning a revelation goddess embodied on earth in her emissaries. But the question remains how vv. 14, 16, 18 are related to what precedes – whether they are part of the source or have been composed by the evangelist. The first suggestion is the simpler, insofar as it means ascribing to the evangelist only the additional verses and parts of verses that have been inserted into the Prologue; whereas in the second case we have to postulate a second, revisionary hand, responsible for adding vv. 6–8, 15 and 17 to the text of the Gospel. Now I believe it to be a fact that several hands have worked on the body of the Gospel, so the second suggestion is certainly a possibility. But before deciding on this, we should consider whether apart from vv. 6–8, 15 and 17 and the Christian additions (in v. 12 and possibly also in vv. 1 and 9) *the whole Prologue can be taken as a pre-Christian written source*; whether in particular the phrase "and the Word was made flesh" could have belonged to such a source. In that case the source will have put aside the idea of earlier bearers of revelation so as to concentrate exclusively on the one definitive revealer, seen in a historical personage of the immediate past. Who could this have been? A source of this kind could scarcely have come from Judaism proper: it must have emanated from Baptist circles where it had been said of John the Baptist that in him the Word had become flesh. This would explain why, taking this source over from hellenistic–Jewish Baptist circles and applying it to Jesus, the evangelist demotes the Baptist into a mere witness to Jesus (vv. 6–8, 15).

Against this there is the other possibility that the source reached only as far as v. 13, and that *v. 14 begins the contribution of the evangelist himself*. In that case, as has already been shown, he will have applied the wording of vv. 10–13 of the source, against its original intention, to the story of Jesus, and may even have taken vv. 4f. in this sense. Even if we see vv. 14, 16, 18 as the composition of the

Christian evangelist, we have to explain the phrase "and the Word was made flesh" as written in the same perspective as the source of vv. 1–13; for it certainly contains the conception of the historical embodiment of the revealing deity in his emissary. The wording of the verse suggests this both in the phrase "he dwelt amongst us", which is reminiscent of Sir. 24 (cf. above, 21) and in the title "only-begotten" (vv. 14, 18) which has no special place except in gnosticism and may well actually have originated in syncretic gnostic circles.[35]

I will not pursue any further here the other ways in which hellenistic terms and ideas appear in vv. 14, 16, 18.[36] But a word needs to be added on the extent to which the *Christology of the whole of John's Gospel* belongs to the context of certain ideas expounded by Reitzenstein in his latest publications and qualified by him as Iranian, specifically the notion of the redeemed redeemer – the divine being, the heavenly "man" who descended to earth as God's emissary, took human shape and after fulfilling his mission as revealer returned to the heavenly world, elevated and transfigured, to take up the office of judge – and all this because he is "the Man". I do not think Reitzenstein is right to place the synoptic Son of Man sayings in this context, because the determinative features of the redeemed redeemer are missing. But it does lie behind the Johannine Son of Man sayings, where it is expressly stated that the Son of Man is the Pre-existent One: "No one has ascended into heaven except he who descended from heaven, the Son of Man" (3:13); "then what if you were to see the Son of Man ascending where he was before?" (6:62). It is affirmed that the Son of Man must be exalted or transfigured: "so must the Son of Man be lifted up" (3:14; also 12:34; cf. 8:28); "the hour has come for the Son of Man to be glorified". As Son of Man Jesus is judge: "he has given him authority to execute judgement because he is the Son of Man" (5:27). And it is expressly stated that the redemption of the faithful depends upon the exaltation of the Son of Man: "and I, when I am lifted up from the earth, will draw all men to myself" (12:32).

The proposition so characteristic of this motif, that the divine being sojourns unrecognized on earth, pervades the whole Gospel, and is given a strongly polemical and ironic flavour: 8:14–19; 6:42; 7:26f.; 9:29f. On the point of departure from the world, the heavenly emissary (it is constantly emphasized that he is *sent*) looks back on his work, and commends to his Father the community he is leaving behind – just like the departing "Plan" of the Mandaeans in the 20th item of the Oxford collection of the Mandaean liturgies.[37] Accordingly I think John 1:14, 16 and 18 should also be understood on the basis of this motif, even if these verses are regarded as the evangelist's own composition.

I will not deny that I find the first suggestion more plausible – that the whole Prologue has been adopted from a Baptist document. The evangelist is responsible for vv. 6–8, 15, possibly 17, plus the other additions – nothing more. The Baptist sect is robbed of its hero in that what was said of him is now asserted of Jesus and he is made to witness on Jesus' behalf. This idea, which accords with Reitzenstein's discussion,[38] must be argued in more detail in another connection. The strength of the baptist/gnostic influence upon the Gospel of John may be gauged from the foregoing remarks. Here I will simply point out that in chaps. 3 and 5, after various propositions emanating from this circle have been enunciated the theme of witness reappears and the Baptist is once again brought on stage to witness on behalf of Jesus. If my supposition is correct, then in the Gospel of John we have fresh proof of the extraordinarily early impact of eastern gnostic speculation upon early Christianity, a thesis which the man to whom these reflections are gratefully dedicated (Hermann Gunkel), with a rare breadth of vision and a fine scholarly flair, was one of the first to advance.

NOTES

1 Only after this article was completed did I have access to Rendel Harris, "The origin of the prologue to St. John's Gospel" (1917). In spite of many similar observations this study differs totally from mine both in its method and in its conclusions, so that there is no need for me to come to grips with it in detail. Harris' main conclusion is "that the first and foremost article of Christian belief is that Jesus is the Wisdom of God, personified, incarnate, and equated with every form of personification of Wisdom that could be derived from or suggested by the Scriptures of the Old Testament".

2 E. Meyer, *Ursprung und Anfänge des Christentums* I (1921) 314–22. H. Leisegang, *Pneuma Hagion* (1922) 55–8.

3 I intend to deal with the text-critical questions in another connection. [In his original article, Bultmann quotes from the Gospel in Greek. Most of his quotations from other Greek sources, especially the Septuagint, are also given in Greek. I have translated all of these, giving a transliteration of the original only where this seems indispensable for an understanding of the argument. On the other hand, I have omitted most of the notes that give references to secondary literature. Tr.]

4 Like Heitmüller and Bauer I regard the words "that was made" (*ho gegonen*) as corrupt, in my view an interpretative gloss intended to conceal what is as it happens a purely imaginary misunderstanding of the text.

5 Some account will be given below of the reasons for bracketing these words as an interpolation.

6 The present tense, "shines", in the parallel clauses is certainly harsh, since one would naturally expect the past. And quite apart from the parallel clauses, it seems to me illegitimate to take the "shines" as referring to the author's own

present, since this would require "does not overcome" in v. 5, rather than "has not overcome". All in all, v. 5 must refer to the past, and the present "shines" must be atemporal, like "enlightens" in v. 9 (if this is not to be attributed to the redactor).

7 See my *History of the Synoptic Tradition* (Oxford and New York, 1963) 114f.

8 Cf. W. Schencke, *Die Chokma* (*Sophia*) *in der jüdischen Hypostasenspekulation* (Kristiania, 1913).

9 Against B's *ektēsamēn* ("I acquired") (the Hebrew text is deficient) S, it is true, reads *hēgēsamēn* ("I led"). But it makes no material difference whether one prefers *ektēsamēn*, or follows Smend in reading *hēgēsamēn*, taking the meaning to be "I had power over peoples and nations".

10 Cf. *History of the Synoptic Tradition* (1963) 101.

11 Cf. Sir. 15:1, which follows the portrait of the seeker after wisdom and concludes,

The man who fears the Lord will do this,
and he who holds to the *law* will obtain wisdom.

Cf. also Bousset, *Die Religion des Judentums*², 136:1; 396:2; Schencke, op. cit., 34f.; and, e.g. *Genesis Rabbah*, chap. 1: God creates the world after consulting the *Torah*, whereas according to the old conception, it was *wisdom* who advised him (F. Weber, *Jüdische Theologie auf Grund der Talmud und verwandter Schiften*², 14ff.)

12 On the text see Rothstein, in Kautzsch, *Die Apokryphen und Pseudepigraphen des AT* I, 220.

13 There is an allusion, but not a significant one, in 4 Esdr. 4:8.

14 I leave aside the question whether or how Job 15:9ff. is connected with this particular myth. Cf. Gunkel, *Genesis*³, 33f.; Schencke, op. cit., 7–10, Reitzenstein, *Das mandäische Buch*, 48.

15 *chrēsamenoi, v. 1. ktēsamenoi* (those who *acquire* it).

16 Arguably *1 Enoch* 91:10 carries this idea over into eschatology: "And the righteous will rise from sleep, and wisdom will rise and be given to them."

17 Possibly it was Luke, no longer understanding the saying, who added the "all". Matthew, equally uncomprehending, changed the "children" of wisdom into "works" (Matt. 11:19). Prov. 8:32 and Sir. 4:11 should not be used as examples of the term "children of wisdom", for here it seems to be just a form of address used in catechesis.

18 See the works cited by Schencke, above, n. 8.

19 Cf. *Pirqe Aboth*, 6:10.

20 As "favourite" or "master builder"? See immediately below; cf. also Schencke, op. cit., 23f.

21 Cf. Wis. 9:10: "from the throne of thy glory send her".

22 *v.l. genetin* (mother).

23 Similarly Ps. Clem. *Hom.* XVI 11f.

24 This cannot of course be conclusively demonstrated without taking the *whole Gospel* into consideration.

25 *Leg. alleg.* II 86. In calling the Logos God (*De somn.* I 229f.), Philo hedges the title in with all sorts of provisos, insofar as he belongs to "those who are improperly called gods". In any case I think it is possible that the phrase "and the Word was God" in John 1:1 was added by the redactor to his source. If so, he will have

taken up the preceding sentence again with the words, "He was in the beginning with God". In that case the "he" (*houtos*) will have been intended antithetically and polemically. However, I place no weight on this suggestion.

26   On the significance of the world-creating word in the Egyptian theogony and cosmology, and especially on Ptah as "the heart and tongue of nineness", cf. Erman, *Die ägyptische Religion*[2] (1909) 46f. Thoth also appears as a creator deity and as the "word of Re". And in the hellenistic period Hermes-Thoth is the Logos both in his role as creative power and as the bearer of knowledge.

27   Luke 11:49: "I will send them prophets and apostles".

28   Is Ps. 1 based on the same sort of wisdom sermon as is contained in the pieces quoted above? There are parallels to the picture of the fruitful tree on the water's edge in Sir. 24:12–22, 30; *Odes Sol.* 38:18ff.

29   This is how wisdom herself speaks in Prov. 9:4.

30   This is how wisdom herself speaks in Prov. 1:20.

31   Cf. Sir. 6:24f., 29f.

32   Cf. Sir. 6:28.

33   Cf. W. Baumgartner, *ZAW* 34 (1914) 173.

34   In my view the only natural way of taking the continuation, "coming into the world" is as qualifying "every man". But this may have been added by the redactor as an expansion of "was". In that case he will have taken the sentence to refer to the entry of the Logos into the world in the figure of Jesus. But if so it is not easy to see either how the light "was on the point of" coming into the world (Heitmüller), not why the light in this sentence is characterized as that "which enlightens every man".

35   Bousset, *Hauptprobleme*, 161, 171, 267, n. 2; *Kyrios Christos*[2], 157. We should also remember the report of Damascius that the Babylonian Mummu, interpreted as "the mental world" is called "the only son" (*monogenēs*) of the two other primitive beings (*De princ.* 125).

36   My colleague G. Hölscher has pointed out to me that Persian influence may be discernible in the conceptual coupling of "grace" and "truth", as indeed in the corresponding OT coupling *hesed w^eemet* (steadfast love and faithfulness), that is to say, in those passages in the more recent parts of the OT in which the pair are strongly hypostatized; e.g., Ps. 89:3, 15; 57:4; 61:8; 40:12; Prov. 20:28; 3:3; 14:22; and esp. Ps. 85:11ff. The two concepts would correspond to the Persian hypostases Vohumanō and Asha, which appear frequently in Zoroastrianism, typically in connection with Ahura Mazda.

37   Lidsbarski, *Mandäische Liturgien*, 190f.

38   *Das mandäische Buch*, 62, esp. n. 3.

2

*The Prologue of John**

PAUL LAMARCHE

It is to be feared that the meaning of this passage, potentially so rich and varied, has been obscured over the centuries by more recent interpretations. Here we shall be attempting to get back beyond these, perfectly legitimate though they are, so as to recover the original conception. To assist our enquiry we will keep two guidelines constantly in mind: first the relationship of the Prologue to the thought-world of the New Testament and secondly the explanation of its apparent anomalies. That we are actually in a position to detect a closer link between the Prologue and the preoccupations of the apostolic age than is normally acknowledged augurs well for the accuracy of our interpretation. On the other hand, the Prologue contains several anomalies which have to be accounted for. Certain difficulties in the train of thought may possibly arise from the adaptation of a primitive hymn, to which, according to one theory, the evangelist made a number of additions.[1] But it remains true that our first task is to interpret the text as it is, more particularly to explain on the level of the final redaction the problems arising from the difficulties it presents in its finished state: the two references to John the Baptist; certain odd and disconcerting conjunctions; the sense of the word "Logos"; the problem of punctuation in vv. 3–4 (before or after the *ho gegonen*);[2] the doublets in vv. 12–13.

How should one approach this formidable passage? Since the origin and precise meaning of "Logos" are disputed and the term has subsequently been overlaid by any number of interpretations, let us leave this christological title on one side for the present, only returning to it once we have got sufficiently far in our study of the Prologue as a whole. Instead of attempting, as it were, a reconstruction from the outside, we shall try to find a leading thread through this maze. Guided by this, and passing from one difficulty to the next, we shall

---

* First published in *RSR* 52 (1964) 497–537. Translated by John Ashton.

eventually (this text does after all hang together), after a number of detours, find a way through.

In the middle of what is often quite a disconcerting succession of clauses there is one short passage where the connection is easier to grasp and defend than elsewhere. This is in vv. 10–13. First, two short parallel phrases recount the rejection of the Logos by the world and by "his own". Many exegetes have suggested that the term "his own" refers to Israel;[3] if they are right, then it is reasonable to give to "world" the meaning it has in some other passages in the Johannine and Pauline writings,[4] that is to say, the Gentile world. This double interpretation, which appears the most natural one, will find confirmation as we gradually progress in our understanding of the Prologue.

Though both reject the Saviour, Israel and the Gentiles remain apart. The long sentence that follows (vv. 12–13) has a different theme: it tells of the acceptance of the Logos by the Christian community. Commentators have been struck for a long time by the strange and repetitive style of this passage and many hypotheses have been put forward to account for it. We must take especial note of the efforts of the textual critics to give a unified interpretation of the double formulaě in these verses.[5]

1 *Interpretation of verses 10–13*

After coming down firmly on the side of the *textus receptus* for vv. 12 and 13a, and deciding in favour of the (better attested) plural in v. 13b, we now have to attempt to interpret the passage. At first sight the repetitiveness of the style contrasts with the conciseness of the rest of the Prologue and its insistence on the divine sonship of the faithful appears to turn the Logos-hymn in a new direction. In fact we have already seen how vv. 10–11 probably refer to the rejection of Christ by the Gentiles and the Jews, which results in their remaining apart. Verses 12–13, on the contrary, celebrate the situation of the faithful, and scholars have rightly seen in them a mixture of Greek expressions and Semitisms. But we must be careful not to excise either one of these series of formulae, whose conjunction is actually full of meaning. By their common faith, Christians of both Gentile and Jewish origin recognize that the barrier that kept them apart has been destroyed (cf. Eph. 2:14); now they are a single people, whose double origin is indicated figuratively by *literary* doublets,[6] of Greek and Semitic origin, grouped together in the unity of a single sentence and a single community!

In 13a, however, the Semitic formula "blood ... flesh" and the Greek "will of man" are not so much juxtaposed as interwoven by the hook-word "will". Isolated, and put in the plural, the word "bloods" (*sic*!) is given, it would seem, a new meaning.[7] In the universalist context of the Prologue, this word could mean "race".[8] No one belonging to Christ should be either proud or ashamed of his origin, his race, his "blood". As A. Viard has well observed,[9] this is a polemical point against those Jews who were eager to take refuge behind their descent from Abraham (cf. John. 8:33–42). Now in Christ there can no longer be any question of different races, there is no longer either Greek or Jew. Furthermore, in order to be saved, all human beings must transcend their weak and sinful, that is to say, their fleshly origin. And, still more radically, they must transcend every human origin, because salvation is not within their control. Our divine sonship does not derive from any human origin, be it Jewish or Gentile, and antecedes both sinful Adam and the whole of humanity, for it goes back to the plan of God, "even as he chose us in him before the foundation of the world, that we should be holy and blameless before him. He destined us in love to be his sons through Jesus Christ, according to the purpose of his will" Eph. 1:4–5). This explains the use of the past tense to refer to this generation, "those who were born of God", a tense which puzzles the commentators because it appears to conflict with the power to *become* children of God. No doubt this sonship is effected at the moment Christ is accepted through faith and baptism, but that is possible only because of God's plan of salvation for all, thanks to which we were chosen in Christ and constituted "sons in the Son"[10] "before the foundation of the world". From this perspective it can be seen that vv. 12–13 are not a digression, still less an aberration calling for corrections. Together with vv. 10–11, with which they form a unit, they are at the centre of the Prologue.

2 *Gentiles and Jews*

This central position is confirmed by a study of the vocabulary. For if we compare the expressions employed in vv. 1–9 with those in vv. 14–18, we find that the vocabulary of the last five verses of the Prologue is clearly Semitic: flesh, dwell, we (3 times), glory, grace (4 times), truth (twice), law, Moses; the beginning, on the other hand, has a Greek ring to it: life (twice), light (7 times), man (3 times), world, the verb in the 3rd person plural. No doubt this "Greek" vocabulary is not foreign to Semitic thought; in fact it corresponds to the fashion in which a Semite would address himself to Greeks without abandoning his own natural way of thinking.[11] So the first nine verses of the Prologue form a block in which the key-words are repeated without ever getting as far as the concluding verses, and conversely the vocabulary of vv. 14–18 is not found at all in the beginning. This is particularly striking in view of the fact that the themes are closely related. However, it must be observed that the term Logos (as well as three or four other words in common use) occurs in both parts of the Prologue: so in the case of this one term we should probably refuse the dilemma of an exclusively Greek or Semitic influence and recognize its double origin.

Accordingly the two large blocks of the Prologue begin to stand out and its general problematic with them. This is closer to Ephesians than to the Colossians hymn. Through a failure to observe that the perspectives are quite different, the Prologue, especially the opening verses, has too often been compared with the hymn of Colossians. Paul reminds the Colossians, tempted as they are to place certain practices and rituals above Christ – as if Jesus alone were incapable of guaranteeing salvation – that Christ offers a total and radical salvation to any creature who accepts it, because he is the first principle of all creation: consequently his primacy is complete. Ephesians confronts a completely different problem. Like Romans, it is concerned with the need for a clear insight into the apparent incoherence of the history of salvation, and with grasping the unity of the divine plan. Now this is precisely the perspective of the Prologue. According to the blessing of Ephesians, the divine plan foreseen before the creation (Eph. 1:4), a mystery once hidden and now revealed, gathers under the single headship of Christ those of Jewish (Eph. 1:11–12), and those of Gentile origin (Eph. 1:13–14). So too in the Prologue of John, God through his Logos conceived, prepared and effected the salvation both of the Gentile world (John 1:1–9) and of Israel (1:10–11). Right from the beginning, despite certain rebuffs (1:10–11), he planned to unite them in the single community of the children of God (1:12–13).

This then is the controlling idea of the Prologue. Now that it has been set out for what it is we can allow ourselves to be guided by it and tackle the text itself, starting at the beginning.[12]

3 *Interpretation of vv. 1–5*

What meaning is to be given to v. 4a: "what happened[13] in him was (*or* is) life?" Does this refer, as is sometimes asserted, to what has been created in the Word? But most of creation is inanimate, and in any case the use of "life" simply in the sense of "natural life" is uncharacteristic of John. Does it refer then, to what happened in Christ at this birth, that is, through his flesh?[14] This idea, perfectly Johannine, is attractive, but is it possible to use the same verb, *ginomai*, of creation in v. 3 and of the incarnation, if this is right, in v. 4a?

Meaning of v. 3

But does v. 3, after all, really speak of creation? The word used here is not *ktizō* ("create") as in Colossians (1:15) or in Revelation (4:11; 10:6), nor even *poieō* ("do/make"), but *ginomai*, which means not "to be created" but "become/happen". If the central perspective of the Prologue is indeed God's universal plan, it is clear that the very wide meaning of this verb can perfectly express God's activity by means of his Logos throughout the history of the world, starting, of course, from the creation, right up to the incarnation, and including Israel's election and the natural law of the Gentiles. Everything that has happened – the history of salvation as well as the creation – happened through the Logos.

Here are some arguments in support of the very wide meaning that must be given to *ginomai*.

1   The use of this verb in the Prologue as a whole ought to shed light on its meaning in v. 3. No doubt in v. 10 the world has "become", that is, has been "created", unless this refers rather to the world of men which has come about in history; but in any case this is just one aspect of "becoming" in the Prologue. In fact the same verb is used for John the Baptist, who "comes", for Christ, who "came" before John and who "becomes" flesh, for the grace and truth which "come" through Jesus Christ, and for the faithful who "become" children of God.

2   The same (historical) meaning of the word is found in the first verse of Revelation: "The revelation of Jesus Christ, which God gave him to show to his servants what must soon take place (*genesthai*)."[15]

3   The same usage is found in the Septuagint, particularly in a passage in the book of Judith: "For thou hast done (*epoiēsas*) these things and those that went before and those that followed; thou hast designed (*dienoēthēs*) the things that are now, and those that are to come. Yea, the things thou didst intend came to pass (*egenēthēsan ha enenoēthēs*)" (Jdt. 9:5–6).

4   The community rule of Qumran has a number of passages quite close to John 1:3; and these, often quoted, but rarely used to cast light on the Prologue, concern not so much creation as all that happens in the history of salvation. In fact they occur in the context of human action (1QS 11:10), of the working out of God's plan 1QS 11:18–19) and of the revelation of his mysteries: "For without thee no way is perfect, and without thy will nothing is done . . . all things come to pass by thy will. There is none beside thee to dispute thy counsel or to

understand all thy holy design, or to contemplate the depth of thy mysteries and the power of thy might" (1QS 11:17–19).[16]

5   Finally, here is an extract from the Valentinian writing known as the *Gospel of Truth*. It is a paraphrase of the Prologue: "Nothing happens without him, nor does anything happen without the will of the Father" (37:21ff.). Here is the context of this passage: "Each one of his words is the work of his one will in the revelation of his Word. While they were still in the depth of his thought, the Word which was first to come forth revealed them" (37:4ff.).

All these clues, taken together, help us to grasp that verse 3 is essentially concerned with the realization of the divine plan.[17]

The Logos

Now that the meaning of v. 3 has been explained we are in a position to understand the precise sense of the word *Logos*.[18] Legitimate though it may be to use the first verses of the Prologue to "get back to" the Trinity, it is plain that the perspective here is not purely and simply trinitarian but above all "economic" [in the sense of the "economy" of salvation]. We have to do with the "foundation" of the world, and the title of Logos designates not only the *Word*, as we now call him, but Christ the Saviour.[19] There is good reason for seeing in this title an allusion to the Word of the Gospel, anticipated by the Word of the OT, at work in prophecy, in the law and in creation. If, however, the term Logos is to be given the precise meaning that belongs to it here, we must go back still further, beyond the visible manifestations of the Word to the inner Word itself, not that which exists necessarily and eternally in God, but the divine plan of salvation for all, conceived by God "before the foundation of the world", in other words the Word that is Christ, the Second Person of the Trinity, destined to take flesh and to save mankind. So here, in conformity with the leading idea of the Prologue, is the precise sense of the Logos, a sense which takes up one of the meanings of the Hebrew *dabar* (cf. e.g., Ezek. 38:10) and establishes a close link between the Word and the wisdom of the OT. Moreover, if we compare John with the Pauline corpus we find that the Logos corresponds exactly to the mystery which, for Paul, is embodied in the divine person of Christ. And it is probably no accident that in one passage in Paul the words "logos" and "mystery" are found side by side; is it not Paul's mission, "which was given to me for you [the Colossians], to make the word of God (*ton logon tou theou*) fully known, the mystery (*to mystērion*) hidden for ages and generations but now made manifest" (Col. 1:25f.). No doubt the Pauline Logos and the Johannine are not identical; nevertheless the link established by Paul between the Word of God and the mystery can pave the way for a more profound understanding of the Word as mystery – inner word, hidden mystery, plan of God. Similarly the Pauline presentation of Christ as the first-born of all creation, in whom all things were created (Col. 1:15f.) and in whom God conceived his plan of salvation for all (Eph. 1:3–10) can prepare our minds actually to identify Christ with this plan (John 1:1ff.).

By seeing in the Johannine Logos the sense of mystery or divine plan, we rediscover not only the context of Paul's thought but also that of Qumran, not to mention the *Gospel of Truth*: we have already cited some passages close to the Prologue which are pervaded by an atmosphere of plan and mystery; here one more will suffice: "All things came to pass by his knowledge; he establishes all things by his design and without him nothing is done" (IQS 11:11). In this sentence – so close to John 1:3 – what takes the place of the Johannine Logos is the design of God (*mḥšbh*; cf. Jer. 29:11; 51:29; Mic. 4:12; Ps. 33:10f.).

The meaning of vv. 4–5

After these remarks on the Logos and on v. 3 we can now usefully return to v. 4a. The ditch that might have separated vv. 3 and 4, the former interpreted with respect to creation, the latter with respect to the incarnation, has vanished. On both sides, in fact, we have to do with the way in which the plan of God is effectively enacted in the "becoming" of history. This way of referring to the incarnation by speaking of what happened in the Word may seem complicated, obscure and imprecise. But taking the words at their face value with no preconceived ideas one might well see in the formulation of v. 4a not just the incarnation but everything that happened to Christ, his whole earthly life and above all his death, resurrection and glorification. Of all these salvific events accomplished in and through Christ according to the plan of God it is fair and reasonable to say that they are *life*.[20]

One point of textual criticism remains to be cleared up. Should one read the imperfect or the present, "what came to pass in him *was* life" or "*is* life"? Here the oldest witnesses among the MSS, the versions and the Fathers split into two more or less equal groups,[21] so that it is difficult to decide on this point with any certainty. But this question is not really important, since whichever is the right tense of the verb the meaning remains virtually the same. If, provisionally and with some hesitation, we accept the imperfect tense, we must stress that the sense of duration carries on right to the present. Just as in one of the preceding phrases, the divinity of the Logos was expressed in an imperfect which goes beyond past and present, so here we should realize that the salvific events which Christ has assumed both were and have not ceased to be life for us. This extension in time is indicated by what follows, since the sentence ends up in the present tense: "the light shines in the darkness". Clearly this light is Christ, the eternal light who has come to his own in order to enlighten them, and who, having escaped from the darkness of death, now shines more brightly than ever as he continues, through his Church, to enlighten the world (cf. 1 John 2:8 and Acts 26:23). But at this point there seems to be a hitch in the progression of the sentence: after the description of Christ the Word, who is still enlightening mankind, we appear to be thrust back into the past: "and darkness has not mastered him". Where is the continuity of movement at this point, and in the first place what does this phrase mean?

There are two possible meanings: acceptance and understanding, or hostility and assault. Which best fits the context? Most of the Fathers opted for the negative meaning, which does in fact accord better with the fundamental meaning of this verb, and, most important, corresponds with its other occurrences in the Gospel of John.[22] Furthermore, the aorist tense does seem to refer to a specific event in the past. Taken together, these facts suggest an allusion to Christ the Word's successful struggle against the powers of darkness at his death and resurrection. But what is the purpose of such an allusion at this point in the development of the ideas of the Prologue? Starting from the first beginnings, we had already reached the salvation offered in the present by the Word of life – and now we have been thrust backwards and compelled to watch the fight and the victory of Christ. But there is nothing so surprising in this: Semitic literature in general and the Johannine writings in particular contain many such reversals. There is only one real problem left: does this move backwards at the end of v. 5 fit into a well-organized whole? And this leads us to examine the structure of the Prologue.

4 *The Structure of the Prologue*

What kind of structure can be plotted of the Prologue? Is there a step by step chronological progression,[23] a series of successive waves,[24] or is there a concentric pattern?[25] The last solution is suggested by a number of chiastic correspondences: incarnation[26] in vv. 9 and 14; witness of John the Baptist in vv. 6–8 and 15; Word or Son close to God in vv. 1–2 and 18. So N. W. Lund and M. E. Boismard are basically right. But their proposed structure must be corrected by shifting the centre slightly. In our view this is to be found in vv. 10–13; next the significance of each of the two branches must be specified (one concerns the Gentiles, the other the Jews); lastly the manner of the construction must be more closely determined, since the two branches are not linear in form, but each comprises within it a further tiny concentric pattern.

In the first section (1–9) we start with the Logos who was with God from the beginning (1–2) and in and through the history of God's plan (3) we come to the accomplishment of salvation (4–5a). At this point we move progressively backwards in time: from an allusion to the death and resurrection of Christ (5b), witness of John the Baptist (6–8), the incarnation in progress (9). The second section (14–18) is constructed in the same concentric fashion but in the reverse order: we start from the incarnation in progress (14) and after the witness of John the Baptist (15) we arrive at the salvific action of Christ who gives of his fullness (16). Here we begin to go back again, first with a mention of Moses and the law (17) and then by introducing the Son in the bosom of the Father (18).[27] Prescinding from the central section (10–13), the form of this construction is like a W.[28]

Taking account of what has been said so far, we can now offer a translation of the Prologue, with the proviso that the key-word, Logos, must be left untranslated, since there is no French [or English] word meaning both Word and Plan. Here the dominant sense is probably that of "Plan", but to restrict the meaning to this might fail to do justice to the heart of the matter, which is the relation between Word and Plan.

A.	a)	(1) In the beginning was the Logos, and the Logos was with God and the Logos was God. (2) He was in the beginning with God.
	b)	(3) Everything happened through him, and without him nothing happened.
	e)	(4) What happened in him was life, and the life was the light of men, and the light shines in the darkness, and the darkness has not overcome it.
	d)	(6) There came [29] a man sent from God, whose name was John.
		(7) He came for testimony, to bear witness to the light, that all might believe through him.
		(8) He was not the light, but the witness of the light.
	c)	(9) The true light which enlightens every man was coming into the world.
B.	—	(10) He was in the world, and the world happened through him, and the world did not know him.

−		(11) He came to his own home, and his own people did not receive him.
+ +		(12) But to all who had received him he gave the power to become children of God, to those who believe in his name, (13) who not of bloods, nor of the will of the flesh, nor of the will of man, but of God were engendered.
A′.	c′)	(14) And the Logos became flesh, and dwelt among us, and we have seen his glory, glory which he has from his Father as his only Son, full of grace and truth.
	d′)	(15) John bears witness to him and cries: "That was he of whom I said: He who comes after me has passed in front of me, for ahead of me he was.
	e′)	(16) Yes, of his fullness we have all received, grace upon grace.
	b′)	(17) For the law was given through Moses; grace and truth come through Jesus Christ.
	a′)	(18) No one has ever seen God; the only Son, who is in the bosom of the Father, he has made him known.

5 *The role of John the Baptist in the Prologue*

One final question is worth raising: what are we to make of the double mention of John the Baptist in the Prologue? It is often said that these two passages have been inserted into an older narrative. But this does not resolve the fundamental problem, since on this hypothesis one would have to ask oneself what was the reason for adding these verses. In any case the presence of this double mention requires explanation. As has often been rightly stated, John may have wished to show honour to his previous master, whilst at the same time trying to draw over to Christ the laggard disciples of the precursor. But one may go further. In the realization of the plan of salvation for all John the Baptist plays an important role. The version of his preaching given in the Gospels is marked by a striking universalism. This can easily be seen by comparing John the Baptist with the Qumran sect, and to be completely convinced it is enough to reread Matt. 3:9 and Luke 3:8, 10–14.[30]

Given this basic truth, the occasional remarks concerning the Baptist's missionary activity, though not as clear and conclusive as we might have hoped, can help us to discern the importance of this feature of his preaching.[31] Offering, along with his disciples, a teaching accessible to the Gentiles, he paved the way for the universalism of Christian salvation. And it is this, no doubt, that the fourth evangelist wishes to affirm in his Prologue. That is why the Baptist whom he presents witnesses to the universality of Christ before Greeks as well as Jews. To the Greeks he appears as a witness of the Light, but since, though representing Israel, he nevertheless refuses to identify himself with the Light, he is implicitly inviting the Gentiles to go beyond the particularism of the Torah. Speaking to the Jews (John 1:15), he points to Jesus as the Messiah who not only came before him but also preceded every prophetic mission as well as the Torah and Israel: the mission of such a saviour could not but burst out of the framework of the Jewish nation. So implicitly John the Baptist is inviting Israel to embrace universalism. Thus his two acts of witness in the Prologue, far from being digressions, belong integrally to the realization of the divine plan to unite in a single nation all those born of God.

Conclusions

Before summarizing the principle ideas of the Prologue let us rapidly review the points in favour of the interpretation that has just been put forward.

(a) Points in favour

Without the key to the Prologue, there are several passages difficult enough to tempt us to use what manuscript evidence is available, weak though it is, in order to emend the text or else, as in vv. 3–4, to evade the problems posed by the majority of ancient witnesses. This essay has at every point – in vv. 12, 13a, 13b, 3–4 and 4a – followed the textual evidence with the utmost objectivity. Not only does the interpretation offered here fit these supposedly difficult passages perfectly well, but it also provides an explanation that justifies their presence and gives them the sense which is required. This is a very strong argument in its favour. Accordingly explanations are given of the redundancies of vv. 12–13, the plural "were engendered" in 13b, the apparent conflict of tenses (past fact, future power) v. 12. Verse 4 is interpreted by what precedes and what follows, the punctuation between vv. 3 and 4 is justified, the present "shines" takes its place in the general development of the passage; and it becomes clear why the Fathers, accustomed to understand v. 3 of the creative activity of the Logos and looking for a purely chronological order in what follows, were so hesitant about what meaning to give to v. 4.

In addition, our interpretation is supported by a series of literary data that at first sight are quite surprising – parallelism of ideas between vv. 1–9 and 14–18 and yet a completely different choice of words. To explain these facts as due to chance is unsatisfactory; a proper solution must account both for the meaning and for the precise placing of every single word. Only then can what at first looks like a maze be transferred into an intelligible pattern.

Lastly, this interpretation, instead of basing itself on ideas more characteristic of the second century than the first, is in perfect accord with the general problematic of the NT. Nowadays the problem of the union of Jews and Gentiles within the same Christian community is no longer as acute as it was in the earliest times; which is why we are all too easily tempted to treat the question as of slight importance. This would be a mistake, not only because there is in every Christian both a "Jew" who is "assured" of possessing the gift of God and a "pagan" who expects everything from God's grace, and these tendencies must somehow be held together; but also because to ignore this problem is to risk misunderstanding the real meaning of numerous passages of the New Testament.[32] This would entail passing over those splendid passages which introduce us to the unity of God's salvific plan. Although the terms of the question are no longer the same, it is more than ever necessary to rediscover in the holy Scripture the great fundamental truths concerning the unity of the divine plan, creation in and through Christ, the role of the Logos in history, the universality of salvation. These great passages illuminate one another; we have attempted to interpret the Prologue of John in the light of Ephesians and we are thereby enabled to establish a link between the Pauline "mystery" and the Logos. Such comparisons, which remove anachronisms and restore to the texts their proper intellectual and socio-historical context, constitute a reliable and fruitful method of exegesis.

(b) Resumé

In presenting a broad and summary outline of the teaching of the Prologue and the development of its ideas, it is best to begin by placing it in the context of the plan of salvation for all. There are two main sections, one addressed to the Gentiles (vv. 1–9) the other to the Jews (vv. 14–18). Then one can see that the Logos refers to Christ the Saviour as he was foreseen by God the Father in the Son and as he accomplished the divine plan. The opening words of the Prologue, "in the beginning", do not refer to the Trinity, which has no beginning, but to the history of the world, and one must return to the beginnings of this history in order to get a reliable picture of the divine plan. In vv. 1–2 the propositions linked by hook-words and held together in an inclusion by the repetition of "in the beginning" speak of a divine being ("and the Logos was God") distinct from the Father ("and the Logos was [turned] towards God"). From v. 3 onwards this plan is brought into effect: everything without exception – the creation, the history of the nations, the conscience of mankind, the provisional Mosaic law, the incarnation, the universalism of the Church – everything is accomplished by the one who is the divine plan. Everything that has happened "through his mediation" (*di' autou*) played its part in the realization of the divine plan, but it is only by the events that happened directly through and in him (*en autǭ*), that is to say in Jesus Christ, that the plan of salvation has been accomplished. These events were and still are for us the source of eternal life, and what is Life itself but Jesus Christ as he lived among men to bring them light, a light which continues to shine and enlighten all men, living as they do in the shadow of death? Christ of course was assailed by darkness, which tried to eliminate him by putting him to death, but the Risen Christ has triumphed over the darkness. This victory of Christ, expressed in a universal language accessible to all, was anticipated by John the Baptist, the precursor of the Messiah and the precursor of the Church's universal mission. On behalf of the chosen people, he announced to the Gentiles that they must go beyond ancient Israel and the law of Moses; it was not in these that the true Light was to be found, since they simply prepared the way for the coming of the Saviour. And this is he, the true Light, coming into the world.

This passage through time takes us back, then, as far as the event of the incarnation, which is where the section devoted to the Gentiles concludes. Before taking up the theme of incarnation with the Jews, the author first (vv. 10–13) describes the rejection of the Logos/Christ by both Gentiles and Jews, whose rejection keeps them apart; then he portrays the community of the faithful who despite their diverse origins are united by their faith: whatever their race or their human ancestry, the power they have received to become children of God shows that from the beginning God has chosen them in Christ to be his adoptive children.

Parallel with vv. 1–9, addressed to the Gentile world, is a second section (vv. 14–18) devoted to Israel. In conformity with God's promises it was to Israel that the Saviour-Messiah revealed himself. But if he came in the kenosis of the *flesh* it was not in order to restrict his activity: the glory he has as only Son extends beyond the limits set by flesh and race. But for the sake of the Jews the language used to express this "salvific" glory is Semitic: the only Son is "full of grace and truth". Whilst recalling the formulae of the OT, his expression goes beyond them in its insistence upon the gratuitousness of the gift that opens the door to universalism. At the same time Israel is invited to associate itself with John the Baptist in declaring that the Messiah "comes after me" but "he has passed ahead of me because before me he was". By his origin and heavenly glorification he goes beyond John the Baptist and Israel and belongs to all men. This does not mean that believing Jews are rejected: the fullness of Christ is in the first place for them, because in employing the first person the evangelist is speaking on behalf of those of his own race. Yet the adjective "all" excludes particularism. In fact grace and truth[33] come from Christ: Moses and his law were only a preparation, a provisional stage, a remote approach on the part of God. And this passage through time takes us back, as in vv. 1–2, to the beginnings, to the only Son in the bosom of the Father.

NOTES

[In one or two minor details I have followed the version of this article used in Lamarche's book on NT Christology, *Christ vivant* (Paris, 1966) 87–140. Tr.]

1 See for instance R. Schnackenburg, "Logos–Hymnus und johanneischer Prolog", *BZ* 1 (1957) 69–109.

2 [Why this Greek phrase, usually rendered "what was made", must be left untranslated here will emerge in the course of the discussion. Tr.]

3 Most ancient and modern authors see "his own" as a reference to Israel (e.g. Cyprian, Cyril of Alexandria, Chrysostom; Zahn, Lagrange, Boismard, Mollat, Cullman, against Irenaeus, Clement of Alexandria, Origen; Loisy, Bultmann, Wikenhauser). In the Old Testament *ta idia* means home, and the home of God is the Temple and Israel. In John *hoi idioi* denotes those who have been chosen (cf. 13:1 compared with 17:9–11 and 15:19); so here in the Prologue it most probably refers to Israel, the chosen people.

4 Cf. 1 John 2:2 and especially Rom. 11:12–15.

5 [At this point Lamarche introduces a section of some dozen pages on the textual criticism of vv. 12–13. There is some very slight support (though none from any Greek MS) for a shorter version of v. 12, omitting the clause "to those who believe(d) in his name", and of v. 13, omitting either "not of blood ... flesh" or "nor of the will of man"; and there is marginally greater support in v. 13 for a singular verb which would give the meaning "was born" (which would have to be taken to apply to the Logos) instead of the much better attested "were born" (i.e., the faithful). Lamarche rejects these variants, and dismisses the hypothesis which M.-E. Boismard, in *RB* 57 (1950) 401–408, builds upon them. Tr.]

6 Apart from certain nuances, to which we will return, the divine sonship of v. 12 corresponds to the divine birth of v. 13. Within these verses, "those who received him" corresponds to "who believed in his name", and "flesh and blood" corresponds to "the will of man".

7 [Problematic in Greek, this plural is equally intolerable in French and in English. Tr.] This word has been causing problems for a very long time. Fathers such as Justin, Irenaeus, the author of the *Epistula Apost.*, Origen (once: *In Matt.*, fr. 11), who apply the verse to the virgin birth of Christ or refer to this in other, similar terms generally avoid speaking of blood (in either singular or plural). So they are careful not to imply that Christ was not born from the blood of the Virgin Mary. The plural might remind us of the union of the "blood" of the man with the "blood"

of the woman. But that would be to attach an excessive importance to it, and in any case it would have been easy to state categorically that Christ was not born "from the union of bloods". If the plural ("were born") is retained, the expression "not from the bloods" points us in a different direction.

8   This is the meaning, in some MSS, in Acts 17:26. But this is a matter of semantics, where authenticity has only a chronological importance.

9   *Ami du Clergé* 68 (1958) 520.

10 The idea of "predestination" is found in other Johannine texts as well, e.g. John 8:42, 47; 10:26; 11:52; 18:37; 1 John 4:6; 5:1; Rev. 13:8; 17:8. There is no contradiction between this and the idea of salvation for all. Nor should one try to set "predestination" against free-will. On the question of Christian *syngeneia* ("kinship"), see E. des Places, *Bibl.* 44 (1963) 304–32.

11 See for example the comparisons which C. H. Dodd (1955) 55f. makes between John and the *Corpus Hermeticum* (18f.) or Philo (55f. and 201 ff.) with regard to life and light. Similarly C. K. Barrett (1955) 131. These comparisons with Greek culture do not miss the profoundly Semitic meaning of these ideas in the Johannine writings.

12 [Here the writer inserts another long (10 page) essay in textual criticism, arguing that the stop should be placed *before* the last two words of v. 3, *ho gegonen*. (The alternative, adopted by the RSV, is to place the stop at the end of v. 3.) Subsequently, K. Aland has put the same case at even greater length: "Eine Untersuchung zu Joh 1:3, 4. Über die Bedeutung eines Punktes", *ZNW* 59 (1968) 174–209. Tr.]

13 [The French "est devenu" could also be translated "became" but not "was made" All three are possible renderings of the Greek *gegonen*. Tr.]

14 This is the meaning favoured by the interpretations of Hilary and Ambrose. M.-F. Lacan has taken up and extended the idea, *RSR* 45 (1957) 61–78. He takes v. 4 to refer to the gift of eternal life by the incarnate Word. In many respects this patristic exegetical study appears to us fundamental.

15 Cf. Rev. 1:19; 4:1; 22:6.

16 The words used in these passages (*hyh* and *'sh*) far from being confined to the idea of creation [*br'*; cf. 1QS 3, 17.25), signify everything that happens and takes place through the initiative of God. This can be confirmed by comparing these passages with other texts from the Community Rule, e.g. 1QS 3:15, the beginning of the section on the two spirits: "From the God of Knowledge comes all that is and shall be (*kwl hwwh wnhyyh*)". See further 8:4, 12 and 9:3: "When these things happen (*bhywt*) in Israel"; also 9:24: "All that happens to him (*hn'sh bw*)"; and 9:26: "he shall bless his Maker (*'wsyw*) and declare [his wondrous deeds] in all that happens (*yhyh*)". [For his translation of these texts, which the English follows closely, but not exactly, Lamarche acknowledged a debt to A. Dupont-Sommer, P. Guilbert and P. Wernberg-Möller. Tr.]

17 As early as 1958 T. E. Pollard had arrived at the same conclusions: "Cosmology and the Prologue of the Fourth Gospel", *Vigiliae Christianae* 12 (1958) 147–53. Besides, this interpretation is likely to be corroborated by a study of the earliest Fathers, who often had more penetrating insight than we do into the Prologue and the Logos. M. Méhat, an expert on Clement of Alexandria, has been kind enough to inform me that this author almost always linked John 1:3 with human and salvation history.

18 In explaining John's choice of this word, one must on no account set Greek against Semitic influences. On the contrary, the two will have given one another mutual

reinforcement, with the result that the term is found both in the Greek and the Jewish section of the Prologue. Yet even the vocabulary of the first section of the Prologue betrays the struggle of a Jewish author trying to be a Greek to the Greeks whilst continuing to think in a Semitic language. So one should not exaggerate the extent of Greek influence on the *meaning* of words in the Prologue.

19 This can be seen clearly from the two other instances of the word Logos in the Johannine writings (1 John 1:1 and Rev. 19:13). From this perspective the Logos might be called the first-born of all creation. In this respect the creed of Eusebius of Caesarea was thoroughly scriptural. But one can see why this profound and complex christological concept gave rise to misunderstandings in the early centuries. Perhaps we should pay more attention to the precise meaning of the Johannine Logos both in the study of Patristic Christology and in current developments in theology.

20 Cf. John 6:63, "the words that I have spoken to you are spirit and life". Now the deeds of the Word are his true words. Observe the absence of the article before "life" both in John 1:4 and in John 6:63.

21 [At this point the author gives a comprehensive list of the witnesses in favour of each reading. Tr.]

22 John 6:17; 12:35; and cf. 8:3.

23 See, e.g., S. Aujedo *Estudios Biblicos* 15 (1956) 295–402 (first step: 1–11; second step: 14ab; third step: 16 and 18).

24 Cf. e.g., M.-F. Lacan, *RSR* 45 (1957) 75–8; and *Lumière et Vie* (July 1957) no. 33, 90–110 (first wave, 1–5; second, 6–14; third, 15–18).

25 See N. W. Lund *ATR* 13 (1931) 41 (A = 1–2; B = 3.4.5.6.10ab; C = 10c.11.12; D = 13; C′ = 14; B′ = 16–17a; A′ = 17–18); and M.-E. Boismard, *Le Prologue de Saint Jean* (1953) 107 (A = 1–2; B = 3; C = 4–5; D = 6–8; E = 9–11; F = 12–13; E′ = 14; D′ = 15; C′ = 15; B′ = 17; A′ = 18). In this respect we may leave on one side the hypothetical reconstructions of a primitive Logos hymn. The problem here is connected but different.

26 The precise meaning of v. 9 is disputed. Is it (a) the Word "was the true light that enlightens every man coming into the world", or (b) "the true light that enlightens every man was coming into the world"? Each rendering has support among the ancient versions, the Fathers and modern exegetes, and the two sides are equally strong. It is the second rendering, however, which is to be preferred. No doubt the Aramaic expression "coming into the world" often denotes mankind, but here the concept of man has already been used, whereas the expression "coming into the world", precisely because of its regular meaning, admirably describes the incarnation. Moreover the same expression is often used by John to refer to Christ's coming on earth, and it would be surprising if there were no link between the present verse and certain passages like John 3:19: "the light has come into the world", or 12:46: "I have come as light into the world".

27 The Son is actually present now in the bosom of the Father; this is underlined by the present participle. Even so, this presence is also (and importantly so) identical with the situation of the Logos who was with God from the beginning (vv. 1–2); for it is this initial situation which made it possible for Christ to reveal the Father to us.

28 Within the two sections it is not properly speaking a question of "parallels", but of a descending movement with an ascending movement to correspond. Moreover the strict parallelism between the two sections is softened by certain variations which introduce an element of lively harmony. For instance, the John the Baptist passage

is longer in the first section than in the second, but the reverse is true of the account of the incarnation.

29 [The French verb "arriver" can mean either "happen" or "come" and so enjoys some of the fruitful ambiguity of the Greek. English is forced to choose between the two. Tr.]

30 See too the interesting article by C. H. Dodd, "Behind a Johannine Dialogue", *More New Testament Studies* (Manchester, 1968) 41–57, where he detects in John 8:33–47 the same atmosphere of thought as we have found in the Prologue. In particular he compares the dialogue on Abraham (John 8:33ff.) with the declarations of John the Baptist (Matt. 3:9 and Luke 3:8).

31 It is quite possible that some of John's disciples came from among the Gentiles. This is the most likely explanation of the ignorance of some of the Baptist's disciples concerning the Holy Spirit, and this is how F. F. Bruce interprets this in his commentary on Acts. For Jews, aware of the messianic promises, would never have answered: "No, we have never even heard that there is a Holy Spirit" (Acts 19:2).

Furthermore, when alluding to those who had sowed in Samaria (John 4:38), Christ may well have been underlining the missionary activity of the Baptist. J. A. T. Robinson (1962) 61–66, makes out a good case for this: "The 'Others' of John 4:38". The most important evidence in favour of this allusion is that Aenon, where John baptized (John 3:23) is probably located in Samaria, not far from Shechem. To this may be added a number of traditions in which it is difficult to disentangle legend from history. Jerome's Latin translation of Eusebius' *Onomasticon* refers to Sebaste, "where the remains of Saint John the Baptist were buried" (*GCS* 11, 155. 21f.). Jerome mentions the Baptist's tomb at Sebaste on other occasions also (PL 22, 491 and 889). Rufinus (*Hist. eccl.* 2, 28 = PL 21, 536) and Theodoret (*Hist. eccl.* 3, 3 = PG 82, 1092) report the violation of the Baptist's tomb at Sebaste. One may assume then that he was buried in this Samarian town by some of his disciples from the region. Finally, according to Clement's *Recogn.* 2, 7f. (= PG 1, 1251f.) and *Hom.* (2, 22ff. = PG 2, 89–92), Simon the magician, who was born at Gitton, near Sheehem (cf. Justin, *1 Apol.* 26, 1–3 = PG 6,368) and who lived in Samaria (cf. Acts 8:9–24) claimed to have been a disciple of John the Baptist. No doubt these traditions are not entirely reliable, but the simple fact that they arose in the first place seems to show that a link was readily made between John the Baptist and Samaria.

32 For example it is only with this problem in mind that one can fully understand the opening of Romans (Rom. 1:3–4), where Jesus is introduced as the Jewish Messiah by reason of his temporal birth and as the Saviour of mankind by his heavenly glorification.

33 In the apocalyptic and sapiential tradition as it appears in John's Gospel, the word "truth", as I. de la Potterie has well shown ("La Verità in San Giovanni" [below, pp. 53–66, esp. 54f. and 58]), is frequently synonymous with "mystery" and denotes the divine plan revealed to men. This is probably the meaning of v. 17: "grace and truth came about through Jesus Christ".

3

*The Truth in Saint John**

IGNACE DE LA POTTERIE

All New Testament scholars will readily concede that the idea of truth is one of the central theological concepts in the thought of John. So it is surprising how few studies have been devoted to this concept. In particular there is only a handful of recent works on the major problem of the literary background of the theme. Yet the exegesis of the passages in which the term *alētheia* ("truth") occurs must depend to a great extent on the solution to this semantic and literary-historical problem.[1]

I *The background of the theme*

1   On this point the commonest view is that of R. Bultmann and C. H. Dodd. According to Bultmann the Johannine concept of truth can only be explained on the basis of hellenistic and gnostic dualism: it denotes the eternal, subsistent reality of the divine insofar as this is revealed to men.[2] Dodd's position is exactly the same, except that he places greater emphasis on the Platonic background and less upon the gnostic antecedents: for John truth means "the ultimate Reality as revealed in Christ",[3] "eternal reality as revealed to men."[4]

This interpretation has been adopted by many authors, in particular by A. Wikenhauser, R. Schnackenburg and A. Augustinović.[5] But a serious difficulty must be raised against it straightaway: if John is dependent on a dualism for which truth is the essence of the divine, how is it that there is not a single instance in which he actually applies the term to God? He tells us that God is spirit (John 4:24), love (1 John 4:8, 16) and light (1 John 1:5) but not that he is truth, unlike the later Platonic and Augustinian tradition. Consequently certain later authors are less positive: they think that this Johannine concept represents a synthesis of the biblical and Greek notions of truth.[6]

The error common to all these different explanations, in our

---

* First published in *RivB* 11 (1963) 3–24. Translated by John Ashton.

opinion, is that of supposing that a choice has to be made between two alternatives: the biblical background or the Greek background. In the Bible, as is well known, *'emet* means basically what is stable and solid: in many cases the word has practically the sense either of faithfulness or of justice[7] – which is certainly no longer true of the Johannine *alētheia*. But in later Judaism, that is to say in apocalyptic and wisdom literature, especially at Qumran,[8] the word takes on a partially new meaning, different both from the old Hebrew meaning and from the Greek. This is where the immediate background of John's *alētheia* is to be sought.[9]

2   What is the sense of the word "truth" in this apocalyptic and wisdom tradition? The term has still a moral significance, as it does in the Bible, but with a different shade of meaning: it is righteousness or rectitude rather than faithfulness. Frequently it also assumes a new significance which directly anticipates the New Testament: it then denotes the *revealed truth*, the teaching of wisdom. In fact the word "truth" is often synonymous with "mystery" and accordingly denotes the divine plan which is revealed to men. As early as Daniel (10:21) the "book of truth" is that which contains the divine plan for the times of salvation. The same association between the two terms is found very distinctly in the Book of Wisdom (cf. 6:22). The chief text is 3:9. The preceding verses describe the lot of the just at the moment of judgement; v. 9 continues: "Those who trust in him will understand truth." How is this verse to be explained? It should not be understood in the sense of the Hebrew *'emet* ("they will experience the *faithfulness* of God"), nor in the Greek, Platonic sense ("they will contemplate the very *reality* of God"), but in a sense we could call apocalyptic: "The just will understand truth" at the moment of judgement, in other words they will comprehend the *divine plan*, whose whole wisdom will be finally revealed to them.[10] The same meaning appears in the apocrypha (e.g. *1 Enoch* 21:5) and in the writings of Qumran. The author of one of the hymns exclaims: "I praise thee, Lord, for thou hast made me understand thy truth and granted knowledge of thy marvellous mysteries" (1QH 7, 26–27); the sect recommends to its members "discretion regarding the mysteries of knowledge" (1QS 4, 6).

Besides the truth/mystery parallelism, we find associated more than once the concepts of truth and wisdom. So in Proverbs: "Buy truth and do not sell it; buy wisdom, instruction and understanding" (23:23). And in the Greek text of Ecclesiasticus the sage addresses to his disciples this magnificent exhortation: "Strive even to death for the truth, and the Lord God will fight for you" (Sir. 4:28).

In these writings, with different shades of meaning in each, it may be said that truth is at once a theme of revelation and a theme of wisdom. It denotes the revelation of the mystery of God and also his revealed teaching itself, wisdom. This teaching takes on the force of a religious norm, which explains all the moral connotations of the concept of truth (e.g. in the opposition between the "sons of truth" and the "sons of iniquity" at Qumran). As a result the term can sometimes take on an extremely wide meaning: at Qumran it comes to denote the ensemble of the religious ideas of the sons of the Covenant, as may be seen from the various names they bestow on themselves: "the community of truth" (1QS 2, 24–26), "the privilege of possessing the truth" (1QM 13, 12), "a foundation of truth for Israel" (1QS 5, 5).

3   In view of the importance of the question, we must demonstrate clearly, even if sketchily, that John's terminology is really derived from this apocalyptic and wisdom background. It is true that he does not use the terms "mystery" or "wisdom"; but all the Johannine expressions that include the word "truth" are connected with this tradition. Thus the formulae: "walk in the truth" (2 John 4; 3 John 3, 4);[11] "do the truth" (John 3:21; 1 John 1:6);[12] "in truth"[13] which are already found elsewhere in the Bible; similarly the expression "spirit of truth", already found in the Testaments of the Twelve Patriarchs (*T.Jud.* 20:1, 5) and at Qumran (1QS 3:6, 18, 19; 4:21, 23; 13:10). None of these expressions is found in Greek or hellenistic texts.

An even more convincing proof of our thesis is furnished by John's manner of expressing himself (which has received little attention), and first of all the close connection he establishes between the theme of truth and that of the *word*: "Your word is truth", says Jesus to his Father in the high-priestly prayer (John 17:17). This points us in the direction of the OT and Judaism, where the expression "word of truth" occurs frequently:[14] all these passages belong to the wisdom tradition. It is also because of this connection between word and truth that Jesus can say in John 8:40: "I have told you the truth." Now we know that in John the verb used here, *lalein* ("to speak"), is used of revelation. So this verse proves that for John the word "truth" does not denote the typically Greek idea of divine reality but the word of God, the revelation Jesus comes to impart to mankind.

The same verse 8:40 also says that the truth revealed by Jesus is that which he has heard from the Father. Here too we have to do with a fundamentally Jewish expression. In hellenistic and gnostic dualism the truth is not a word that is listened to but the divine reality which is seen and "contemplated" at the conclusion of the spiritual ascent. Thus, according to the *Corpus Hermeticum*, the supreme vision consists in contemplating "the beauty of truth" (*C.H.* 8, 3). If Jesus says that he is revealing the truth which he has "heard" from the Father, his way of speaking is totally different from hellenistic dualism; on the contrary it is much closer to apocalyptic. In fact we see in this literature that the men on God's side, beneficiaries of his heavenly revelation, *listen to and hear* the interpretation offered of the mystery by the angel/interpreter (4 Ezra 10, 35; *1 Enoch* 14:24; 14:1, etc.); these rival interpretations are precisely what the Book of Daniel calls "truth" (cf. Dan. 11: 2).

In brief, the conclusion of the first part of our exposition is that the literary milieu to which John is closest in his use of the theme of truth is not Hellenism or gnostic dualism but that of the last books of the Bible, especially the apocalyptic and wisdom traditions of Judaism.

II *The word of the Father and Christ the Truth*

1   As has already been observed, John more than once establishes a connection between the themes of truth and the word of God. In the first letter, he draws a clear parallel between them in two verses whose sense is recognizably the same: "the truth is not in you" (1:8) and "his word is not in you" (1:10).

The same idea is found in the high-priestly prayer, where Jesus prays on behalf of his disciples: "sanctify them in the truth: your word is truth" (John 17:17).[15] Here too the truth of which Christ speaks is the word of the Father. But it is in John 8 that the connection between the two themes is most clearly underlined: in no passage in the Johannine writings do the words *logos* ("word") and *alētheia* ("truth") occur so frequently:[16] here, we may note, the first of these words always refers to the word of Christ. Nowhere in the passage are the two concepts closer than in vv. 31–2: 'If you continue in my *word*, you are truly my disciples, and you will know the *truth*." This is the truth which Christ has heard from the Father and comes to proclaim (8:40); he is in the world to testify to the truth (18:37; cf. 1 John 5:6). So the truth is the revelation which comes to us from the Father and is passed on to us in the actual word of Jesus. To become true disciples of Christ, one must not only believe in his words (cf. 8:31a), one must also continue in his word (8:31b); his word must find a place in us (8:37) and we must go on discovering the truth (8:32).[17] The whole growth of the life of faith is outlined here.

2   What we have said proves that there is a close relationship between the revealed truth and the actual person of Jesus. Other passages state this explicitly. Jesus is not just a vehicle of revelation like Moses and

the other prophets, who remained, so to speak, exterior to their message. The contrast between the revelation of the OT and that of Christ is strongly emphasized at the end of the Prologue: "the law was given through Moses; grace and truth became (real) through Jesus Christ" (1:17). The old revelation contained in the law was an expression of God's wisdom (Sir. 24:22–3; Bar. 4:1), but still an imperfect one: only in Christ has the total and definitive revelation arrived.

What is the object of this revelation, the content of this truth? The following verse tells us: "the only Son, facing the bosom of the Father, he is the one who has revealed [*sic*]."[18] These words describe the sonship of the Word, eternally "facing the bosom of the Father", by whom he was engendered. This divine life, this filial life is what the Word comes to reveal to mankind. So we get an even better understanding of the unusual terminology of v. 17: "the truth became (*egeneto*) (real) through Jesus Christ: the becoming of the Christian revelation is linked to the actual "becoming" of the Word made flesh: it is in him that the divine life has appeared among us (cf. 1 John 1:2).

To conclude, then, what John affirms in these texts is that the revelation of the divine life is made through the actual person of the incarnate Word. That is why he is said in v. 14 to be "full of grace and truth": with the appearance among us of the very Word of God, there appears at the same period of the history of salvation the fullness of truth.

One of Jesus' sayings at the Last Supper rounds off this teaching: "I am the way, the truth and the life; no one comes to the Father but by me" (14:6). Probably none of John's sayings on the truth has given rise to such divergent interpretations as this. The first question to decide is a literary one: what internal relationship is to be seen between the three members of the phrase: the way, the truth and the life. For many authors the last two terms are the most important, telling us where the way is leading; according to this view Jesus calls himself the way to truth and life. This is the exegesis of St Augustine, in which the influence of his Neoplatonic education may be discerned. His interpretation has been excellently summed up by St Thomas: "He is both the way and the way's end: the way in his humanity, the end in his divinity. As man, then, he declares: 'I am the way'; as God, he adds 'the truth and the life'."[19] A similar idea is to be found in some modern interpreters, notably Bultmann. But the literary analysis of the passage demonstrates the impossibility of this interpretation;[20] to see this it is enough to look at the second part of the verse ("no one comes to the Father, but by me") which is parallel to the first:

the main idea is that of the *way*, and this is also true of the first part. The end to which the way leads is not the truth but the Father. The two other nouns ("the truth and the life") are to be regarded simply as an explanation of the declaration of Jesus, "I am the way". So Christ is our way to the Father inasmuch as he is the truth and the life; it is in virtue of these gifts that he fulfils his role of mediator on the way to the Father.[21]

What is the theological significance of this solemn declaration of Jesus? First of all it makes plain that he is essentially the revealer of the Father, the one who passes on to us the words of the Father. But the phrase used here compels us to go beyond this purely functional interpretation. As St Jerome[22] observed, no prophet or apostle could say, as Christ did, "I am the truth". Here once again is the teaching of the Prologue, but expressed with all possible clarity: the identification, pure and simple, between the person of Christ and the truth. To understand and justify this declaration of Jesus, we are forced to contemplate the mystery of his person, the mystery of the trinitarian relationships between Father and Son. The broader context of 14:6 (cf. 14:7–14) as well as the parallel of the Prologue, compels us to say that if Christ is the truth and the life because he can lead us to the Father, this depends on the fact that he himself, in person, is in close communion with the Father: he is in the Father and the Father is in him; the words he speaks he does not speak of his own accord (vv. 10–11); he who knows the Son also knows the Father (v. 7); he who has seen Christ with the eyes of faith has seen the Father (v. 9). So if Jesus is the truth, this depends on the fact that in his own person he reveals to us the mystery of his trinitarian life, the intimate and vital relations which unite him to the Father.

The content of the word *alētheia* is still a *mystērion* ("mystery", "secret"), as it is in the pre-Christian texts from which the word comes, but it is now immensely enlarged and deepened. Let us add an observation of some theological moment: John 14:6 does not belong to a theology of the *divine nature* (which would imply the Greek idea of *alētheia*: truth = essential being) but to a theology of the divine persons. *Alētheia* is used here also because of its intimate association with the word "word" (*logos*). So if Christ can call himself the truth it is basically because he himself is the Word, the incarnate Word of the Father, his only Son.

III *The Spirit of truth*

Among all the Johannine expressions that include the word "truth", none is as common as "the spirit of truth" (John 14:17; 15:26; 16:13;

1 John 4:6); it is not found elsewhere in the New Testament. We should add to these the passages in which the words spirit and truth are so strongly linked that they seem practically equivalent, "in spirit and truth" (John 4:23f.); "the spirit is truth" (1 John 5:6). So altogether there are seven texts which establish a direct relationship between the two words. This is already reason to think that in Johannine theology the function of the Spirit is carried out mainly in relation to the truth of Christ, and consists in arousing faith in Christ and in his truth by rendering this truth present and active in the hearts of the faithful.

Let us examine three aspects of this action of the Spirit, each expressed in an important passage.

1   Let us begin with 1 John 4:6, which represents an older stratum of the teaching we are examining. This verse belongs to a section in which the true believers are opposed to the Antichrists. John requires the spirits to be tested to see if they come from God (4:1). And after having proposed various criteria for discerning the spirits, he concludes: "By this we know the spirit of truth and the spirit of error" (4:6). It is the only passage in the Johannine writings in which we find this dualistic opposition of the two spirits which is now well known through the writings of late Judaism.[23]

What is the function of the Spirit of truth here? A detailed analysis would be necessary to demonstrate it completely convincingly. Let us note simply that 4:6 concludes a small literary unit which begins at 3:24. These two verses form an inclusion, and so it is the same Spirit who appears both at the beginning ("the Spirit which he has given us") and at the end ("the Spirit of truth"). Now 3:24 is clearly a transitional verse between 3:10–23, on the observance of the commandments, and 4:1–6, on the discernment of spirits. Here is the verse in question, in a literal translation: "And he who keeps his commandments abides in God and God in him. And in this we know that he abides in us, by [the action of] the Spirit which he has given us." Between "in this we know" and "by the Spirit" there is clearly an anacolouthon, as is apparent from the change of preposition. This comes from the fact that John is passing to a new subject: having recalled the criterion of communion with God ("by this we know that he abides in us") he adds a more profound explanation of this criterion ("by virtue of the action of the Spirit"). In fact it is through the action of the Spirit that we are enabled to recognize our union with God, because it is the Spirit who makes us keep the commandments; in other words, it is under the influence of the Spirit that we are enabled to believe and to love, and by this we know ourselves to be in communion with God. Accordingly, the sign of God's indwelling in us is actually the Spirit; but he always accompanies this sign with his own action, that is with the external comportment of faith and charity which he causes us to assume in the Church. This criterion of a faith prompted by the Spirit will be the theme of 4:1–6.

If this analysis is right everything becomes clear, and the link between 3:24 and 4:6, the two verses that make up the inclusion, can be properly understood. In 3:24, at the conclusion of the whole of the preceding section (3:10–23), John pointed to the Spirit as the inner source of our faith and charity. In 4:1–6 he no longer speaks of anything except faith: he wants to show that the Spirit causes us to adopt the attitudes of faith in the community and that these are the criteria of his action within us. These criteria are first the believers' confession of faith (vv. 2–3) and their readiness to accept the teaching authority (v. 6b). This is only a development of the theme underlined in 3:24: the Spirit as the source of our faith. But it will be observed that this faith is considered from within the Church, in opposition to the heretics. So the bearing of the concluding verse is plain: if the Spirit is called the Spirit of truth it is because he causes us to confess our faith in Jesus Christ and to submit ourselves to the Church. If this is how we act, says John, we can be sure that the Spirit of truth abides in us.

2   Another aspect of the action of the Spirit is described in the third promise of the Paraclete. The Spirit of truth appears there as the witness of Christ: "But when the Paraclete comes, whom I shall send to you from the Father, even the Spirit of truth, who proceeds from the Father, he will bear witness to me; and you also are witnesses, because you have been with me from the beginning" (John 15:26–7).

The context of this promise is the hatred of the world (15:18–25), and persecutions (16:1–4). This is reminiscent of the words of Christ in the Synoptics on the role the Spirit will fulfil when the disciples are dragged before the courts (Matt. 10:17–26; Luke 12:11–12; Matt. 24:9–11 and parallels). But whereas the Synoptics say that the Spirit will speak or else tell the disciples what they should say, the fourth evangelist alone calls this action of the Spirit a witness. We should also observe that John mildly contrasts the witness of the Spirit with that of the disciples: "the Spirit of truth ... will bear witness to me; and *you also* will bear witness." So the witness of the Spirit must be distinct from that of the disciples: the Spirit will bear an *inner* witness in their hearts, so that they in their turn may be able to witness to him before men.

This makes perfect sense of the following verse: "I have said all this to keep you from being scandalized" (16:1). The scandal is a profound crisis of faith, of the kind some of the disciples went through after the great eucharistic discourse (6:61). The role of the Spirit of truth will be to protect the disciples effectively in this trial, that is to prevent them from being shaken in their faith. So it is a question of a completely interior action.

But then why call it a witness? Is not a witness essentially something public and external? To understand John's language here, we must remember one of the most important features of his theology – that the whole life of Jesus is presented in the Fourth Gospel within the juridical framework of what is called "the great trial". It is not simply a question of the historical trial that took place in Jerusalem, but of something much more profound that this signifies, namely the vast theological trial in which Jesus Christ is confronted by the world. Just as the concept of trial is spiritualized and generalized, so too the concept of witness is spiritualized and interiorized with it:[24] in John what is witnessed is not just historical events seen in the light of faith, as in Acts, but the actual person of Jesus. The man who bears witness does so to his faith in Christ: all witness is essentially geared to faith, a call to faith, an invitation to believe.

So it is to be expected that the interior activity of the Spirit in the conscience of believers should be called "witness" by John: this is his way of indicating that this activity is conducted in a juridical context of opposition and crisis and that its purpose is to confirm the disciples, in the midst of their trials, in their faith in Jesus.

Finally, let us observe that in the First Letter John once again speaks of this witness of the Spirit in the celebrated passage about the three witnesses (1 John 5:6). It can be shown that this witness of the Spirit, allied to that of the water and the blood, that is of baptism and the Eucharist, is nothing but the action of the Spirit in the genesis of the faith of the new Christians: it consists in bringing them to a knowledge of the truth of Christ.[25] Here too the action of the Spirit is geared to faith.

3   Let us now move on to the last passage concerning the action of the Spirit with regard to the truth: it is perhaps the most important of all: "When the Spirit of truth comes, he will guide you into all the truth; for he will not speak on his own authority, but whatever he hears he will speak, and he will reveal to you the things that are to come" (John 16:13).

To help us to understand the formula "guide you into all the truth" we have two other expressions, which are, as it were, a commentary on it. The first is that the Spirit "will speak whatever he hears". This is the only place in the NT where this verb (*lalein*, "to speak") is used to denote the activity of the Holy Spirit. In using this word John probably wants to suggest that the action of the Spirit is a sort of continuation of that of Jesus, which was a revelation (expressed with the words *logos* and *lalein*). In 16:25 Jesus declares that he will no longer *speak* in parables, but will make an open revelation concerning his Father: this is an allusion to the future action of the Spirit. The difference between the revelation of Christ and that of the Spirit consists in the fact that the first was still veiled, in parables, whereas the second will be open, in the full light of day: in this second phase of revelation the role of the Spirit will not be to bring a new revelation, but to display in a clear light the words of revelation of Jesus. This was already the sense of 14:26: "the Paraclete ... will bring to your remembrance all that I have said to you", that is to say, he will cause them to understand the true significance and bearing of the words of Jesus. So we may sum up the meaning of the expression "whatever he hears he will speak" as follows: the action of the Spirit will consist in repeating in the Church the words spoken by Jesus.

But this is no ordinary repetition, as we can see from the triple occurrence, in the same verse, of the expression *anangelei humin* ("he will declare to you").This is like a *reprise* and it constitutes the most important element of the promise. The compound verb *anangellein* does not mean simply "announce", as it is ordinarily translated, but rather "to announce or reveal something which up to now has been unknown or secret".[26]

The word occurs frequently in the LXX of Isaiah and Jeremiah, and also in the apocalyptic literature in the special sense of "revealing the hidden meaning of a dream or mystery".[27]

The verb is wonderfully well-suited to characterize the activity of the Spirit regarding the revelation of Jesus. It is also found in a verse already cited (16:25), where the contrast between "in parables" and "plainly" shows that we are actually in the literary genre of apocalyptic. Now in this literary tradition *anangellein* does not imply the proclamation of a completely new revelation, but the interpretation or clear explanation of a previous revelation, which had been mysterious and obscure. This is precisely what the role of the Spirit is to be: his task will be to interpret, through the Church, the revelation of Jesus, still not fully understood; he will have to reveal to them its true meaning and all that it implies. At the same time "he will reveal the things that are to come" (v. 13); in other words, in the light of the words and works of Jesus the Spirit will give the understanding of the eschatological order, of the new economy of salvation, of the "new order of things that has issued from the death and resurrection of Christ".[28] As it has been excellently put by H. van der Bussche, commenting on the role of the Spirit in this verse: "To give the Christian meaning of history, to uncover in all things traces of the divine plan (Acts 20:27), to project upon every event in every epoch the living light of revelation: that is the mission of the Holy Spirit among the disciples."[29]

All this, nothing less, is what is meant by "guiding into all the truth". It is clear then that in the economy of revelation the role of the Spirit remains essentially subordinated to that of Christ, who is the only revealer; the task of the Spirit will be to cause the message of Jesus to penetrate into the hearts of the faithful, to give them the understanding of faith.

Let us conclude this third section with one last remark: in John 14:6 Christ said of himself, "I am the truth"; but in 1 John 5:6 John writes that "the Spirit is the truth". There is no inconsistency here on the part of John. These two verses do not mean that there are actually two revealers, but that there are two times of revelation as in the revelations of the apocalypses: the first is the time of Christ, who brings revelation objectively and historically, the second the time of the Spirit, who illuminates the truth of Christ and renders it subjectively present in us. These two definitions are to be taken together if we want to have a complete idea of the Johannine truth: the truth is not simply the revelation of Jesus: it is that revelation illuminated by the Holy Spirit. Without the action of the Spirit there is no true interior awareness of the truth.

[The author adds a final section, omitted here because of lack of space, entitled "Truth and Christian Life".]

Conclusion

This all too brief exposition is at any rate enough to have established that the idea of truth is truly at the heart of John's theology. This is easy to explain, because John's theology is above all a theology of revelation. It will also, we hope, have been noticed how essential it is to determine precisely the literary and historical antecedents of this theme: by positing as a background the dualistic notion of truth one easily arrives at a mystery of gnostic conception of revelation, hard to reconcile with the incarnation of the Word. But if John is situated within the later development of the apocalyptic and wisdom tradition, then the right place is given to the essential activity of the Word made flesh and of the Holy Spirit in the transmission of the truth: the truth, for John, is not the divine essence; it is Christ himself, the Word of the Father, and the Spirit.

The Johannine idea of truth, then is quite different from the intellectualist conception of the Greeks, for whom the truth was the reality, the essence of being, that is revealed to the spirit. In hellenistic dualism, this reality is transferred to the sphere of the divine, and consequently cannot be attained except by escaping from the world, and fleeing to the realm of light; but the cosmic dualism underlying this conception is liable to cut the world off from God.

For John, on the other hand, truth is found in the word of the Father turned to mankind, incarnate in Christ, illuminated through the action of the Spirit. What men are required to do with respect to the truth is not to win it by intellectual endeavour; it is to receive and enter into it in faith, to submit to it and to live by it. This Christian disposition is perfectly expressed by the Church every year in its Easter liturgy: "that as we come to know your truth, we may also attain it by worthy conduct" (Secret of Fourth Sunday after Easter).

NOTES

1   The only study devoted entirely to the Johannine concept of truth is already dated: F. Büchsel, *Der Begriff der Wahrheit in dem Evangelium und in den Briefen des Johannes* (Gütersloh, 1911); but its fundamental defect is precisely that it ignores the historical problem of the origin of the Johannine term: consequently Büchsel's interpretation of the theme remains vague and imprecise. In a more recent work, *Johannes und der hellenistische Synkretismus* (Gütersloh, 1928) 83–97, he touched on the problem of comparative semantics: *alētheia*, he declared, has the same meaning in John as among the Greeks, but this is to be explained not as a direct derivation but as the result of an influence from Judaism already long permeated by Greek thought. This affirmation, at least as regards the concept of truth, would be very difficult to prove.

2   R. Bultmann, "Untersuchungen zum Johannesevangelium: *Alētheia*", *ZNW* 27 (1928) 113–63, reprinted in *Exegetica* (Tübingen, 1967) 124–73; art "*alētheia*" in *TDNT* I, 232–51; Bultmann (1971), and (1955) 26f. His constantly repeated expression in defining *alētheia* is "the self-revealing reality of God".

3   *The Johannine Epistles* (London, 1946) 145.

4   Dodd (1953) 170–8 (cf. 177): "It means the eternal reality as revealed to men – either the reality itself or the revelation of it – To conclude: the use of the term *alētheia* in this gospel rests upon common Hellenistic usage in which it hovers between the meanings of 'reality' or 'the ultimately real' and 'knowledge of the real'." Let us illustrate this idea with some texts from the Platonic tradition: Albinus (a philosopher of the second century A.D.): "The first God is ... the divinity, the essence, *the truth*, because he is the principle of every truth, as the sun is the principle of every light" (in C. F. Hermann's edition of the works of Plato, coll. Teubner VI [1907] 164); the *Corpus Hermeticum*: "Then what is truth, father? – Thoth, the One and Only, he who is not made of matter, who is not in a body, who is without colour, who is eternal" (*Exc. Stobaei* II, A, 15); Gregory of Nyssa: "God is Truth" (*Life of Moses*, II, 19; PG 44, 332C).

5 A. Augustinović, "*Alétheia* in the Fourth Gospel", in *Studii biblici franciscani liber annuus* I (1950/1) 161–96 (cf. 165, n. 13): "John is therefore in the tradition of Greek philosophico-religious philosophy"; R. Schnackenburg, *Die Johannesbriefe* (Freiburg, 1953), 24–26 and *passim*; C. Senft, art. "Vérité" in *Vocabulaire biblique* (Neuchâtel, 1954) 299; A. Wikenhauser, *Das Evangelium nach Johannes*[3] (1961) 181f.

6 H. Schlier, "Meditationen über den johanneischen Begriff der Wahrheit", in *Festschrift M. Heidegger* (Pfullingen, 1959) 195–203: "But in the Gospel of John, which brings the basic Greek and Hebrew meanings together in a new unity, *alétheia*, formally speaking, is what is revealed and established as the right and valid" (195). Cf. J. Leal S.J., *Evangelio de San Juan in La Sagrada Escritura. Nuevo Testamento, I. Evangelios* (Madrid, 1961) 842–4: "In John the concept of truth goes beyond the limits of the Old Testament and has a mingling of the Greek and Hebrew meanings" (844). Similarly F. Büchsel (see above, n. 1).

7 Cf. my article "De sensu vocis *'emet* in Vetere Testamento", *Verbum Domini* 27 (1949) 336–54; 28 (1950) 29–42; a different interpretation is defended by S. Porubčan, "La radice *'mm* nell' A.T.", *Rivista Biblica* 8 (1960) 324–36; 9 (1961) 173–83; 221–34.

8 Cf. F. Nötscher, "'Wahrheit' als theologischer Terminus in den Qumran–Texten", *Festschrift W. Christian* (Vienna, 1956) 83–92.

9 I have demonstrated this point in greater detail in "L'arrière-fond du thème johannique de vérité", in *Studia Evangelica*, TU 73 (Berlin, 1959) ed. K. Aland *et al.*, 277–94. Compare K. G. Kuhn, "Die in Palästina gefundenen hebräischen Texte und das NT", *ZTK* 47 (1950) 192–211; W. F. Albright, "Recent Discoveries in Palestine and the Gospel of John" in *The Background of the NT and its Eschatology. Studies in honour of C. H. Dodd* (Cambridge, 1956) 153–71.

10 Cf. "L'arrière-fond du thème johannique de vérité", 280f. This exegesis of Wis. 3:9, first put forward, probably, in the commentary of C. J. W. Grimm (1866), has subsequently been adopted by the majority of exegetes.

11 *Jub.* 21:2; 25:10; *T.Levi* 18:8 (some MSS); *2 Enoch* 66:6; 1QH 16:7.

12 *Jub.* 20:9; 30:23; 36:3; *T.Reub.* 6:9; *T.Iss.* 7:5; *T.Ben.* 10:3; *Pss.Sol* 17:17; 1QS 1, 5; 5, 3; 8, 2.

13 The simple formula "in truth" is found three times in John: "sanctified in truth" (John 17:19); "love in truth" (twice: 1 John 3:18; 2 John 1). It is also found in composite formulae: "in spirit and truth" (John 4:23f.); "in deed and truth" (1 John 3:18); "in truth and love" (2 John 3). The expression "in truth" is not Greek but Semitic: it is found frequently in the LXX and in the writings of hellenistic Judaism (*Ep.Arist.* 260; *Pss.Sol.* 6:9; 10:4; 14:1; 15:3; *T.Jud.* 24:3; *T.Dan* 2:1, 2; *T.Lev.* 18:5); it also occurs in the New Testament (Matt. 22:16; 2 Cor. 7:14; Col. 1:6; Eph. 6:14).

14 See in the OT: Ps. 118:43; Prov. 22:21; Qoh. 12:10; for the Jewish or Jewish Christian writings see *1 Enoch* 104:9; *T.Gad* 3:1; *Odes Sol.* 8:8; 12:1; for the NT (where "the word of truth" denotes the preaching of the gospel); 2 Cor. 6:7; Eph. 1:13; Col. 1:5; 2 Tim. 2:15; Jas 1:18.

15 Several witnesses have a reading generally rejected by modern editors: "sanctify them in thy (*sou*) truth". There are good reasons for believing that this reading is right.

16 *Logos*: 6 times in 8:31–55; *alétheia*; 7 times in 8:32–46.

17 For the suggestion of the *progressive discovery* of the truth implied by the future

tense (cf. also 15:8), see my article "*Oida* et *ginōskō. Les deux modes de la connaissance dans le quatrième évangile*", in *Bib* 40 (1959) 709–25 (cf. 720f.).

18 This translation of the words *eis ton kolpon* is justified by John's consistent use of the preposition *eis* everywhere in his writings; see "L'emploi dynamique de *eis* dans S. Jean et ses incidences théologiques", *Bib* 43 (1962) 366–87.

19 St Thomas, *Super evangelium S. Johannis lectura, ad loc.*, ed. Marietti (Rome, 1952) n. 1868.

20 See especially the valuable analysis of J. Leal S.J., "Ego sum via et veritas et vita", *Verbum Domini* 33 (1955) 336–41.

21 The origins of the metaphor of the way used here by Jesus have been perfectly described by S. Amsler, *L'Ancien Testament dans l'Église* (Neuchatel, 1960) 42, n. 2: "The phrase, 'I am the way, the truth and the life' (John 14:6) takes up the terms applied by Judaism to the law.... What Jesus is asserting by this allusion is that from now on, as the mediator of revelation and salvation, he himself is replacing the law." In the LXX there occurs the phrase "the way of the truth" (Gen. 24:48; Tob. 1:3; Wis. 5:6; Ps. 118 [119]:30) and the parallelism between the ideas of the way and the truth.

22 St Jerome, *In Eph.* 4:21 (PL 26, 507A[539B]): "The truth did not lie in any of the patriarchs, in any of the prophets, in any of the apostles, but only in Jesus. For all others knew only partly, prophesied only partly and saw riddlingly in a mirror (1 Cor. 13). In Jesus alone did the truth of God manifest itself and declare confidently, 'I am the truth' (John 14:6)."

23 In the *Testaments of the Twelve Patriarchs* (*T. Jud.* 20:1, 3, 5) and in the Qumran writings, especially in the section of the Community Rule on the two spirits (1QS 3:13 4, 26).

24 For greater detail cf. my article, "La notion de témoignage dans Saint Jean", *Sacra Pagina* II (Paris–Gembloux, 1959).

25 Art. cit., 202–8.

26 Cf. Zorell, *Lexicon graecum Novi Testamenti*, s.v.

27 Dan. (Theodotion) 2:4, 7, 9 (*bis*), 11, 16, 24, 25, 26, 27; 5:12, 15; *3 Bar.* 1 (ed. James 84, 20).

28 See the Jerusalem Bible.

29 H. van den Bussche, *Le discours d'adieu de Jésus* (Maredsous, 1959), 126.

4

*God's Agent in the Fourth Gospel**

PEDER BORGEN

I *The State of Research*

In his discussion of christological ideas in the Fourth Gospel, C. H. Dodd finds that the status and function of the Son as God's delegated representative recalls the language of the OT prophets. Certain peculiarities, such as the Son's complete and uninterrupted dependence on the Father, and the dualism between higher and lower spheres, suggest to him that this aspect of Jesus' human career is a projection of the eternal relation of the Son and the Father upon the field of time.[1] This interpretation by Dodd does not take seriously the idea of the Son being commissioned and sent, but rather dissolves the idea of agency into an eternal and "Platonic" idea of relationship.

R. Bultmann, on the other hand, rightly places the commissioning and sending of the Son in the very center of the message of the Gospel. He also finds certain points of contact between the Johannine ideas and the prophets of the OT. But John, according to Bultmann, goes beyond the thought of a prophet and interprets gnostic mythology about divine and pre-existent agents, commissioned by the Father and sent to the world. The Mandean literature is Bultmann's main source for his hypothesis.[2]

Close parallels found in the *halakah* encourage the investigation of the extent to which John's Christology and soteriology are moulded on Jewish rules for agency. K. H. Rengstorf had made a promising beginning at this point, although he does not think that the idea of agency plays any central role in the Johannine idea of Jesus as the Son of God.[3] Also Théo Preiss and C. K. Barrett draw attention to the similarities between John and the *halakah* at certain places. Significantly enough, Preiss discusses the idea of the Son as commissioned by the Father within the wider framework of the juridical aspects of Johannine thought. The importance of judicial ideas in John has been

---

* First published in *Religions in Antiquity*, ed. J. Neusner (1968) 137–48.

stressed by N. A. Dahl as well.[4] In spite of the work of these scholars, the field is open to examine the degree in which halakhic principles of agent are reflected in the Fourth Gospel.

II *Principles of Agency*

(*a*) The basic principle of the Jewish institution of agency is that "an agent is like the one who sent him."[5] This relationship applied regardless of who was the sender. Thus, for example "the agent of the ruler is like the ruler himself."[6] Consequently, to deal with the agent was the same as dealing with the sender himself:

> With what is the matter to be compared? With a king of flesh and blood who has a consul (agent) in the country. The inhabitants spoke before him. Then said the king to them, you have not spoken concerning my servant but concerning me.[7]

The saying in John 12:44 is a very close parallel to the saying by the king in the quotation from *Siphre*:

John: he who believes in me, believes not in me but in him who sent me;
Siphre: you have not spoken concerning my servant but concerning me.

Another saying which expresses the same idea, that dealing with the agent is the same as dealing with the sender himself, is found in all four Gospels.[8] The Johannine version occurs in 13:20:

> he who receives any one whom I send receives me;
> he who receives me receives him who sent me.

There are also other similar sayings scattered throughout John:

  5:23: he who does not honor the Son does not honor the Father who sent him;
12:45: he who sees me sees him who sent me;
 14:9: he who has seen me has seen the Father;
15:23: he who hates me hates my Father also.

The halakhic principle that "an agent is like the one who sent him" usually meant that the agent was like his sender as far as the judicial function and effects were concerned. There were, however, rabbis who developed it into a judicial mysticism saying that the agent is a person identical with the sender.[9] Thus not only his authority and his function are derived from the sender, but also his qualities. *Qiddushin* 43a formulates this mysticism in the following way: the agent ranks as his master's own person.[10]

In the Fourth Gospel the personal identity between the Son and the Father is stated in several different ways. One formula is "I and the Father are one" (10:30) and another formula is "the Father is in

me and I am in the Father" (10:38; cf. 14:10–11 and 17:21–3). In
10:36–8 it is explicitly stated that it is the agent, the Son in the capacity
of being sent into the world, who is one with the sender. Similarly,
in 17:20–3, the unity between the Son and the Father shall make it
possible for the world to recognize the Son as agent of the Father,
"so that the world may believe that thou has sent me". Moreover,
in 10:37–8 and in 14:10–11 the oneness between the Son and the
Father is made manifest in Jesus' words and works which also are
said to be the works of the Father.

(*b*) Although John interprets the relationship between the Father and
the Son in such legalistic terms, it is a legalism that is not seen
in contrast to personal "mysticism". Thus Preiss' term "judicial
mysticism" is a very apt one, and the personal element is further
deepened by the fact that it was the *Son* who was the agent of the
Father.[11] It should be added that the idea of the Son–Father relationship also implies that the Son is subordinate to the Father. This
subordination fits very well to the principles of agency, since here the
thoughts of unity and identity between agent and sender are modified
by an emphasis on the superiority of the sender. The principle is
stated in John 13:16 and *Gen. R.* 78:

John: a servant is not greater than his master; nor is he who is sent
         greater than him who sent him.[12]
Gen. R.: the sender is greater than the sent.

Matt. 10:24, cf. Luke 6:40, offers a parallel to the first part of John
13:16: "nor (is) a servant above his master". What in Matthew and
Luke is said about pupil–teacher and servant–master relationship is
in John specifically applied to agency.

(*c*) Another important area of agency centers around the specific
mission of an agent. It was a legal presumption that an agent would
carry out his mission in obedience to his sender[13] as can be seen from
Erubin 31b–32a, *Qiddushin* 2:4 and *Terumoth* 4:4:

It is a legal presumption that an agent will carry out his mission (*'ôśh*
šlîḥôtô)[14]
I appointed you for my advantage, and not for my disadvantage.[15]
If a householder said to his agent (*lšlôḥô*), "Go and give heave-offering",
the agent should give heave-offering according to the householder's mind
(*kr'tô šl b'l hbyt*).[16]

In accordance with this principle, Christ was an obedient agent
who did as the Father had commanded. He said, "I have come down
from heaven, not to do my own will but the will of him who sent

me" (John 6:38). Likewise, the Christ always did what was pleasing to the one who sent him (8:29).

(*d*) The Johannine idea of the mission of Christ as God's agent is seen within the context of a lawsuit. The statement in *Baba Qamma* 70a is of special interest for this question:

> Go forth and take legal action so that you may acquire title to it and secure the claim for yourself.

The principles reflected in this rule are also found in the Fourth Gospel. Although there is no scene of commissioning as pictured in the halakhic statement ("go forth", etc.), the commissioning itself is referred to in these words: "I came not of my own accord, but he sent me" (John 8:42); "For I have not spoken of my own authority; the Father who sent me has himself given me commandment what to say and what to speak" (John 12:49); "For he whom God has sent utters the words of God" (3:34); "My teaching is not mine, but his who sent me" (7:16); "... he who sent me is true, and I declare to the world what I have heard from him" (8:26); "... I do nothing on my own authority but speak thus as the Father taught me. And he who sent me is with me ..." (8:28–9); "... the word which you hear is not mine but the Father's who sent me" (14:24).

According to the *halakah* the sender transferred his own rights and the property concerned to his agent.[17] On this basis the agent might acquire the title in court and secure the claim for himself. The will of the sender, the Father, in John 6:39 makes just this transfer clear: "This is the will of him who sent me, that all that he has given me (*pan ho dedōken moi*) ..." The transfer is even more pointedly stated in 17:6: "thine they were, and thou gavest them to me" (*soi ēsan kamoi autous edōkas*).[18]

The next step is the actual acquiring of the title in court and the agent's securing of the claim for himself. John 12:31–2 pictures such a court scene:

> Now is the judgment of this world,
> now shall the ruler of this world be cast out;
> and I, when I am lifted up from the earth,
> will draw (*helkusō*) all men unto myself (*pros emauton*).

There is close resemblance between the two phrases "I will draw all men to myself" (John) and "secure the claim for yourself" (*halakah*). In both cases the agent himself is to take possession of the property since the ownership has been transferred to him. John uses a different verb, "draw" (*helkysō*) and not "secure" (*ôʾpîq*) but the Johannine term comes from judicial context. The very renders with all probability the Hebrew *mšk* to draw, pull, seize.[19] Thus the Septuagint frequently translates *mšk* by *helkyein*.[20] And in the halakah of Judaism *mšk* has received the technical meaning of "to take possession of" (by drawing or seizing an object).[21] Thus the meaning of the phrase in John 12:32 and *Baba Qamma* 70a is the same.

Moreover, the legal acquiring of the title can be seen in John 12:31-2, although pictured in a negative way. The world and the ruler of this world are judged and cast out from the heavenly court.[22] The ruler of this world is judged not to have any just title to or claim upon God's people.[23] Thus it is implied that God's agent has the title and therefore can secure the claim for himself.

Although the ownership, for sake of the lawsuit, is transferred from the sender to his agent, the agent is, of course, still an agent of the sender. Thus as a matter of fact, the sender takes possession of the property when the agent does. The meaning of John 6:44 is to be understood along this line: "No one can come to me (i.e. the agent) unless the Father who sent me (*ho pempsas me*, i.e. the sender) draws (*helkysē*) him." In other words, the coming to the agent, Christ, is the same as being in the possession of the Father, and only those who are included in the Father's claim come to his agent. Against this background it is logical that the rabbis discussed if an agent in such cases is to be characterized as partner to his sender.[24]

(*e*) As Jesus has completed his mission (John 4:34; 5:36; 17:4; 19:30) he is to report to his sender. John 13ff. is dominated by this theme of Jesus' return to his Father: "Jesus, knowing that the Father had given all things into his hand, and that he had come from God and was going to God ..., etc." (13:3). And just as the judgement scene in John 12:31-2 was pictured in a proleptic way before its completion on the cross (19:30), so also is the Son's report given ahead of time in the form of the prayer found in John 17: "I glorified thee on earth, having accomplished the work which thou gavest me to do" (17:4).

It is in accordance with the *halakah* that an agent who is sent on a mission is to return and report to the sender. The return is mentioned in *P. Hagigah* 76d: "Behold we send to you a great man as our shaliach, and he is equivalent to us until such time as he returns to us." Although a contrast between human and divine agency is drawn in *Mek. Ex.* 12:1, the passage illustrates the point of return and report by an agent to his sender: "Thy messengers, O God, are not like the messengers of human beings; for the messengers of human beings must needs return to those who send them before they can report.

With thy messengers, however, it is not so, ... whithersoever they go they are in thy presence and can report: we have executed thy commission." John does not draw this contrast between human and divine agents but applies rather the human principle of return and report also to God's agent, Jesus Christ.

(f) One question remains, namely, the actual effectuation of Jesus' mission after his return to his Father and beyond the limitation of his work in Israel. John found the solution of this problem in the halakhic rule that "an agent can appoint an agent" (*Qiddushin* 41a).[25] Consequently at the completion of his own mission, Jesus said: "As thou didst send me into the world, so I have sent them into the world" (John 17:16).

At the last evening before his departure, Jesus therefore first made clear to the disciples the principles of agency, John 13:16, 20, and then in his prayer reported to the Father about the sending (chap. 17), and then after his resurrection the actual commissioning of the disciples took place: "Peace be with you. As the Father has sent me, even so I send you" (John 20:21). Accordingly, the unity between the Father and his agent, the Son, is extended to these agents of the agent: "... as thou, Father, art in me, and I in thee, that they also may be in us, so that the world may believe that thou hast sent me" (John 17:21).

Thus there are striking similarities between the halakhic principles of agency and ideas in the Fourth Gospel, as (a) the unity between the agent and his sender (b) although the agent is subordinate, (c) the obedience of the agent to the will of the sender, (d) the task of the agent in the lawsuit, (e) his return and reporting back to the sender, and (f) his appointing of other agents as an extension of his own mission in time and space.

III *Heavenly Agent*

On the basis of the analysis of agency in John one might be tempted to draw the conclusion that the Fourth Gospel represents the socalled normative and rabbinic Judaism,[26] and not mystical Judaism which E. R. Goodenough so forcefully championed.[27] Such a conclusion would be premature. The study so far has not explained the fact that Jesus according to John is not just a human and earthly agent but a divine and heavenly agent who has come down among men. Bultmann's hypothesis of gnostic mythology would offer an explanation of this point, since the gnostic agents were divine figures who were sent down to earth.[28]

The close similarities between agency in John and halakhic principles point in another direction. The question can be formulated in this way: Where do we find *halakah* applied to the heavenly world and man's relation to it? It is the merit of G. D. Scholem to have brought to the foreground the Merkabah mysticism and to have made manifest its halakhic character. Here we find a combination of *halakah*, heavenly figures and the heavenly world as is the case with the idea of agency in the Fourth Gospel.[29] H. Odeberg, G. Quispel, N. A. Dahl and P. Borgen have suggested that the Fourth Gospel reflects early stages of Merkabah mysticism.[30]

Since Philo also is influenced by early Merkabah mysticism, his writings can throw light upon ideas in John.[31] In connection with the concept of agency, the Johannine idea of the vision of God can serve as a good point of departure for a comparison with Philo. According to John 12:45 God's agent mediates the vision of God: "he who sees me sees him who sent me." Moreover, in John the agent from God is a heavenly figure and the only one who has seen God:

> Not that any one has seen the Father
> except him who is from God:
> he has seen the Father (John 6:46).

John 6:46 as well as 1:18 ("No one has ever seen God; the only God (Son), who is in the bosom of the Father, he has made him known") are an interpretation of the theophany at Sinai. According to Exod. 33:20 there was a significant modification made to this theophany. Moses was not allowed to see the face of God; for no man can see God and live. John adds that one heavenly figure has had this full vision of God, namely the divine Son, the one who is from God.[32]

The closest parallel to this heavenly figure is the idea of the heavenly Israel, "he who sees God". The idea is found in Philo, *Conf.* 146 and *Leg. all.* I 43:

> But if there be any as yet unfit to be called a Son of God, let him press to take his place under God's First-born, the Word, who holds the eldership among the angels, their ruler as it were.
> And many names are his, for he is called, "the Beginning", and the Name of God, and His Word, and the Man after His image, and "he that sees", that is Israel.
> ... the sublime and heavenly wisdom is of many names; for he calls it "beginning" and "image" and "vision of God".

Two observations support the theory that there is a connection between the Christ of the Fourth Gospel and the angel Israel. First, although there is no explicit etymological interpretation of the word Israel ("he who sees God") in John, the idea of Israel is tied together with the idea of vision in the interpretation of Jacob's vision, John 1:47–51. Nathanael, the true Israelite is to see what his ancestor, Jacob/Israel saw. And the reference to the Son of Man (John 1:51) probably presupposes the idea of the heavenly model of Jacob/Israel.[33]

Secondly, important parallels can be seen between John and Philo as the many other names of the heavenly figure. Both John and Philo identify him who sees the Logos (John 1:1, 14 and *Conf*. 146, cf. the heavenly wisdom in *Leg. all*. I 43). He is furthermore called the Son, in John the only Son *monogenēs*, John 1:14; 3:16, 18) and in Philo the firstborn Son (*prōtogonos*, *Conf*. 146). It should be added that both John and Philo at times characterize the Logos and the Son as God.[34]

Two other parallel terms for the heavenly figure are Philo's "the Man after God's image" (see *Conf*. 146 and *Leg. all*. I 43) and John's "the Son of Man". The kinship between these two terms can be seen from the fact that both John and Philo associate this heavenly man with vision, with ascent into heaven, and with the second birth in contrast to the first birth.

At this point the ideas found in *Quae. Ex*. II 46 are of particular interest. Philo here says that when Moses, at the theophany at Sinai, was called above on the seventh day (Exod. 24:16), he was changed from earthly man into the heavenly man, and the change was a second birth in contrast to the first. John's ideas in 3:3–13 seem to be a polemic against the very idea expressed by Philo. John says that the vision of God's kingdom[35] and the second birth from above are not brought about by ascent into heaven to the Son of Man. It is rather the heavenly man's descent which brings about the second birth.[36]

The conclusion is that John and Philo have in common the idea of a heavenly figure as the one who sees God, associate this figure with Israel, and also have in common several of the other terms and concepts which are crystallized around the same heavenly figure.

Although Philo in *Conf*. 146 says that Israel, "he that sees", mediates the vision of God, he does not apply the halakhic principles of agency to the concept. At this point John differs and says that the heavenly figure, the only one who has seen God, is sent as God's agent to mediate the vision. It is of interest to note that John in 8:16–18 applies also another judicial principle to Christ and his mission. Here the OT and halakhic rule of two witnesses has been applied to the idea of Jesus as the Son of the (heavenly) Father: the Father and the Son both witness.[37]

IV *Conclusion and Perspective*

Thus the ideas of the heavenly figure who sees God (Israel) and ascent/descent are found in both Philo and John. Similarities have also been found between John and rabbinic *halakah* about agency. The Fourth Gospel, therefore, shows that no sharp distinction can be drawn between rabbinic and hellenistic Judaism.[38]

It has been suggested above that the Jewish background reflected in John should be characterized as early stages of Merkabah mysticism, in which we find such a combination of *halakah*, heavenly figures and the heavenly world. A strong support for this conclusion is found in a text from Nag Hammadi, as reported by Doresse:[39]

> It [the Ogdoad] comprises a glorious palace, a throne erected upon a chariot surrounded by cherubim with faces like those of a lion, a bull, a man and an eagle. The chariot, we are told, has been taken for a model by the seventy-two gods who govern the seventy-two languages of the peoples. There are also seraphim in the forms of dragons, who perpetually glorify their lord. Near to Sabaôth stands a first-born who is named Israel, "the man who sees God".

This text shows close parallels to the ideas discussed from Philo and John, such as the heavenly Son, the firstborn who is the same as the heavenly Israel, the man who sees God.[40] It is significant that this heavenly figure has its place in the heavenly palace near the throne erected upon a chariot. Thus the influence of Merkabah traditions is unmistakable, a fact which shows that the same is the case with regard to the ideas discussed in John and Philo.[41]

Furthermore, the text from Nag Hammadi gives clear evidence for the fact that Jewish Merkabah traditions have influenced the gnostic movement. It is therefore quite probable that the ideas of heavenly agents in gnostic/Mandean literature similarly have been influenced by Jewish principles of agency and Jewish ideas of heavenly figures. In that case the gnostic agents do not explain the background of God's agent in the Fourth Gospel, as Bultmann thinks.[42] The Fourth Gospel rather gives a clue to the Jewish background of the gnostic/Mandean mythology.

Not very long before the death of the eminent scholar Dr E. R. Goodenough, I had the privilege of conversing with him about Philo of Alexandria. In the course of the conversation he said that it was the task of the younger generation of scholars to explore what light the Merkabah mysticism could throw upon Philo's work and upon Philo's relationship to rabbinic Judaism and the NT. The present study is meant to be a contribution towards the fulfillment of this charge given by Dr Goodenough.[43]

Peder Borgen

NOTES

1 C. H. Dodd (1953) 254–62.

2 R. Bultmann (1971) 251–2; (1925) 104–9.

3 K. H. Rengstorf *TDNT* 403–5; 421–2; 435–6.

4 Preiss (1954) 9–31; C. K. Barrett (1955) 216, 474); N. A. Dahl (1962) in this volume, pp. 122–40; P. Borgen (1965) 158–64.

5 *Mek. Ex.* 12:3; 12:6; *Berakoth* 5:5; *Baba Metzia* 96a; *Hagigah* 10b; *Qiddushin* 42b, 43a; *Menahoth* 93b; *Nazir* 12b, etc.

6 *Baba Qamma* 113b.

7 *Siphre* on Numbers 12:9, cited in K. H. Rengstorf *TDNT* I, 416.

8 See Matt. 10:40; cf. Matt. 18:5; Mark 9:37 and Luke 9:48. The parallels are discussed in C. H. Dodd, "Some Johannine 'Herrnworte' with parallels in the Synoptic Gospels" *NTS* 2 (1955/56) 81–5.

9 The phrase of judicial mysticism as clue to central ideas in John is suggested by Preiss (1954) 28.

10 "He ranks as his own person." Translation in *The Babylonian Talmud*, Nashim VIII, ed. I. Epstein (London, 1935) 216. Hebrew text in *Der Babylonian Talmud mit Einschluss der vollständigen Mischnah*, by L. Goldschmidt, V (Leipzig 1906) 845.

11 See Preiss (1954) 24–5: "The formulae suggestive of mystical immanence so typical of Johannine language are regularly intermixed with juridical formulae ... Jesus reveals himself to be one with the Father as a result of the strict fidelity with which he waits upon him and utters his words and performs his task as ambassador and witness. (The bond between the Father and the Son) *coincides* with the bond formed by the obedience of a witness ... Jesus is in the Father and the Father in him because he does the work of the Father (10:30, 37, 38). Inasmuch as he is the Son of Man sent as a witness from the height of heaven, ... Jesus is according to rabbinical law "as he who sends him".

12 See also John 15:20.

13 Cf. K. H. Rengstorf, *TDNT* I, 41.

14 *Etrubin* 31b–32a; cf. *Ketuboth* 99b; *Nazir* 12a.

15 *Qiddushin* 42b; cf. *Baba Bathra* 169b; *Ketuboth* 85a; *Bekoroth* 61b.

16 *Terumoth* 4:4. Cf. the medieval collection, *Shulhan Aruq, Hoshen Mishpat*, 188:5: "Stets wenn der Vertreter (*šhšlîḥ*) von dem Willen des Vertretenen (*mdʿt hmšlḥ*) abweicht, is das Vertretungsverhältnis gänzlich aufgelöst." See M. Cohn, "Die Stellvertretung im jüdischen Recht," *Zeitschrift für vergleichende Rechtswissenschaft*, 36 (1920) 206.

17 See M. Cohn, *Zeitschrift für vergleichende Rechtswissenschaft*, 36 (1920) 165–7; L. Auerbach, *Das jüdische Obligationsrecht*, I (Berlin, 1870) 567–9.

18 Variants of the phrase occur in John 17:2, 6, 7; cf. 13:3.

19 So also A. Schlatter (1930) 176, and R. Bultmann (1971) 231 n. 2. These scholars have not, however, focused the attention upon *mšk* as a judicial term.

20 Deut. 21:3; Neh. 9:30; Ps. 9:30 (10:9); Eccl. 2:3; Cant. 1:4, etc.

21 *Baba Metzia* 4:2; *Baba Metzia* 47a; 48a; 49a. Cf. Ph. Blackmann (ed. and trans.), *Mishnayoth*, IV (London, 1951) 579.

22 See N. A. Dahl (1962) below, p. 135; C. K. Barrett (1955) 355–6 ("The devil will be put out of office, out of authority. He will no longer be *archōn*; men will be freed from his power").

23 Cf. that the children of Abraham have as Father God and not the devil, John 8:39–47.

24 *Baba Qamma* 70a, from which the above quotation was taken, discussed this very question: "He was surely appointed but a shaliach. Some, however, say that he is made a partner ..."

25 There was discussion among the rabbis on this question, and some offered specific qualifications as to circumstances under which an agent could appoint an agent. See *Gittin* 3:5–6; *Gittin* 29b.

26 The champion of "normative" Judaism is G. F. Moore, *Judaism*, I–III (Cambridge, Mass., 1927–30).

27 See especially E. R. Goodenough, *Jewish Symbols in the Greco–Roman Period*, I (New York, 1953) 3–58.

28 See reference in n. 27.

29 G. D. Scholem, *Major Trends in Jewish Mysticism*, 3rd rev. edn (New York, 1961); *Gnosticism, Merkabah Mysticism and Talmudic Tradition* (New York, 1960) 9–19.

30 H. Odeberg (1929); G. Quispel, "L'Évangile de Jean et la Gnose", in *L'Évangile de Jean, Recherches Bibliques* III (Lyon 1958) 197–208; and N. A. Dahl (1962) below; P. Borgen (1965) have especially emphasized Jewish mysticism as background for John.

31 Concerning elements of Merkabah traditions in Philo, see K. Kohler, "Merkabah", *The Jewish Encyclopedia*, Ed. I. Singer, VIII (New York, 1947) 500.

32 Further discussion of ideas from the theophany at Sinai in the contexts of John 1:18 and 6:46 in M. E. Boismard, *St. John's Prologue* (Westminster, Md., 1957) 136–40; S. Schulz, *Komposition und Herkunft der Johanneischen Reden* (Stuttgart 1960) 40f.; N. A. Dahl (1962) below, p. 129; P. Borgen (1962) 150f.

33 See especially N. A. Dahl. (1962) below, pp. 132–4 and notes with numerous references. It is even possible that the etymology of Israel meaning "he who sees God", is implied in John 1:47–51. It would be more of pure speculation to try to find allusions to the etymology also in John 1:18, that "No one has seen God" should render Hebrew *ľ 'îš r'h'l*. Concerning other places in which the idea of Israel and the vision of God are associated in John, see P. Borgen (1965) 175–7.

34 John 1:1, 18; *Somn.* I 228–30 and *Quae. Gen.* II 62.

35 For the idea of seeing God's kingdom, see Wisd. 10:10.

36 This analysis of John 3:3–13 gives support to the interpretation suggested by H. Odeberg (1929) *ad loc.*, that v. 13 is a polemic against the idea of visionary ascent among Merkabah mystics. So also N. A. Dahl (1962) below, p. 137; see also E. M. Sidebottom (1961) 120–1.

Commentators have overlooked the importance of *Quae. Ex.* II 46 for the interpretation of John 3:3ff.

37 See C. H. Dodd (1953) 77 and Str-B II, *ad loc.*

38 Also E. R. Goodenough, "John a Primitive Gospel", *JBL* LXIV (1945) 145–82 rightly stresses the Jewish background of John. He draws, however, too sharp a distinction between legalistic rabbinism and hellenistic (mystical) Judaism.

39 J. Doresse, *The Secret Books of the Egyptian Gnostics* (New York, 1960) 167. (See also 176f.)

40 See N. A. Dahl (1962) below, p. 133 nn. 21, 22; H. Jonas, "The Secret Books of the Egyptian Gnostics", *The Journal of Religion* XLII (1962) 264.

41 See references to the works by J. Doresse (n. 39) and N. A. Dahl in this volume, pp. 122–40.

42 See references in note 41.

43 See also E. R. Goodenough, *Jewish Symbols*, I, 8 and n. 6.

5

*Towards the Interpretation of John's Gospel**

A Discussion of
The Testament of Jesus
by Ernst Käsemann

GÜNTHER BORNKAMM

This quietly innocuous title is one which a conservative religious writer might equally have chosen. At first glance it gives no indication of the position and significance the most recent of Ernst Käsemann's works is bound to hold in current and future Johannine scholarship. For this book is by no means a straightforward exegesis of the high-priestly prayer. With chapter headings drawn from chapter 17 ("The Glory of Christ", "The Community under the Word", "Christian Unity") it gives an exceptionally sharply-drawn and concise sketch of certain central theological categories belonging to the whole Gospel, whilst leaving aside detailed questions of literary analysis, religious background and the history of traditions. The nature of the Shaffer lectures, delivered at Yale Divinity School, made these omissions unavoidable, and they certainly contribute to the clarity of the book's theses. In addition the author's conviction comes through that the huge labours of Johannine scholarship have not only left the historical and theological problems unresolved but have scarcely allowed the nature of these problems to be appreciated. It is still true that "the Evangelist whom we call John appears to be a man without definite contours. We can hear his voice, a voice distinct from the rest of primitive Christianity, and yet we are unable to locate exactly his historical place." (1f.)

Directing some fierce invective against the mainly harmonizing tendencies of traditional Johannine exegesis, Käsemann exposes the distinctiveness and uniqueness of the Fourth Gospel and at the same time asks crucially important questions regarding the theological content of this remarkable book. The sheer passion with which he

* First published in *EvT* 28 (1968) 8–25. Translated by John Ashton.

presents his thesis gives his work a fascinating but at the same time disquieting power that the reader finds it hard to escape. The book is unquestionably destined to give a new direction to the debate on the Fourth Gospel, one which will last for a long time. It confronts the "challenge" (2) of the Gospel; and so it would be the greatest possible disservice to theology simply to tap it on the shoulder, as it were, and to correct a few details here and there in a well-meaning attempt to keep the debate cool and thereby guide it back onto conventional lines even before it has properly taken off. At any rate this is certainly not the intention of the critical remarks that follow.

I

The theme of the work is Johannine eschatology under the aspects of Christology, ecclesiology and soteriology (3). Adhering closely to Käsemann's own words, so as to enable his remarkably uncompromising views of the Gospel to emerge clearly, we shall start by giving an outline of the content of the book; then in a second part we shall append some critical reflections.

The author is right to start by singling out the motif of "the glory of Jesus" in John 17 as the key-word of the whole Gospel. In his earlier (1969) essay, "The Structure and Purpose of the Prologue to John's Gospel", Käsemann picked out the *doxa* ("glory") of Jesus as the central concept of the Prologue: he emphatically denied that the real point of John 1:14 is the incarnation of the divine Logos. Contrary to traditional teaching on the incarnation, the evangelist is chiefly interested, according to Käsemann, not in the humanity but in the divinity of the incarnate Logos.

The incarnation of the Logos as expressed in John 1:14a stands completely in the shadow of the statement that follows: "and we have seen his glory"; it is this that gives the incarnation its proper content. The meaning of the incarnation is simply that the divine Word, originating in heaven, "descended into the world of man and there came into contact with earthly existence, so that an encounter with him became possible" (9). Accordingly the author asks of those traces of lowliness which are undeniably present even in the Fourth Gospel, whether they represent more than "the absolute minimum of the costume designed for the one who dwelt for a little while among men, appearing to become of them, yet without himself being subject to earthly conditions" (10). Properly speaking there is no trace in John of a truly human Jesus, persecuted by the world and exposed to suffering and death. So in the light of John 1:14 and the confession of Thomas (20:28f.) that rounds off the Gospel it is meaningless to speak of a genuine paradox. The truth is that the Johannine Christ is throughout *"God striding over the earth"* (9, 13, etc.). According to other christological conceptions in the New Testament (esp. Phil. 2:6–11), the earthly man is rewarded for his obedience by being exalted; here, on the contrary, his obedience culminates in his return to the Father (10). Consequently, "the glory of Jesus is not the result of his obedience ... On the contrary, obedience is the result of Jesus' glory and the attestation of his glory in situations of earthly conflict" (18f.). "Obedience is then the manifestation of the divine Lordship, of the divine glory, in the realm below which is alienated from God. For Christ obedience is the attestation of his unity with the Father during his sojourn on earth" (18). So it is a mistake to speak of Jesus as moving on from lowliness to exaltation. For "he does not really change himself, but only his place. Human fate is thrust upon him so that in a divine manner he may endure it and overcome it" (12). For the revealer the world is only "a point of transit, and humiliation means simply being in exile" (12). John uses Jesus' life on earth "merely as a backdrop for the Son of God proceeding through the world of man and as the scene of the inbreaking of the divine glory" (13).

This, according to Käsemann, is what makes it possible to understand "the preponderance of the so-called present or realized eschatology", with "no imminent expectation" and no "cosmic drama of the end-time as in apocalypticism" (13). For John, "Eschatology is no longer the force that determines Christology; the opposite is the case. Christology determines eschatology and eschatology becomes an aspect of Christology. In Christ, the end of the world has not merely come near, but is present and remains present continually" (16). "The *praesentia Christi* is the centre of his proclamation" (15).

John's Christology, then, breaks the bounds of traditional eschatology, and accordingly John gives a completely new meaning to Jesus' passion. No gospel writer could pass this over completely; but in John's scheme of things the passion was bound to create problems, since it was impossible to fit it organically into the work as a whole. Consequently the passion narrative has a strange feel to it. The evangelist's solution "was to imprint the features of Christ's victory upon the passion story" (7). There is no longer any room for a theology of the cross (51). Rather, the aspect of *doxa* controls both passion and incarnation and binds them tightly together, the latter as a projection of the glory of Jesus' pre-existence and the former as a return to it (20). Passing unmolested through a death that simply means the end of all earthly limitations, the heavenly emissary makes his victorious and exultant ascent (19:30) back to where he had come from: he has fulfilled his mission and is now recalled into the realm of freedom (20): nothing has changed except the place and the scope of his manifestation (18, 20). So coming and going, descent and ascent, mission and return are central motifs of Johannine Christology (20).

The soteriological significance of this is unfolded in Jesus' miracles and discourses (21–4). The miracles are not just a concession to human weakness[1] but belong to the radiance of God's self-manifestation; at the same time they are not to be detached from the person of Christ, and he himself wishes to be understood in and through them as the true gift of God. Similarly, the monologues of Jesus' discourses revolve endlessly round the theme of the relations between Father and Son within the divinity and the essential nature of Jesus *qua* revealer – a theme which is thoroughly dogmatic here, not just a by-product of soteriology (23).

Out of the Christology of the Gospel, central, absolute and all-consuming, there naturally proceed further characteristics of Johannine theology. These are treated in the chapters that follow under the headings, "The Community under the Word" (27–55) and "Christian Unity" (56–73). It is no accident that the basic ideas are best expressed in predominantly negative propositions. I confine myself here to the following characteristics. There is no question in John of any *ecclesiology* in the proper sense. If one insists on speaking of community (as the author himself does) in spite of the absence of the concept of *ecclesia*, then it is obvious straightaway that there is no trace in the Fourth Gospel of the elements that constitute the life of a community – worship, sacraments, church officer, charisms, etc. The memory of Peter as the representative of the historical circle of the disciples does, it is true, pierce through, but the ecclesial significance of the prince of the apostles is overshadowed by the mysterious figure of the beloved disciple (28f.). He, along with various personages not otherwise known (Philip, Nathanael, Nicodemus, etc.) – including, significantly, a number of women – plays a much more important role than the group of disciples already known from the Synoptists. Absent too are the other honorific titles: "family" or "people of God", "heavenly building", "body of Christ". The focus is now exclusively on the disciples, and only as individuals. They are given peculiarly esoteric names, such as "friends of Jesus", "the beloved of God", "the elect", "those who are sanctified", though historically they are the same people. This is the group, moving "like a phantom, between heaven and earth" (30), that carries the Spirit.

All this enables us to understand John's relationship to *tradition*. Of course even he has to work with traditions. And there is no contradiction in his Gospel between spirit and tradition. But it is of paramount importance that in dealing with the tradition he knows – that is, with a hitherto untended tradition of his own, no longer simply the synoptic tradition – he treats it with greater freedom, even violence, than any other NT author. Not interested in the name or position of those who passed it on, he allows it weight only to the extent that it preserves the voice of Jesus and is able to give witness in the present – in other words, only a context of prophetic proclamation. The only function of the tradition is to draw attention to Jesus; when it is actually mistaken for the voice of the Good Shepherd it is dangerous, and unless it leads to the true faith that has seen, heard and found its own way to Jesus, it has not been understood (36ff.).

Here too we get a clearer vision of John's general understanding of *history* (36ff.). This is not accessible through our own categories, whether they be those of historical enquiry, existentialism or salvation history. For John sees history exclusively in terms of his own incarnational and christological teaching. Not for him "a history which arranges the world's epochs and signifies its immanent path" (34). "Historicity is not really an attribute of the world as such" (35). It is only revelation that has a history, viz. "the history of the Logos who overcomes or increases the world's resistance to its Creator" (35). And this is not history in the sense of an ongoing historical process, but only as the sphere of his epiphany, his presence and his return to the Father, so that the world encountered by Jesus in his role as revealer is simply a matter of backcloth and stage-props and is otherwise of interest only because of its response to his presence. Such other characters as appear on the stage are normally nothing but puppets manipulated "from above" (36). Everything is controlled by this dogmatic reflection. "Compared with the reality of everyday life, all of this is quite artificial" (36). And again: "Judged by the modern concept of reality, our Gospel is more fantastic than any other writing of the New Testament" (43).

It follows necessarily that John can no longer offer a picture of the so-called historical Jesus (44). Instead he has to portray him as the Logos, uninterruptedly united with the Father, mediating the presence of the Creator, an alien and constantly misunderstood figure in a world which is nothing but a temporary lodging for this heavenly wanderer. This conception concentrates exclusively on Jesus' glory and victory; a future eschatology has no more place or sense in it than does a theology of the cross: what moves into the centre in its stead is a *protology* (21): "What is missing is the great Pauline paradox, that the power of the resurrection can be experienced only in the shadow of the cross, and that the reality of the resurrection now implies a position under the cross" (52). Hence the enormous curtailment of historical and salvation-historical perspectives. John's sacrifice of history leads straight to a clear-cut though "naive" christological *docetism*, as Käsemann never tires of stressing (cf. 26, 45, 70, 77). Nothing could be more wrong-headed, in his view, than to attach the label "anti-docetic" onto the Fourth Gospel (45).

The fourth and last chapter completes and rounds off this picture. Here is where the leitmotif of the *unity of Christendom* derived from John 17 is assigned its place in the history of theology. The theme of unity is first encountered in Paul's teaching on the one body of Christ. Paul understands it exclusively in relation to the multiplicity of historical charismata in the members of the body; but by the time of the deutero-Pauline writings it has become a mark, guaranteed by heaven, of the Church's truth and essence, contained in the baptismal confession (Eph. 4:5) and confirmed in orthodox doctrine (1 Tim. 3:15) as the pillar and foundation of the truth (56f.).

John's understanding of unity is completely different, since with perfect consistency he bases himself upon one of his own theological premises, namely the unity of Father and Son (57). This is what makes Jesus *the* revealer of the heavenly world, who has appeared in the earthly world in the *Word* for the purpose of cutting the faithful off from the world, where they were scattered and not at home, and establishing them in unity in heaven. Thus everything focuses on those who are chosen and loved; they, not the world, are the objects of God's love: we should not be misled by the isolated saying in John 3:16, drawn as it is from a fund of traditional Christian formulae (60). The same holds for Jesus' title of "Saviour of the World", which is far from adequately characterizing the Johannine Christ. So too the Johannine love-commandment has a completely different sense from that of the Jesus of the Synoptic Gospels. Founded as it is upon the relationship between Father and Son and confined to the circle of the disciples, the meaning of love is esoteric and opposed to the world. It cuts the disciples off from the world. It is no longer the love of one's neighbour preached by the historical Jesus. A neighbour has no title to such a love, for it involves no self-surrender to others. As a mark of the elect who cut themselves off from the world it is one with their faith: "Faith means the acceptance of the Word and love means self-surrender to the Word in service" (62). Of decisive importance too is John's uncompromising dualism, which accounts for the "iron and ice of this so-called apostle of love" (63). No doubt the world is and remains God's creation but only as "the arena of divine history" and "the realm of his call' (63). Yet we need to be rescued from it. The disciples, it is true, have been sent into the world, but they are hated and persecuted by it: they are reborn and as such representatives of the heavenly world (63). Accordingly, Christian unity means simply "the solidarity of the heavenly" (67). In Jesus' signs and symbolic discourses, earthly unity serves as nothing other than the "realm which can reflect the heavenly reality, namely the realm of the divine Word" (69), "for the heavenly reality invades the earth with explosive power in order to unfold itself in representations as its earthly counterparts" (69).

Basing himself on the conclusions he has reached in chaps. 2–4, Käsemann attempts to solve the difficult problems of the history of religions and theology and to give the Gospel its proper historical place. He does not, it is true, engage in a closer examination of the questions at issue; for instance, he avoids classifying the Gospel as a product of gnosticism. Yet he is forced to conclude "that John prepares for the gnostic proclamation or else already stands under its influence. For gnosticism regards the gathering of the souls scattered on the earth as the goal of world history" (73). In fact precisely in reference to the chapter on Christian unity it has to be said that in recent discussion there have been few descriptions of the gnosticizing tendencies of the Gospel of John as sharply drawn and comprehensive as this one. The book is full of attempts to place the Gospel in its historical context. These all point to the conclusion that the Fourth Gospel already presupposes the consolidation of the Christian Church within the period of early Catholicism but resists the movement of the Church in the direction of institutionalization and sacramentalism. Its historical setting, according to Käsemann, is a hellenistic, conventicle Christianity of an "enthusiastic" type, whose present eschatology brings it near to the "enthusiasts" so strongly attacked in 1 Cor. 15 and 2 Tim. 2:18 and whose Christology is close to docetism (cf. 15f., 24, 31f., 38f.). It is "the relic of a Christian conventicle existing on, or being pushed to, the Church's periphery" (39). In this modified form Käsemann is taking up again the theses he put forward in his inaugural lecture at Göttingen, "Ketzer und Zeuge", (1951).[2]

All things considered, the theological problem posed by the Church's assumption of this Gospel into the canon could not be set out more sharply. Historically speaking this decision was a mistake (76). The Fourth Gospel was a long way from measuring up to the criterion of apostolicity (74) and certainly cannot be called orthodox. In fact, "against all its own intentions, misled by the picture of Jesus as God striding over the earth, the Church assigned to the apostles the voice of those whom it otherwise ignored and one generation later condemned as heretics" (75). So the acceptance of this book into the Church's canon was "through man's error and God's providence"

(75). Was this error, asks Käsemann, a fortunate one? (76). His reply is indirect and indefinite. What is definite, indeed quite uncompromising, is his vehement protest, throughout his book, against any apologia that wishes to assimilate this Gospel to those of the Synoptists: on this point Käsemann makes it quite clear that the theological judgement on the Gospel should not be left hanging in the air. It is much more important to confront the problem of the nature of the canon, its diversity and indeed its oppositions and contradictions, which cause every attempt at developing a standard biblical theology to come to grief. So the reception of the Fourth Gospel into the canon does not resolve the problem of its theological authority. This resides rather in the challenge it presents to surrender oneself continually to the word of Jesus and to evaluate every Christian church in the light of the one question, Do we know Jesus? (76f.). Admittedly, the voice of the truly human Jesus is not to be heard in chapter 17. But how far the Gospel of John can make good its claim to present Jesus' last will and testament can only be determined by answering the question "who Jesus is for us and whether he and he alone leads us to the Father" (78). This is how the book ends: "It is precisely John's dangerous and fascinating theology that calls us into our creatureliness through his christological proclamations. In doing so, does he not actually show us the one final testament of the earthly Jesus and his glory?" (78).

II

The very comprehensive picture of Johannine theology sketched in Käsemann's book should restrain any reviewer from criticizing his clearly outlined theses simply on the basis of particular statements occurring here or there in the Gospel. Käsemann could justifiably rejoin that any statement found in the Fourth Gospel must be read within the precise context he himself has delineated. Nevertheless, despite the many accurate and brilliantly expressed observations to be found in his book, it is just because of this general context that I find myself unable to agree with his interpretation as a whole. In explaining my reasons I must restrict myself to certain aspects of particular importance.

1 *The meaning of the farewell discourses*
In Käsemann's interpretation of the Fourth Gospel remarkably little weight is attached to the farewell discourses of chapters 13—17, situated by the evangelist between Jesus' earthly career and the passion and Easter narrative.[a] The mere extent of these (almost a fifth of the

entire Gospel!) is enough to show their importance; but what really counts is their thematic content. Käsemann's failure to give them more prominence is particularly surprising in view of the fact that he heads his chapters with terms drawn from John 17. It is true that several quotations from chapters 13—17 are to be found at various places in his book and that towards the beginning he makes some very pertinent observations on their literary form, one which the evangelist himself has exploited (4f.). And he correctly observes also how strange it is that the farewell discourse of a dying man – his *testament* – should be placed in the mouth of the Prince of Life. It is also true that what is involved here is not just an episode in Jesus' career, but an episode in the history of the community, in that the discourses are to be understood as Jesus' final provisions, now that he himself has his place with the Father, for ensuring the consolation of the community and protection against the dangers which beset it. Even so, I cannot admit that this situation and what it involves have been adequately explained or that its significance for the Gospel as a whole has been appreciated.[3]

Jesus' departure is not just the external occasion of these discourses: rather, his return to the Father, while his disciples remain behind on earth, is actually their theme. Moreover in this picture of the disciples on the eve of Jesus' death is to be descried the situation of the faithful on earth, its essential nature, the path it must follow till the end of time. Such traces of history as there are recede completely into the background: the names of the various disciples who intervene at certain points are of no consequence. This is not a matter of an isolated temporal happening, but of the basic problematic of time and history that confronts the faithful in all ages. The finality of the end of Jesus' earthly life and the trials that ensue for the faithful, shocked, grieving and distressed, are reflected here more profoundly than anywhere else in the NT. Jesus departs, the world remains. Not it, but its era comes to an end.

These discourses carry the astonishing message that Jesus' departure, which puts an end to the human association the disciples had enjoyed with him on earth, founds and inaugurates a new and different association, one that his presence on earth was unable to provide: it is the foundation and commencement of a new era, an era that will have no end. This is part of the message of the Johannine Christ, that his glory shines out in his death. His farewell is transformed into the birth of faith. So Jesus' death is not merely a passage through to glory but in the proper sense a *breakthrough*. A new future opens out to the faithful, the chance of remaining with him, on the strength of his promise to come to them and to abide with them. The fulfilment of this promise is the task of the Paraclete, who will wait until Jesus' departure from earth before he comes and leads them into all truth. This event is not one that can be placed in an apocalyptic pattern or inserted into the conceptual framework of salvation history, because in what is said about Jesus in these very discourses, Easter, Pentecost and Parousia coalesce.

Given that this is the central theme of the farewell discourses, can one really agree with Käsemann that the one who is speaking here is not the one who is about to die (5)? Surely not. Admittedly there is no longer any reference in this Gospel to the torments of the passion or to Jesus' dread of death – though there is a counterpart to the Gethsemane story in 12:22ff.[4] Nevertheless the one about to die does indeed speak in the farewell discourses, insofar as his words reveal to the faithful the benefits of his death. The passion narrative that follows is also, if looked at in the same light, the story of the one who has completed his work on earth (19:30). But it is equally true that this gives us a new insight into Jesus' career on earth before his passion. It is the task of the Spirit Paraclete to bring this into remembrance. But this does not mean simply recapitulating the historical facts. The reminding, the re-presentation, is identical with the glorification of Jesus.

I cannot understand Käsemann's assertion that the passion narrative must have been in some sense an embarrassment to the evangelist because it does not accord with the picture of a God striding over the earth. According to Käsemann, John made things easier for himself by more or less forcibly stamping his narrative with the seal of victory. But John – though he takes a completely different path from the Synoptists – makes perfectly clear the significance for him of a theology of the cross. The actual concept of glory itself, anchored as it is in this Gospel to the paradox of the crucifixion, is in my view sufficient proof of this. Admittedly the Jesus of John's Gospel is glorified whilst still on earth. But the community realizes that it is only after Easter that it can use this language or understand its significance. This is acknowledged even in the Prologue (1–14). This means *in retrospect*. Of this perspective, which is of paramount importance, Käsemann, surprisingly, has nothing whatever to say. In other words, he fails to bring out that the faith that lies behind the Johannine picture of Christ is not in the first place grounded in the earthly Jesus but upon him who died on the cross.[b] If this is right then it means the collapse of the only level on which, according to Käsemann, John presents the story of Jesus, namely as a mythical account of God striding over the earth.

In my opinion, John has given ample indication that this is how he wishes to be read, by placing, throughout his Gospel, anticipatory glimpses of Jesus' approaching death. It is wrong to assert (7) that there are only a few of these and that the passion narrative only comes into view at the end of the narrative, to which it forms a postscript. The opposite is the case. One has only to mention the witness of the Baptist (1:26–9) and the numerous places throughout the Gospel, from the story of Cana on, in which there is a mysterious allusion to the "hour" of Jesus (2:3; 7:30; 8:20), culminating in 12:23ff. and 13:1 and in the equivalent teaching of the farewell discourse (13:31; 17:1). Then too there is the story of the purification of the Temple, placed right at the beginning of this Gospel – once again with a mysterious allusion to Jesus' death (2:13ff.), as well as the discourse appended to the dialogue with Nicodemus on the descent, ascent and paradoxical elevation of the Son of Man (3:12–15; cf. 6:63ff., 12:32f.). These allusions become clearer with the Good Shepherd discourse, the raising of Lazarus (already placed within the context of the passion narrative, cf. 11:45ff.), the anointing at Bethany (12:1ff.) and the saying on the grain of corn that has to die in order to yield its fruit (12:24f.). Equally important in this connection are the anticipatory references to the approaching revelation of the Son of Man that occur first in the call of Nathanael (1:51), and then at the conclusion of the feeding miracle and the discourse on the bread of life (6:61ff.; cf. also 8:28). Mention must also be made of the repeated use of the direct "we" form that belongs to the witness of the later community (1:14; 3:11f.; 9:4).^c

When all these anticipatory references are taken in conjunction with the earliest form of the Johannine farewell-discourses, which are without parallel in the other Gospels, then it is clear that this Gospel is to be understood *by looking back*: what gives it its intelligibility is the witness of the Paraclete, who testifies to the one glorified in his death and claims thereby to pronounce sentence on the world.

2 *John and his tradition*

Although what has been said so far must be allowed to stand without reservation, even so one should not conceal from oneself the abiding difficulties of Johannine exegesis. The vantage-point from which, as we learn from the farewell discourses, John views the history of Jesus is certainly of great importance; so too is the hermeneutical perspective from which his Gospel is to be understood. Still, it would be a mistake to think that this provides us with a master-key for the interpretation of the whole book. The complexity and difficulty of the problems which John poses to exegesis are clearly determined by the fact that this evangelist, like the others, is reproducing certain traditions, whilst at the same time seriously reworking these for his own purposes. So it is necessary to take a closer look at the tradition he had in front of him and his relation towards it.

This means touching on obscure and much-debated issues that can scarcely be treated satisfactorily here. We can certainly recognize a preformed tradition in the miracle stories, Jesus' signs. There are weighty reasons for thinking that there are far-reaching differences between this pre-Johannine tradition and the synoptic tradition. This is proved by the strikingly few agreements between the narrative and discourse material of John and the Synoptists. Admittedly there are some. But even at points where the two overlap, as in the account of the nobleman's son (4:46ff.), the feeding narrative (6:1ff.) and the story of Jesus' walking on the lake (6:16ff., where the pericopae follow in the same order as in Mark 6:30ff., 45ff.), in certain of Jesus' sayings, and above all in the passion and Easter cycle, the divergences are so considerable that it is hard to suppose that John had a first-hand knowledge of the Synoptic Gospels and decided for himself what to retain and what to omit. This means that there is no place for the long-debated question whether John was setting out to replace or to supplement the first three Gospels. It is more plausible to suppose that the relatively few points of agreement go back to a common fund of traditional material, which may occasionally occur even in John in a very early form,[5] but have generally been developed independently and (especially in the miracle stories) taken a shape in which the miraculous element has been heightened.[6] In all probability the portrait of Christ as it appeared in the tradition lying behind John corresponded in many respects to the portrait of God striding over the earth which Käsemann has projected for the Gospel as a whole.

Of course this does not mean that one can make the tradition bear the brunt of the blame for these accounts and the Christology they evince, thereby relieving the evangelist of responsibility and making him out to be simply a critic of what was handed down to him. It would be quite wrong to affirm that John worked upon this tradition only for want of anything better. He certainly adopted it as his own and was influenced by it to a remarkable degree.

But equally incontrovertible is the thoroughgoing critique to which John subjects this tradition, his constant readiness to read the miracles as signs pointing to Jesus himself, to warn against a faith based on miracles alone, and to castigate the persistent incomprehension or unbelief arising from an over-attachment to the earthly Jesus. So it is no accident that the miracle stories are often linked at least implicitly and potentially, sometimes quite explicitly, with one of the great "I am" sayings (6:35; 9:5; cf. 8:12; 11:25). Nor is there anything accidental in the frequent shift from the past tense of the narrative to the present tense of the discourses, or in the way that pericopae beginning, as in the Synoptic Gospels, in a narrative style suited to the context, tail off without any clear ending and with no further mention of the characters of the story. Relevant in this connection are the peculiar "faults" (in the geological sense of the word) that occur in the dialogues preceding Jesus' discourses. Examples are the beginning of the dialogue with Nicodemus (chap. 3), the account of Jesus' meeting with the Samaritan woman (chap. 4), the healing of the cripple (chap. 5), the feeding of the five thousand (chap. 6) and finally in the episode concerning the Greeks (12:20ff.). The train of thought that has been started suddenly takes off in new and surprising directions, like a path that breaks off at a precipice or climbs steeply up to inaccessible heights.[7]

The elements of pre-Johannine tradition discernible in the Gospel are not, then, to be dismissed as an awkward residue which the evangelist could not quite manage to discard. At the same time it should be evident that *both* the thoroughly traditional portraiture of the earthly Jesus *and* the critique to which John submits the tradition stem from a common root. Both are to be understood from the standpoint adopted in the farewell discourses, in other words from the testimony of the Paraclete. This opens up what from now on is the dominant perspective, that of Jesus' significance for salvation: which means that the evangelist did not have to abandon the earthly Jesus but was able to offer a fresh version of the story, one that keeps close to the tradition whilst never ceasing to give a critical interpretation of it. Hence the unevennesses and the extremely dialectical[8] character of the Fourth Gospel. There remain a number of snags and oddities. But this much seems to me certain. If one follows Käsemann in interpreting John's version of the story of Jesus undialectically as a simple, straightforward story of God striding over the earth, a story infected with docetism and robbed of the reality of the crucifixion, then what one has encountered is not John but the pre-Johannine tradition.

Even from the point of view of history the thesis that the Christology of John is naively docetic seems to me to be false. The opening of the First Letter of John, alluding to and improvising upon the Prologue of the Gospel, contains an unmistakeable onslaught upon docetism, and this is how the Church correctly came to interpret John 1:14.[9] However justified Käsemann may have been in protesting against taking the first half of the verse ("the word was made flesh") in isolation and offering a precipitate modernizing interpretation of it as "a paradoxical incognito", still it is equally mistaken, it seems to me, to place exclusive emphasis upon the second half of the verse ("we have seen his glory"), spoken from the perspective of the post-Easter community, and thus to insist upon a choice.[10] It is obvious that for John the thrust of 1:14 is not towards affirming that Jesus was *God*, but that the Logos of God, God himself, has manifested himself, the incarnate one, in the man *Jesus*,[d] even if the programme contained in this sentence is carried through in the body of the Gospel very differently from the Jesus tradition we know from the rest of the NT, with a distinctively Johannine style and vocabulary and in a manner tied to and conditioned by its own historical presuppositions.

One should therefore go further than Käsemann in attempting to determine the history of religions background of the Fourth Gospel. The vague recourse to hellenistic enthusiasm is unsatisfactory. Even if earlier hypotheses[11] have become increasingly questionable and in need of a fresh critical examination, the question whether John paved the way for gnosticism or was influenced by it should not remain unanswered. John *presupposes* gnosticism. What precisely this is has not yet been sufficiently determined, and my assertion may require certain modifications. Nevertheless it must be allowed to stand. As is sufficiently recognized, an abundance of gnostic ideas and concepts have been taken over and adapted, especially in the Johannine discourses,[12] so much so that there is no need to keep dithering over the solution to this particular problem. Käsemann is cautious here and he does not discuss the history of religions problem at any length; even so, his book is more successful than many other works that simply pile up parallels as they highlight the many points of contact between Johannine theology and gnosticism. The recognition that the Fourth Gospel presupposes gnosticism is important for its interpretation, not least because this conceptual world discloses a horizon of problems and perceptions that are simply not broached by the rest of the early Christian tradition. In the language and insights of gnosticism the evangelist finds not just a terminological tool-kit, but the means of expressing his own genuinely new understanding of revelation and salvation. Furthermore the fact that John speaks from within the same conceptual world is important for grasping the significance of his differences from gnosticism. Heading his attack, obviously, is the confessional formula regarding the incarnation of the Logos in John 1:14, which speaks of something more than a temporary masking or veiling of the divine Word, and whose wording represents for gnostic ears a vastly greater stumbling-block than statements such as those in Rom. 8:3, 1 Tim. 3:16 and the letters of Ignatius. Against Käsemann, I think that John's anti-gnostic stance is also evinced in John 3:16 ("God so loved the world"). Even if this statement did come from a fund of pre-Johannine material – which is by no means proved – that does not affect its central importance. Equally disputable, it seems to me, is the thesis that John, without denying that the world was created, does not allow it really to remain creation (66) but makes it into a mere backcloth or setting for the revelation that is directed at it. Certainly John's gnosticizing language makes this a possible interpretation. But here is where one needs to be alert to the significant differences from gnosticism which the evangelist, despite his use of the same language, succeeds in highlighting. Käsemann himself admits that the world is not disqualified in the Gospel of John in the sense of a metaphysical dualism (63). Rather its refusal to believe qualifies it unambiguously as the enemy of God. Even in its rebelliousness, however, it remains God's creation.[e] That is why the reality in which the unbelieving world moves is a lie and an illusion: it lives on surrogates.[13]

In this connection a word of criticism must be said against Käsemann's understanding of the Johannine concept of creation. It is striking how much use he makes of this theological motif throughout his book, giving it much greater emphasis than can be justified by the Gospel itself (cf. e.g. 51, 55, 62f., 66). This is evidently because he is using the concept of creation to attack an anthropological and existential interpretation of the Gospel and therefore gives it especial prominence. But in doing so he makes it, so to speak, into a separate, independent article of faith, and practically cuts it off from the context in which it occurs in the Gospel, that is to say the specifically Johannine context of the link between revelation and faith.[f]

This is where John's creation motif really belongs: in the realm of the opposition between light and darkness, truth and falsehood, freedom and slavery, life and death, as options available to all mankind, to be grasped or rejected. No doubt when this happens it is not just the decisions men make for themselves that are involved, but the decisions God makes in their regard. This is most decidedly an anti-gnostic understanding of faith, and it is matched by the fact that the most specific and central gnostic ideas are not to be found in the Fourth Gospel, which has nothing about the heavenly origin and divine nature of the redeemed and the gathering of the sparks of light.[14g] In the Gospel the separation of the faithful from the world is not a cosmic event, nor is it the object of a ritual and sacramental enactment.

All this goes to show that even the Gospel's undeniably "gnostic" traits, the absoluteness of the demands of revelation, the hostility to the world, the esotericism, etc., are not, properly understood, gnostic at all. What they obviously do assert, with unprecedented, unremitting and perhaps exasperating one-sidedness, is that purely *as* world the world is impure and that the only road to salvation is a union with God and Jesus disclosed in the word and seized on by faith. And this is the typical reproach that the world receives from the faithful. The world is and continues to be affected and concerned by what happens to them. In this sense Jesus is and continues to be "the light of the *world*" (8:12), and his victory is and continues to be the judgement that convicts the world (16:8ff.). So even the esotericism of the Gospel has a proclamatory function.

3. *The precariousness of anachronisms*

One last point deserves brief mention. In his critical judgement upon John, Käsemann employs a number of categories drawn from the subsequent history of heresy and dogma (e.g. naive docetism, inner-trinitarian reflection, even early Catholicism).[h] These are indeed capable of shedding light on some states of affairs and outlining certain problems clearly. But they are dangerous in the sense that they can easily conceal the most fundamental problem of all: what historical and theological significance is there in the fact that such astonishingly different conceptions had room to exist side by side in the early Church, whereas later they could no longer do so? We cannot satisfactorily account for this state of affairs by noting simply that an appeal to the "riches of Scripture" (with a well-attested satisfaction that is often enjoyed at the expense of a responsible theological judgement) is regularly accompanied by a global repudiation of theological decisions which the Church arrived at later in the course of her history. Even where Scripture is concerned we cannot shrug off the task of a theological assessment of truth and error. Nevertheless it remains highly precarious to rush into a verdict based on the criteria of the later Church. This would soon lead to the conclusion that in the wake of practically every NT author, be it Matthew, Luke, Paul or John, there soon emerges a questionable theology – even a heresy. We must have a clear realization of these possible consequences and that means recognizing that theology is always a high-risk activity.

Nevertheless the first task is still to arrive at a critical understanding of the manifold varieties of early Christianity with an eye to their original intention, to take on board the questions that arise from their extremely diverse historical settings, and then to present freshly, in one's own language and according to one's own way of thinking, the gospel of Christ. Käsemann's important book is of considerable help in promoting a sharp awareness of the pecularities and puzzles of Johannine theology. But his presentation, strikingly uncompromising as it is, is too one-sided to give an accurate account of the Gospel's peculiar dialectic. Still, the powerful thrust of this book is not likely to go unheeded. This will not be the last time that we are forced to make a fresh start in the field of Johannine studies.

NOTES

1 Against Bultmann (1955) 56.

2 *Exegetische Versuche und Besinnungen* I (1960) 168–87 [No ET].

3 In what follows I take up some points that are also developed in my articles, "Der Paraklet im Johannesevangelium", *Geschichte und Glaube* I (Munich, 1968) 68–89; "Die Zeit des Geistes" (ibid.) 90–103.

4 Cf. R. Bultmann (1971) 428 n. 1; M. Dibelius, "Gethsemane", in *Botschaft und Geschichte* I (1953) 262. Original English in *The Crozer Quarterly* 12 (1935) 193ff.

5 I will confine myself here to mentioning first, the saying concerning the destruction of the Temple (John 2:19) which the evangelist (secondarily, it is true) interprets of Jesus' body (cf. R. Bultmann [1971] 126 n.1): and second, the date John assigns to the crucifixion. On the question of the antiquity of the Johannine tradition see too R. Gyllenberg, "Die Anfänge der johanneischen Tradition", *Neutestamentliche Studien für R. Bultmann* (1957²) 144ff.

6 On this see especially E. Haenchen, "Johanneische Probleme", in *Gott und Mensch, Gesammelte Aufsätze* (1965) 78ff.

7 These are just a few examples from a rich store of such "faults". They illustrate a constant stylistic device in the Gospel, one which stems from the subject-matter.

8 [*Höchst dialektisch:* this is a phrase Käsemann (1969) 144 uses in a pejorative sense to criticize C. H. Dodd's interpretation of the Prologue. Tr.]

9 The first clear and explicit attack upon docetism comes, it is true, in 1 John; but the sharp formulation of John 1:14a obviously has a similar aim of affirming the identity of the divine Logos with the historical man Jesus of Nazareth, an identity contested by docetism but crucial for the Christian faith. On this point see R. Schnackenburg (1965) 268 and R. Brown (1966) 31f. No conclusion should be drawn concerning the reduction in importance of the incarnation of the Logos from the general antithesis between spirit and flesh in 3:6 and 6:63. See my article, "Die eucharistische Rede im Joh Ev", *Geschichte und Glaube* I (Munich, 1968) 60–67. For John the incarnation is not just the vehicle of revelation but the actual revelation itself (cf. Bultmann [1971] 65f.). The difference between John and Ignatius is well brought out by H. Köster in *ZTK* 54 (1957) 56–69: for Ignatius the redeemer unites the spheres of flesh and spirit, man and God. This idea of a substantial unity between the two spheres is the basis of Ignatius' sacramental teaching but is totally unJohannine. For the anti-docetic use of John 1:14 in the early Church, see Irenaeus, *Adv. haer.* I, 10, 3, etc. Cf. W. von Loewenich, *Das Johannes–Verständnis im 2. Jahrhundert* (1932) 119ff., esp. 128. 1 John is actually quoted more often.

10 [The debate alluded to in this paragraph is between Bultmann (1971) who stressed the first half of 1:14 and Käsemann (1969) 152–9 who stressed the second. Tr.]

11 [This alludes to the views of Bultmann. Tr.]

12 There are weighty reasons for believing, against Bultmann, that the Johannine discourse source was already Christian.

13 Cf. R. Bultmann (1955) 15ff.

14 The gnosticizing language of 1 John 3:9 goes beyond anything in the Gospel.

ADDITIONAL NOTES

[a] Käsemann responds to this criticism in the first of the retaliatory notes mentioned in our introduction (above, p. 9). He says that he has given as much space to the farewell discourses as "the taut line" of his analysis would allow: "Even so", he continues, "I think I have clearly delineated the problem posed by these discourses and their significance. The key question is this: How can the basic christological message of the Gospel be reconciled with the fact that this is the only place in the Gospel where the anthropological theme of the faith under threat is given any extensive development? My answer is that Jesus' departure allows for fundamental observations concerning the presence of the exalted Christ among his own. Thus the "anthropological" thematic also serves Christology. Even more important is the fact that Jesus' death, like the miracles and the Easter events, is not treated along strictly historical or, in the ordinary sense, salvation-historical lines. Rather it offers a paradigm of what the faithful repeatedly experience. According to John, Christians cannot live upon a single, once-and-for-all happening. Their faith is continually under threat from the apparent departure of the Lord, and if it is to "abide" has to rely on the coming of the Paraclete in the Word. This was precisely the lesson of 6:66f. regarding dealings with the earthly Jesus. The need and necessity stay the same. How then can Bornkamm assert that the time of Jesus ends with his departure (p. 87)? How can the farewell discourses be *retrospective* (cf. p. 88)? They make a promise for the future. The "reminding" of the Paraclete points to the historical Jesus as a model of what is still of immediate importance and actuality. What is "new" since Easter is not the encounter with the glorified Jesus as such, but only the knowledge (through the Spirit) that Jesus' exaltation, as well as being his own ultimate destination, is also the key to his earthly life. This already stood under the sign of glory. Bornkamm goes against the evangelist's intentions by historicizing both Jesus' passion and the farewell discourses, and thus assimilating them to the synoptic account (18 n. 2; cf. Käsemann [1968] 5).

[b] According to Käsemann, this opposition betrays a failure to recognize that there is no real antithesis in John between the earthly Jesus and the Jesus exalted on the cross: "... to me both incarnation and cross seem to be 'projections' or manifestations of the pre-existent Logos. Accordingly I feel equally unable to lay any stress on 'the fruit of death'. Finally, I disagree with the statement (above, p. 87) that 'Jesus' death is not a passage through to glory but in the proper sense a breakthrough'. For it is as just such a breakthrough that 1:14 characterizes the incarnation. Jesus' death has no special significance except as the return to the infinite glory of pre-existence" (49 n. 53; cf. *Testament*, 20).

[c] "Bornkamm's statistics", counters Käsemann, "might seem rather to support me than to tell against me. Obviously no Gospel can entirely ignore Jesus'

death. But the question is not how often reference is made to it and its attendant circumstances. Rather we have to ask how it is interpreted. 7:30 and 8:20 testify primarily to the exaltation of the earthly Jesus, and also predict his subsequent arrest. In 12:1ff., 23ff., 32 and 13:1 death is understood as the path to glory. The same is true of 2:19f. and 3:14, which (like 10:11) make use of traditional material. For the formula "give his life" refers to the external act of love. None of this goes anywhere towards a theology of the cross. It simply shows that John uses previous ideas about Jesus' death as a starting-point for his own interpretation. The only exceptions are 1:26, 29, and it is no accident that these are put in the mouth of the Baptist and thereby marked out as traditional sayings of the community" (22 n. 7; cf. *Testament*, 7).

d To say that in 1:14 Jesus is portrayed as the Logos of God and not as God is not very illuminating, suggests Käsemann, in view of 1:1f and 20:28 (28 n. 10; cf. *Testament*, 9).

e This, asserts Käsemann, is not so: "John's thinking here seems to be dialectical. The world remains creation insofar as it has been brought into existence through the Word. But its refusal of belief, which is an act of rebellion against the Lord, reveals that in its present situation, which is one of darkness, falsehood and transience, it belongs to the realm 'below'. So the faithful, though indeed *in* the world, are not *of* it. In practice it is only as reborn believers, who have passed from death into life, that they represent creation. For in John this receives its character not from the initial act of creation, but from the working of the Word. For him creation is the world within the sphere of the activity of the Word, and does not include the world as a simple reality existing previous to and alongside this. Relevant here is the fact that John, unlike the early Christian milieu in which he lived, no longer represents an unbroken universalism. 'The proclamatory function of Johannine esotericism', of which Bornkamm speaks (above, p.94), is not in question. But this should not make us lose sight of the Gospel's predestinarianism. The proclamation is not directed to the world as such but to the elect scattered throughout the world" (132 n. 18; cf. *Testament*, 64).

f Käsemann professes astonishment at this charge. From the opening lines of the Gospel, the Logos is seen as the instrument of God's creative act, an idea, Käsemann asserts, "which encompasses and pervades the whole Gospel and so cannot be made out to be an independent article of faith" (something which Bornkamm accuses him of doing). If there was any substance in this charge Bornkamm should direct it against the Gospel itself. But this would be to rob the teaching on the Logos of its depth and breadth. This, as Bultmann saw, not only establishes man's essential creatureliness but exposes the cosmic gulf separating truth from falsehood and light from dark. "Disagreement on this point actually reveals an utterly different conception of the Gospel and puts at risk its radical otherness (*Radikalität*)." Here Käsemann invokes the Bultmannian principle of *Sachkritik* (material criticism of the content) which allows the exegete to use the subject-matter of a work to control and interpret his interpretation. "On no account", he declares, "is the Gospel's radicality to be flattened out or put on a par with the rest of early Christian teaching. Throughout the history of the Church the singularity of this Gospel has been continuously emphasized. Equally continuous has been the offence it has caused. (And incidentally this is our only clue to the historical situation of the evangelist.) I am surprised, I must confess, that my critics have paid so little attention to this central point" (109 n. 55; cf. *Testament*, 51).

^g On the contrary, says Käsemann, this motif, or at least a variant of it, is discernible in the idea of the gathering of the scattered (cf. John 11:52): "Similarly, the idea of election is a variant of the statement concerning the heavenly provenance of the redeemed. They are born 'from on high'. Finally, one should remember that for John faith means remaining together in a heavenly union. This at any rate is a 'cosmic event' that brooks no existential interpretation. If Bultmann's discourse source is not accepted, then it is no longer possible to ascribe gnosticizing terminology and motifs to pre-Johannine tradition. The Gospel is more gnostic than Bornkamm himself is prepared to admit. It is curious that he should reproach me at the same time for failing to give sufficient prominence to the sort of facts that a 'history of religions' approach would be interested in" (150 n. 39; cf. *Testament*, 72).

^h In a very long note Käsemann protests vigorously against the charge of anachronism. Above all he is anxious that the true state of affairs (*Sachverhalt*) be properly acknowledged, most particularly what he, as a Protestant, sees as the deplorable retreat of "apocalyptic theology" in the face of ecclesiology.

In the second place Käsemann admits an interest in certain embryonic tendencies, already discernible in the NT period, that foreshadowed the later Church. Though himself convinced that there was a pre-Christian gnosis, he allows that this is a hotly-debated question. On the other hand, he points out that there is as yet no consensus about the meaning of this term, unlike his own preferred terms: early Catholicism and docetism. He suggests that a metaphysical dualism is not in itself sufficient justification for the use of the term "gnosis" and asks slyly whether it too, borrowed as it is from church historians, may not be anachronistic.

It is widely acknowledged that the first two Letters of John are anti-docetic, and Käsemann asks whether this is not yet another anachronistic category. Besides, does not anti-docetism presuppose docetism? Even today the un-examined premises of an intellectual movement may later be seen to be dangerous and so prompt a reaction. "So the anti-docetism of the Letters does nothing to disprove the presence of docetism in the Gospel itself, which I have backed up with all sorts of weighty arguments." Having offered an alternative reading of John 1:14a, Käsemann wonders why people evade the issues this raises. To be flexible with regard to terminology does not mean that one should compromise with the facts. And in any case since it is clear that the explanation of later dogma is to be sought somewhere in early Christianity, there is some justification for retaining the very terms Bornkamm criticizes. The real anachronism would be to set up such a stark opposition between subsequent church dogma and the kerygma of the early Church as to exclude the latter from all discussion of the development of doctrine (62 n. 69; cf. *Testament*, 26).

6

*Source Criticism and Religionsgeschichte in the Fourth Gospel**

J. LOUIS MARTYN

The time available for this working paper made necessary the familiar choice: either to work with some care on perhaps two or three passages, or to try a bird's-eye view of a part of the Johannine landscape. Had I chosen the former route, the passages would probably have been drawn from the passion narrative, where (1) the discipline of source criticism, (2) the comparative study of religious ideas, and (3) the informed quest for John's place in the history of early Christian thought seem to me to intersect in unusually productive ways. I suspect that current divergent opinions regarding John's attitude toward Jesus' death might be at least set in better order by such labor.[1]

As it is, I have chosen the more general alternative which necessarily leads to the more sketchy result. But it suits my present purpose well enough: simply to suggest some of the gains that may be had if one will be reckless enough to try to ride uphill and downhill on three horses at once, and, much of the time, by night.

I *Hypotheses and Probes*

I can indicate the area under conscious purvue and the general approach by stating two working hypotheses and two critical probes.

HYPOTHESIS 1:   Fortna's Signs Gospel (SG) is reasonably similar to the Fourth Evangelist's narrative source.

I do not find Fortna's analysis equally compelling in all of its parts. Toward the end of this paper I will cite one or two instances of

* First published in *Jesus and Man's Hope*, vol. I, ed. D. G. Buttrick (1970) 247–73. The notes have been abridged slightly.

disagreement. There are others. But it is not to be expected that a source analysis of John will be uniformly convincing to anyone save its author, and probably not even to him. In the main I find Fortna's work to be a solid working hypothesis. One of the questions posed in this paper – stated below – is whether the placing of Fortna's work as one hypothesis alongside others will lead to increased or lessened confidence in it and/or modifications in it.

HYPOTHESIS 2: Between the production of SG and the writing of the Fourth Gospel (4G) lie dynamic developments of various sorts which played important roles in causing the Fourth Evangelist to handle SG as he did.

One might think that so obvious a hypothesis is superfluous, but a survey of recent literature indicates the contrary. To cite a single example, I must say that *in regard to this hypothesis* Bornkamm's generally telling review of Käsemann's *Testament of Jesus* is a step backward.[2] For it is one of the numerous and distinct services of Ernst Käsemann, curiously overlooked in Bornkamm's review, to renew and make potent in our time the voice of F. C. Baur.[3]

> Nothing is gained when someone conjures up an inaccurately pictured ghost of the terrible "Tübingen School", only to pose as a modern St. George when he has laid it again in its grave. Much will be gained if we can re-learn how to analyze "the concrete, the individual, the peculiar" in the history of early Christian thought, and only after having done that to attempt a synthetic picture which is therefore drawn on the basis of the stubborn details rather than drafted according to modern desires for a balanced harmony.[4]

A careful reading of Käsemann's Johannine studies will cause one at the very least to re-examine an assumption, conscious or unconscious, that John wrote in response almost exclusively to forces internal to himself, caring very little whether his work would be read or not.[5] The Fourth Gospel does belong *somewhere* in the history of early Christian thought, even if we are not able to fix that "somewhere" as easily as in the case, let us say, of Galatians (which is problematic enough itself). And the chances of our finding its historical locus are vastly increased if we will listen for clues to the *dynamism* of the setting. John is not fighting mad as he writes – contrast Paul in several instances – but neither is he pronouncing the benediction at the graduation exercises of Ephesus University, even if, as a modern parallel, a commencement speaker might be tempted to enlighten *some* graduating seniors regarding their true parentage (John 8:44a).

In short, there are numerous data in the Gospel which indicate that John is a theologian with *opponents* perhaps every bit as active and aggravating as those Paul knew in Corinth. In part and in some sense of the term John apparently writes in order to *win*. Käsemann has helped us to see this.

PROBE 1: Do the two working hypotheses intersect in ways which are illuminating to one or both of them?

Again we are dealing with the more-or-less obvious. The surveyor knows that a point fixed by measuring along a single line is more reliable if it is confirmed by the intersection of two reasonably drawn lines. To be specific, if it is reasonably clear that John is a theologian with opponents, it is equally clear that the scholar who searches for clues to the identity and beliefs of those opponents will need as many scientific controls as he can get. One recalls how the pendulum has swung almost off its mooring in the various attempts to identify Paul's opponents at certain points in his work. The relative success – so it seems to me, at any rate – in the case of the Corinthian correspondence is due in no small part to the fact that *literary criticism* has provided us with *several documents* representing successive *stages* in the volatile give-and-take, perhaps even including snippets of the opponents' work. Will Fortna's source-critical labors provide a similar helpful control for a renewed attempt to distinguish *stages* in the Johannine tradition?

But, to return for a moment to hypothesis 2, it is putting Fortna and Käsemann together which has caused me to formulate it as I have (Between ... dynamic...). I can scarcely believe that John expended the massive effort necessary to re-think and re-shape – perhaps one should say recreate – SG (and other available traditions), and to do so *as* he did, merely because some inadequacies in SG offended his theological sensitivities.[6] In other words we are dealing here not with two stages (SG and 4G), but rather with at least three: the writing of SG; subsequent and thus chronologically intervening developments, including activities on the part of "opponents"; and the writing of 4G. This being so, an adequate understanding of the third stage will require careful consideration of *both* its predecessors.[7]

PROBE 2: Do the two hypotheses intersect in ways which are illuminating with regard to both the general history of religious ideas (*Rlg*) and the history of early Christian theology (*Thg*)? Conversely, are they supported by what we already know of *Rlg* and *Thg*?

In an age which seems thoroughly entranced with redaction criticism, for the sake of quickly acquired theological pay dirt, one needs, perhaps, to recall that patient labors in the general history of religious ideas and in the history of specifically Christian thought are themselves carried out by *Neutestamentler* for the sake of theological precision, gained by observations similar to those proper to *Redaktionskritik*.[8] That is to say, each of the three disciplines under consideration here

– source criticism, *Rlg*, and *Thg* – forms a basis for possible redaction criticism or something similar to it. Therefore, mutual criticism among the three is imperative. But to limit ourselves to the two working hypotheses, it will be sufficient, perhaps, to say that these will acquire added probability to the extent that (a) SG proves to be readily identifiable *religionsgeschichtlich* and *theologiegeschichtlich*, (b) the intervening stage or stages posited between SG and 4G and (c) John's own contribution are similarly identifiable, or at least comprehensible.

It may be further clarifying for me to add that the impulse to attempt the present paper came to me when I began to ask myself how three recent monographs might fit together, or not fit together, on the Johannine shelf: Käsemann's *The Testament of Jesus*, Meeks' *The Prophet-King*, and Fortna's *The Gospel of Signs*. Käsemann seeks to fix the historical place of John's theology – mainly Christology – by means of carefully and boldly constructed *theologiegeschichtlich* comparisons. Meeks explores an aspect of John's Christology partly by following a similar approach (*Prophet-King*, 60ff.), but mainly by placing great weight on *religionsgeschichtlich* comparisons, an avenue Käsemann explicitly leaves aside (*Testament*, 66). The results reached in these two monographs are not entirely harmonious, to say the least.[9] Now Fortna has propounded a far-reaching source analysis, relying very little on either of these kinds of conceptual comparisons, but making some concluding observations which do indeed speak to the questions of *Rlg* and *Thg*, and which are now being expanded in papers and in a forthcoming *redaktionsgeschichtlich* monograph.[10]

However, the major point here is not the need for ecumenical, scholarly interchange, but rather the methodological imperative to allow *mutual critique* among the three disciplines. Points which are fixed by the supportive intersection, so to speak, of two or, better, of all three are surely worth very serious consideration.

It should be obvious that in a relatively brief working paper one can make only a modest beginning in the very large task to which the two hypotheses and the two probes point. Three factors lighten the load somewhat and enable me at least to make an attempt.

I do not take it as my task, at the present juncture, explicitly to test Hypothesis 1. An initial testing was provided by the oral examination of Fortna's work in dissertation form. Further evaluation will doubtless be provided by reviewers and others.

With regard to Hypothesis 2, I will consciously impose a limitation. In stating that hypothesis I have spoken of *various* developments taking place between the production of SG and the writing of 4G. The range of these developments may be rather large. Were one proceeding on the basis of the present state of Johannine research, rather than following a more inductive path, several possibilities would demand attention. *Perhaps* between SG and 4G arose:

(A) a struggle with followers of John the Baptist
(B) a hardening of battle lines between synagogue and church
(C) inner-church problems, such as:
  1 overemphasis on the anticipated glories of Jesus' future coming
  2 loss of a sense of contact with and memory of the earthly Jesus, with concomitant danger that Christianity might devolve into a mystery religion
  3 docetism
  4 growth of a hardening and institutionally oriented orthodoxy which pits itself with increasing fervor against the growth of Hellenistic enthusiasm in the church
  5 theological developments which are not truly christocentric.[11]

It can be seen that the range of possible developments is large indeed. I do not intend to attempt even a survey of the whole picture, but rather to look for *some of the intervening developments which seem fairly directly and simply reflected in the Evangelist's handling of SG.* If the results of my sketch are taken as an over-all view, they will be misinterpreted.

Finally, I shall not be mechanical in relating the two probes to the two hypotheses. For the timing being I am content to pose a series of questions and to allow the probes and hypotheses to form a general methodological context.

II *Questions and Developing Answers*

A. WHO IS JESUS?

We may begin at a point many interpreters identify as the very center of Johannine theology: the remarkable and massive concentration on Christology. When we raise the question which is surely a key to the Gospel – Who is Jesus? – do we hear answers along the line which affect the degree of probability attaching to our hypotheses?

The Signs Gospel

Fortna finds in SG a single-minded focusing on Christology which appears to be even more exclusive than that often attributed to 4G. The reader of SG is *not* told that a new age has dawned or is about to dawn. He is *not* taught that suffering and sin are now destroyed

(Jesus does not perform miracles in order to alleviate suffering or to attack sin and evil), that the Spirit is bestowed on believers, that in Jesus Christ God has begun to build an *ecclesia*, that in the *ecclesia* the sacraments are centrally important. He *is* told again and again who Jesus is: the Christ, the Messiah of Israel.

On the face of it, source criticism is not strongly supported here by *Rlg* and *Thg*. Fortna speaks of SG's uniqueness in this regard, vis-à-vis not only first-century Christian literature (234), but also Jewish apocalyptic (228). It is a kind of christological oddity, and its being such does not especially increase one's confidence in the source analysis. On the other hand, 4G is itself nearly as single-mindedly oriented to Christology. Käsemann is fully justified in thinking of John when he quotes Zinzendorf: "I have but one passion. That is He and only He." Furthermore, when one ponders the question, What percentage of the religious literature of the hellenistic age has come down to us?, he will be very slow to label any document a *religionsgeschichtlich* "bastard".

More important are observations which may be made regarding SG's optimistic assumption that a simple recounting of Jesus' signs will lead the reader to confess him as Messiah. Fortna points here to Old Testament traditions about Elijah, Elisha, and Moses, and he refers his reader to Dieter Georgi's pages on *theioi andres* ("divine men") in Jewish tradition. There are, then, several possible recognizable conceptual milieux for SG's sign-working Messiah, a figure who apparently raised not only Lazarus, but also himself from the dead. The milieux are all OT–Jewish in character.

Post-SG Developments

With only a pinch of imagination one can pursue the question of Jesus' identity into the intervening period between SG and 4G. For the moment I will limit myself to three suggestions, each of which is given some strength, I think, by the intersection of source criticism and *Rlg*:

1 "To the Bet ha-Midrash!"

Some of the persons exposed to SG, specifically some of the potential Jewish converts for whom, at least in part, it was written (Fortna, 234) reacted quite reasonably by saying, in effect: "Very well, if your claim that Jesus was the Messiah [note the tense] is to be sustained, it must stand up under careful and extensive midrashic examination, carried out by those whose training equips them for such work." (Consider John 5:39; 6:30ff.; 7:17, all non-SG passages.)

We see a similar reaction in the case of Trypho; and there are numerous data in Christian documents which indicate that many early Christian preachers not only encountered such Jewish reactions, but also accepted the demanding challenge, as did Justin in the second century.

The challenge has epistemological implications, notably those evident in the assumption that one can "book a through train" from rational midrashic discussion to dependable conclusions. God gave the Torah. He stands, therefore, at the *beginning* of the line extending from Moses.[12] If he acts today, he will do so in forms that are consistent with, and perhaps even pre-given in, the Torah. When he gave the Torah, he did not keep anything back. Hence, one can pronounce judgment on the basis of authoritative midrash.

2 "Moses is the one who ascended and received the heavenly secrets."

A bit more exotic, on the face of it, is a second possible intervening development, corresponding, I suppose, to SG's portrait of Jesus as the Elijah-like, Elisha-like, Moses-like, prophetic *theios anēr*. The opponents evidently countered such a portrait by identifying themselves as followers of *Moses himself*, who on Sinai ascended to heaven where the heavenly secrets were imparted to him.

The Jewish data which support such a possible development, as well as the relevant Johannine data, have been carefully collected and sifted by Wayne Meeks.[13] What calls for emphasis here is the fact that the Johannine data suggesting such a reaction on the part of SG readers fall outside SG. In this important matter, then, Fortna's source criticism and Meeks' work in the history of religious ideas are mutually supportive. And again we see an intervening development which involves extra-church opponents.

3 "You are Ditheists!"

We are not to assume, of course, that Jewish opponents did all of the talking in the interval between SG and 4G, or that the Johannine theologians limited their counter-response to a simple repetition of SG's materials. There are data in 4G which suggest that at some point(s) the Johannine church so elevated Jesus as *the theios anēr*, the God striding across the face of the earth,[14] as to evoke from Jewish opponents the charge of ditheism. That is to say, the Johannine community apparently used SG and embroidered on it in ways which caused the Jewish opponents to see perhaps in it, and certainly in the use being made of it, an abrogation of monotheism.

Religionsgeschichtlich we *may* see a move here which corresponds in some *rough* way to a move from the materials (proper to SG?) by which van der Woude and Hahn investigate the Prophet to those

105

(added in the interval between SG and 4G?) cited by Wetter as he made a similar attempt.[15] But I am not at all sure about that. Perhaps it merits further investigation. I want only to suggest that such passages as 5:18ff., 8:53 and 10:33 reflect a charge which Jewish opponents hurled at the Johannine community with considerable reason, between the writing of SG and that of 4G.

It may also be relevant to note that the "Logos Hymn" could have played a part in such developments. For it moves implicitly in the direction of ditheism, as Conzelmann has recently pointed out.[16]

With regard to the opponents, there are numerous possible parallels. Perhaps one should consider some of the Rabbinic references which show polemic against those who hold the doctrine of "Two Powers in Heaven", though it would not be necessary to limit the field at this point to Rabbinic data.[17]

The Fourth Gospel

1 Confronted by opponents who enthusiastically exclaim, "To the Bet ha-Midrash", and knowing quite well the simple implications in SG regarding the relationship between signs and faith,[18] John appears to react in several ways:

(*a*) He makes the frequent failure of the signs an important theme in his Gospel.[19] John 12:37ff. shows the Evangelist pondering the development of dominant Jewish opposition which has characterized the interim since the writing of SG. The signs are now seen as the dividing *krisis* (judgment) rather than as simple occasions for faith.

(*b*) He corrects SG in such a way as to deny that the question of Jesus' identity can be settled by midrash.[20]

(*c*) He makes clear that this all-important question is not, Was he Messiah?, but rather Who *is* he? I have pointed out that Bornkamm (1968) steps back from the heritage of F. C. Baur in that he does not ask about the dynamic setting of 4G. But he does provide some very helpful comments, including an accurate listing of four aspects of John's critical stance toward his tradition. The first two are relevant here:

> So it is no accident that the miracle stories are often linked at least implicitly, sometimes quite explicitly, with one of the great "I am" sayings (6:35; 9:5; cf. 8:12; 11:25). Nor is there anything accidental in the frequent shift from the past tense of the narrative to the present tense of the discourses (above, pp. 90f).

(*d*) John senses the epistemological naïveté present both in SG and in the arguments of the opponents; hence he emphasizes:

1 What Bornkamm (ibid.) lists as a fourth aspect of John's critical stance

toward his tradition: *Verwerfungen* (geological faults) which make clear that there are no "through trains" from this side.

2 the role of Paraclete in perception. Note that John points forward to the five paraclete sayings by three times appending to an SG passage an emphatic note about the transition from ignorance to true understanding (2:17; 2:22; 12:16). In each of these cases the transition involves perceiving the true relationship between "the scripture" and Jesus' deeds/words. The verb *mnēsthēnai* ("to remember"), absent from SG, is very important to John as an epistemological-hermeneutical key.

3 the dualism of *present* election. There are numerous facets to this emphasis. John accomplishes it in part by employing what Bornkamm calls the language and perspective of gnosis (118): the exclusive character of the claim to revelation, the enmity to the world, the esoterica. But he employs such language and perspectives in order to sharpen the epistemological issue. Unlike the author of SG, John is interested in exploring various patterns which can arise when the verbs "to see" and "to believe" are related to one another.[21] (Note e.g. 6:36f.) Perhaps Peder Borgen's ingenious exegesis of v. 36 is correct;[22] either way the point here is the same: *seeing* and *believing* cannot be properly related to one another apart from the motif of *present election*. God does not stand only at the beginning of either creation or Torah-revelation (Sinai).[23]

(*e*) I am inclined to think that John's introduction and shaping of Son of Man tradition, wholly absent from SG, and his – so I think – creation of two-level dramas are also to be listed here, i.e. as adjustments of SG in the face of inadequacies in it which have been revealed in the course of Jewish opposition to it.[24]

2 Confronted by opponents who not only are disciples of Moses (9:28; cf. 5:39, 45), but also claim that Moses received the heavenlies on the occasion of his Sinai ascent, John counters quite dogmatically:

No one has ever seen God (1:18), except, of course, the Son, and he who has truly seen the Son (14:8f.). No one has ascended to heaven, except the Son of Man, *not even Moses* (3:13).[25]

John's exegesis of the "Logos Hymn" (i.e. 1:14–18) cannot be fully grasped, I think, unless one (a) gives due weight to *both* of the emphatic elements, v. 14 *and* vv. 17–18, and (b) notes that the literary seam preceding v. 14 coincides with a disjuncture in *religionsgeschichtlich* background.[26] For our present purposes it is, perhaps, enough to say that John is considerably more interested in Moses than was the author of SG, and that the reason for this increased interest apparently lies with the intervening volatile developments vis-à-vis the synagogue. Unlike the author of SG, John finds it necessary to deny claims made for Moses.

3   To the charge of ditheism, a charge nowhere reflected in SG, John constructs a careful response.[27] Here it is important to see that John does not place the lengthy sermon of 5:19–47 immediately after the healing (raising – v. 8) sign of 5:1–9a. Nor is it the sabbath conflict as such which introduces this long speech of Jesus on the relation of the Son to the Father. The transition is accomplished, rather, by 5:18b. One is not surprised, therefore, to find that the sermon in 5:19–47 is preached *at least* in part to those who do not honor the Son at all, while claiming nevertheless to honor God (v. 23). Verse 21 (cf. 26) may very well be an indirect challenge to those who regularly recite the *Shemoneh Esreh*, the second benediction of which reads in part:

> Thou art strong ... Thou livest forever, bringing the dead back to life ... Thou supportest the living and revivest the dead ... Blessed be thou, O God, who bringeth the dead back to life.

Why do the addressees not honor the Son? From their point of view they refuse to do so in order to remain rue monotheists (v. 18). John is also a monotheist. Therefore he is at pains to show his opponents – among other things – how he combines monotheism (which the Jews in their own way represent) with the duality of Father and Son: The Son can do nothing of himself; he does only what he sees the Father doing".[28]

Here we may receive a valuable clue to John's place in the history of Christian thought. There is a theological "both ... and" in 4G, and there is a theological "both ... and" in 1 John. The two are related, yet significantly different. The Evangelist's "both ... and" is directed to opponents (Jews) who want the Father without the wondrous Son, and who hurl at John the charge "Ditheist!" The Epistle writer directs his "both ... and" to inner-church opponents who want Christ without Jesus, and against whom he hurls the charge "Docetist!" Apparent ditheism and unreflecting docetism (Käsemann's term) are coupled in the Johannine community until first one development and then another cause them to be separated and individually handled vis-à-vis disparate opponents. or, to put it another way, the unreflecting docetism of SG and of the "Logos Hymn" – Käsemann's term may be somewhat more satisfactory for SG than for 4G, though I suspect it is suggestive for both[29] – has come home to roost by the time of the First Epistle. Paradoxically, docetic opponents must now be faced by a member of a community which at an earlier date had to find a way simultaneously to honor *the theios anēr* and, being largely Jewish, to remain monotheistic.

Results thus far:

Posing the question of Jesus' identity in these ways leads, I think, to (a) increased confidence in the hypothesis of SG, to (b) the view that dynamic and influential developments do lie chronologically between SG and 4G, to (c) the conclusion that some of these developments constitute a sharp debate between John's church and a mostly hostile Jewish community, and to (d) the conviction that John's own theological stance is in part formed by this post-SG debate.

B. CAN ONE FOLLOW MOSES AND JESUS?

The Signs Gospel

The question does not come up in the mind of the author; thus it is neither posed nor answered as such. Assumed, however, is a clear continuity between Moses and Jesus. Indeed, there is good reason to believe that when SG was produced, the community of messianic believers was, in John's city, a group within the synagogue fellowship. John 1:45 is typical of a simple and unsophisticated strain in SG:

We have found the one of whom Moses and the prophets wrote . . .

Intervening Developments

I have already suggested that John was far more interested in the Moses-Jesus question than was the author of SG, and that the reason for his being so lies in certain intervening developments. Of these developments, 9:28 is typical. To the question, Can one follow Moses and Jesus?, the answer is now a resounding, No![30] With this come two further moves on the part of the opponents: excommunication of those confessing Jesus as Messiah,[31] and trial and execution of Jewish-Christian evangelists who continue the mission among Jews.[32]

The Fourth Gospel

Here again, in light of what has already been said, no lengthy comment is needed. It is John, not the author of SG, I think, who knows and ponders the two awesome moves just mentioned, and who hears "the resounding No!" In light of these developments he works out a profoundly dialectic stance toward the Moses-Jesus issue.[33]

C. WHAT SIGNIFICANCE HAS JESUS' DEATH?

I have remarked above (in the initial paragraph of the paper) that the disciplines of source criticism, *Rlg*, and *Thg* seem to intersect in unusually productive ways as one pursues them through the Johannine passion narrative. In the space and time remaining let me offer a few suggestions.

The Signs Gospel

The reader of SG makes his way through what Fortna calls the Exordium, the Baptist's testimony, the conversion of the first disciples, and all seven of the signs without encountering a single note which is preparatory for Jesus' death. There are no *Streitgespräche* ("controversy dialogues") no hostile murmurings, not even any opposition to the faith awakened by Jesus' signs. We certainly have no guarantee that Fortna's reconstruction presents the whole of this hypothetical document; indeed he explicitly avoids such a claim.[34] Nevertheless, one who works with SG as an hypothesis is clearly justified in pointing out the absence of a correspondent to Mark 3:6. The signs produce faith, not a death plot.

Thus, the weight of showing motivation on the part of Jesus' enemies in the passion story is placed squarely, and virtually exclusively, on the confrontation provoked by Jesus' cleansing of the Temple. Even here, however – that is, within the limits of the Temple cleansing pericope itself – the accent may fall not so much on Jesus' death as on his resurrection. To the authorities' demand for a legitimizing sign Jesus responds, "Destroy, this temple, and in three days, I will raise it up." To the author of SG this old piece of tradition (Bultmann argues well) is a clear reference to Jesus' death and resurrection, perhaps implying that he will raise himself from the dead.[35] In any case the saying refers primarily to Jesus' chief *sēmeion* ("sign"), the one which shows his messiahship more clearly than any other: his resurrection.[36]

It would seem reasonable to conclude that the author of SG was not greatly interested in Jesus' death, and did not see great significance in it. To paraphrase Käsemann's statement about 4G and apply it to SG, the passion comes into view only at the very end, is provided with virtually no preparation, and is overshadowed by Jesus' signs which find their proper climax in his resurrection.[37]

Intervening Developments

These are somewhat more difficult to identify in this case than in the earlier instances. As before, one tries, of course, to look forward from SG and backward from 4G. Doing so here suggests that some factors caused the death of Jesus to be far more important to John than it was to his predecessor. Let me suggest that two intervening developments already mentioned played roles here also:

1   It is clear that John's church knows the experience of Christian martyrdom. The prophecy of 16:2, spoken virtually from heaven (17:11f.) by the departing Lord points to just such a development, and redaction criticism will indicate it to lie chronologically between SG and 4G. Jewish Christians have somehow been brought to their deaths by Jews. A priori it is not likely that such experience would fail to leave some kind of marks on the tradition of the passion narrative. We shall see in a moment whether that may be the case, but let me mention 11:16 and 12:10 which lie outside the passion story and are non-SG.

2   In a rather different way another development already discussed may belong here: the polemical claim that Moses is the one who ascended into heaven. It is difficult to say with certainty which is claim and which counter-claim, but that there is polemic seems clear enough.

The Fourth Gospel

1   We begin with the cleansing of the Temple, because with respect to the passion, John's handling of this pericope is his most obvious alteration of SG, and because some interpreters have taken the re-location – it is a re-location on virtually any theory of tradition-history — to indicate John's interest in Jesus' death. In handling this pericope John did at least four things: (1) He moved it to a position very early in the Gospel, separating it rather completely from the passion narrative. (2) He introduced the motif of literalistic misunderstanding on the part of "the Jews". (3) He portrayed the opposite to such literalistic misunderstanding: the perspective which is provided in a memory informed by Jesus' resurrection. I have spoken above about the epistemological weight John attached to the verb *mnēsthēnai* ("to remember"), pointing ahead to the coming of the Paraclete. By introducing this motif so early in his Gospel, John signals that the whole of the story is to be understood from Jesus' glorification backwards (so also Bornkamm, 114). (4) It is not entirely surprising, then, that John ignores the verb *lysate* ("destroy") whereas he twice repeats and thus highlights the verb *egerō* ("I will raise") (vv. 20 and 22). In this way he accents the hermeneutical importance of the resurrection, looking forward again to 14:26.

These alterations show two things: first, that John places the so-called "Book of Signs" not in the shadow of Jesus' death – the cleansing pericope no longer has about it even the small odor of death it possessed in SG – but rather in the light of Easter and of the coming of the Paraclete. Second, that having removed SG's sole passion-motivation pericope from its passion setting, John will have to show the adversaries' motivation in some other way.

2   The second of these points calls for exploration. How does John portray the motivation for Jesus' passion-adversaries?

(*a*) While SG lacks a note corresponding to Mark 3:6, 4G does indeed have one, namely 5:18. We have already noted that this verse is the major link by means of which John makes his way from the drama of the paralytic to the lengthy speech about the Son's relation to the Father. Now we note that it is also the first of a weighty series of references to Jesus' death, by means of which John points forward to 11:53, a verse he took from SG; 5:18; 7:1; 7:19; 7:20; 7:25; 8:22; 8:37; 8:40; 8:44; 11:50; 11:51.[38] Furthermore, John extends the same line beyond the verse taken from SG: 12:10 ("also"); 12:24; 12:33; 18:14; 18:31; 18:32; 19:7.

John takes the verb *apokteinai* ("to kill") from SG only once (11:53). Elsewhere, about 11 times, he either draws it from other traditional materials or introduces it himself, alternatives which may amount to very nearly the same thing if, as the hypothesis has it, SG is John's narrative source. Add to this that the seven references employing *apothnēskein* ("to die") are all non-SG, and it would seem reasonable to conclude that John is far more concerned with Jesus' death than was the author of SG. But is it equally obvious that by constructing the long lines leading up to and away from the SG verse (11:53), he is providing a picture of the Jewish motivation for killing Jesus, a picture to replace the one portrayed in SG by the cleansing of the Temple pericope.

(*b*) Several factors suggest that John's portrait of this motivation is drawn in light of the first of the intervening developments mentioned above, the appearance of ditheism, the charging of Jewish-Christian evangelists as Beguilers, and their execution. This development seems clearly reflected in the climactic motive-describing references to Jesus' death, the first and the last:

> 5:18 For this reason the Jews sought all the more to kill him, because ... he was speaking of God as his own Father, thus making himself God's equal.
>
> 19:7 The Jews answered him [Pilate], "We have a law, and according to our law he ought to die, because he made himself the Son of God."[39]

And the same development is dramatically portrayed in relation to the death references in John 7.

3   An alteration of SG very nearly as obvious as the re-locating of

the Temple cleansing, and from a literary view-point its counterpart, is the sewing together of the Lazarus story and the portentous convening of the Sanhedrin. Again John's editing is multifaceted. Consider one facet. In SG, the Lazarus story ended with the optimistic note characteristic of the signs in that document: "... those who came to Mary and who saw what he did believed in him." Typically, John accepts this positive reference to believers; but he then turns immediately to speak of others who show themselves to be informers against Jesus. Recall the healed paralytic and his action in chapter 5:

5:15	11:46
the man went away and told the Jews that it was Jesus who had healed him.	But some of them went to the Pharisees and told them what Jesus had done.

This parallelism, plus the notes struck somewhat obliquely in 12:10–11 and 12:19, point to the same conclusion: the experience of martyrdom on the part of highly successful Jewish-Christian evangelists has strongly colored John's presentation of the death motif in the first half of his Gospel. In light of the developments since the writing of SG, it is important for the one who thus dies to know that, like Lazarus, he has already passed from death to life by Jesus' word.

But I suspect that the experience of martyrdom is reflected also in the passion narrative itself. For the same motif, in the form True Mosaic Prophet/False Beguiling Prophet, plays an important role in the trial scenes, as Meeks has shown. And the key verses in this regard appear to be John's additions to SG. This may be one of those junctures at which *religionsgeschichtlich* research intersects source criticism in such a way as to modify slightly the latter's results. I have in mind John 18:19. Fortna gives this verse to SG with some reservations, expressed by enclosing it in parentheses (242). In his discussion of it (120) he calls it "very likely pre-Johannine, showing none of the signs of John's characteristic dialogues".

Against its stemming from SG is the fact that there is no prior reference to Jesus' *didache* ("teaching") in that document. Correspondingly, in favor of viewing it as John's own addition are factors recently mentioned by Meeks. At the parallel point in synoptic tradition, the High Priest asks Jesus whether he is *ho Christos* ("the Messiah"). This question would have been well suited to SG; perhaps it originally stood in SG at this point, though that can be no more than a guess. In any case it would have been in character for John to substitute for some such question the picture of the High Priest querying Jesus about his *didachē* ("teaching") and his *mathētai* ("disciples"). For of the false prophet it is required to determine whether he teaches words which have not come from God (Deuteronomy 18:20) and whether he has "led astray" others (Deuteronomy 13:1–6).[40]

(Perhaps a similar confluence of source criticism and *Rlg* would lead one to delete "Now Barabbas was a robber" [18:40] from SG. See Meeks [1967] 67f.).

From the foregoing, it will be obvious that with Bornkamm[41] and Meeks[42] I find some of the statements Käsemann has recently made about John's attitude toward the passion less than convincing. But they are also far from being entirely wide of the mark. If comparison with SG shows that John carefully introduced quite a number of remarks that point ahead to the passion (contra *Testament*, 7), thus supplying a distinct motive for the adversaries' deeds, an equally important and well-known pattern is revealed by a linear reading of 4G itself, especially if one bears in mind the synoptic tradition of Jesus' passion predictions: there is a distinct line pointing from such verbs as *apokteinai* ("to kill") to such verbs as *hypagein* ("to go away"). Such a pattern did not escape Bultmann's notice, of course,[43] and it is clearly this pattern which Käsemann has firmly in mind.[44] Käsemann's mistake lies, I think, in his assumption that the *apokteinai* references are traditional and more-or-less excess baggage, while "the comprehensive and, for John, characteristic description of Jesus' death is given with the verb *hypagein*".[45] If Fortna's source analysis is essentially correct, *both* sets of references are largely Johannine.

But so is the pattern which leads from the one to the other and which makes abundantly clear that the Jesus

> who walks on the water and through closed doors, who cannot be captured by his enemies, ... [who] debates with them from the vantage point of the infinite difference between heaven and earth[46]

is not snatched away and killed. On the contrary, he *goes away* in an entirely sovereign manner. Why does John employ so emphatically the verbs *hypagein*, *anabainein*, etc?

A *full* answer to this question may not be attainable. I close with it primarily in order to point up the *complex* character of the *religionsgeschichtlich* factors which are involved in the transition from SG to 4G. On the one side, it should be clear that, in part, the pattern *apokteinai → hypagein/anabainein* is polemically related to the opponents' claims regarding Moses' ascent.[47] But the more obvious and more often commented-upon pattern *katabainein-anabainein* (*"to descend-ascend"*) is scarcely to be viewed in such a manner. The Moses traditions provide no parallel. Indeed the notion of a descending and, therefore, pre-earthly-existent figure is not "at home" either in Jewish apocalyptic or in Jewish mysticism.[48] And while it is true that Wisdom descends, her descent is nowhere tied to a victorious and redemptive ascent. In short, the descent/ascent pattern "has been and remains the strongest support for the hypothesis that Johannine Christology is connected with gnostic mythology".[49] At this point – and it is a very important point for John's theology – comparing 4G with SG supports Haenchen's suggestion:

> The gnostic terminology ... must be investigated to see whether it belongs to the miracle-source or only to the evangelist. I presume the latter...[50]

III *A Sketch of a Sketch*

1 *Source Criticism and Religionsgeschichte*

This sketch – I accent again its partial character – suggests that a significant portion of the developments transpiring between SG and 4G arises from the side of Jewish opponents. There is a synagogue which, having expelled the messianic believers, now stands opposite John's church; its complex and varied response to Christian propaganda, including and, I suppose, centering in SG, is reflected in the Fourth Gospel, dominantly in non-SG passages. Moreover, one of John's concerns as he reshapes SG is to correct those of its deficiencies which the intervening debate has brought to light.

If one is convinced of this much, the next question is: What kind of a synagogue stands opposite John's church? Two points are clear: (1) The Jewish community of John's city follows, at least in large part, the lead of Jamnia (*aposynagogos genesthai* ["to be expelled from the synagogue"] is related to the reworded Birkath ha-Minim). The local Gerousia is through and through Pharisaic. (2) At least some of the Jewish opponents know and treasure exotic traditions about Moses as the one who ascended into heaven, receiving the secrets.[51] But this sort of speculation was very widespread (see Meeks). Its presence, therefore, cannot serve to draw narrow limits for the type of Jewish community in question. The possibility is certainly not to be excluded that some of the opponents represent a form of Jewish gnosis, although it is also possible that elements of gnosis are introduced into the picture by actors other than these opponents. One may recall with uncommon interest the remarks with which Odeberg forty years ago concluded his comments on John 5:19–29:

> 1 With regard to language, terms, expressions used, or problems treated, it may safely be stated that, on the whole, John 5:24–30 is most akin to Jewish, early Rabbinic, terminology. The section, it is true, makes use of

two single terms which are foreign to the Rabbinic terminology, as far as it is known,[52] viz. those of the "voice" and the "Son of God", terms, which are familiar to other circles. Yet, there is no doubt but that the large proportion of terms used and the contiguity of the statements best fit in with Rabbinic modes of reasoning and assertion.

2 With regard to the inner meaning (roughly speaking: the doctrine) conveyed, on the other hand, it must be urged that John moves in a sphere far removed from the Rabbinic world of ideas. The situation in this respect might perhaps be best pictured by one of the two suppositions following viz. 1. either that John himself completely familiar with, brought up in, Rabbinic Jewish learning and schools of thought, tries to convey to Rabbinic readers, by using their terms and language, a doctrine, yea, a spiritual reality altogether different from their world of thought 2. or else that John addresses himself to readers who, although sharing the terms and language of Rabbinic religious thought, belong to a circle different from normative Rabbinic Judaism.

... If, then, we call the religious atmosphere of John "the Johannine (Christian) salvation-mysticism" it might be said that the Johannine salvation-mysticism uses an idiom which is most nearly related to the Rabbinic style and terminology.

It is significant 1. that in the scanty sources of early Samaritan and Jewish Mysticism or Gnosticism we meet with a similar salvation-mysticism, 2. that we are actually able to demonstrate that there existed already in the first and second centuries A.D., in the Judaism that moved within the folds of Rabbinic tradition, several circles of a salvation-mystical character, and 3. that some of these, in ideas and expressions, were more closely bound up with Mandaean mysticism than with any other known mystical religious formation outside Judaism. Certainly John cannot be maintained to be identical with or to have developed from any of these and still less from Rabbinic circles – , but the sources in question afford parallel phenomena to John and make it possible to discern the approximate position of John in relation to Palestinian mysticism.[53]

In short, *religionsgeschichtlich* developments behind 4G are complex. Accepting SG as a working hypothesis promises to bring the complexity into sharper focus, if not to render it more readily understandable, and that fact speaks in favor of the hypothesis.

2 Source Criticism, Rlg, and Theologiegeschichte

With respect to the problem of finding John's place in the history of Christian thought, the sketch leads to at least one conclusion: John belongs in a dominantly Jewish-Christian milieu. Bultmann suggested something similar about the setting of the Semeia-Quelle.[54] But if the lines of thought pursued above are essentially correct, the same must be said about the Gospel itself. As one views the growth of the tradition from SG to 4G, overt concerns with Jewish questions become more, not less central.[55]

Although I have given no preparation for it in the body of the paper, let me underline this conclusion by appending a note on John and Luke. One thinks of comparing these two theologians because F. C. Baur placed both of them at or near the emergence of early Catholicism, and because in his own way Käsemann has revived Baur's thesis in our time. Without suggesting that the thesis is entirely erroneous, I want simply to point out one significant difference between Luke and John.

Centrally characteristic of Luke's stance is the *replacing* of the old frontier, the synagogue, by the new frontier, the market-place of Greco-Roman culture. Luke's church views the Jewish mission as thoroughly closed. The horizon is occupied by a Gentile church which is expanding into the Gentile world. Luke must remind this church of its OT roots, but even as he does just that, he emphasizes that the synagogue frontier is closed.

The author of the Signs Gospel is of quite a different view. He pens "a textbook for potential Jewish converts".[56] And John himself, in spite of the bitter Jewish opposition and persecution, holds that frontier still to be at least partially open.

> Yet there may have been one group of Jews that the Gospel addressed with a certain hopefulness; namely, the small group of Jews who believed in Jesus but as yet had not severed their relationship with the Synagogue. In the 80's and 90's of the 1st century these Jewish Christians were going through a crisis.[57]

In short, John precisely does not substitute one frontier for another. If he belongs to a sectarian milieu, as Käsemann has proposed, I wonder whether that milieu may not be considerably more Jewish-Christian than most interpreters have thought.[58]

NOTES

1 Among the numerous works which might be mentioned are W. Thüsing, *Die Erhöhung und Veherrlichung Jesu im Johannesevangelium* (1960); E. Haenchen (1967); E. Käsemann (1968); and the reviews of this last work by G. Bornkamm and W. A. Meeks cited below in notes 2 and 9.

2 Bornkamm in this volume (1968), pp. 77–98. Pages cited below are from this translation.

3 See particularly Käsemann's "Einfuhrung" for volume 1 (1963) of Baur's *Ausgewählte Werke in Einzelausgaben*, ed. K. Scholder. The pervasive influence of F. C. Baur is apparent in most of Käsemann's works; only to a lesser degree, perhaps, that of W. Bauer.

4 In much of his work Käsemann's overt emphasis is on the first of these two

demands, but the second is surely present. In the American context – as distinct from the Continental and the British – I suspect both must be emphasized. As one surveys the labors of SBL, for example, one is reminded of A. Schweitzer's eulogistic remark about F. C. Bauer, with emphasis on the first words: "He was the last who dared to conceive and to deal with, the history of dogma in the large and general sense..." *Paul and his Interpreters* (1911) vi.

5 In the excellent introduction to his commentary C. K. Barrett discusses the Gospel's purpose by drawing a picture which is stretched against the background of "two urgent problems" faced by the Church at the turn of the first century: eschatology and gnosticism. But the tenor of his discussion is thoroughly set by the following statements:

> ...; it may be doubted whether he [John] was very interested in its publication. It is easy, when we read the gospel, to believe that John, though doubtless aware of the necessity of strengthening Christians and converting the heathen, wrote primarily to satisfy himself. His gospel must be written: it is no concern of his whether it was also read ... [the traditional material] cried aloud for rehandling; its true meaning had crystallized in his mind, and he simply conveyed this meaning to paper...; no book ever was less a party tract that John (115).

I do not suppose Barrett had Käsemann's lecture "Ketzer und Zeuge" in mind as he wrote this last sentence. The lecture was given in Göttingen on June 30, 1951, and the manuscript of the commentary was completed in Durham on December 31 of the same year (with no mention of Käsemann in the index). However that may be, the influence of Baur and of Bauer is dominant on the one side and very nearly absent on the other.

6 One must also bear in mind that according to the hypothesis SG was the *gospel* of John's church, used and no doubt in some sense venerated in its worship.

7 It is a helpful and illuminating exercise to relate Schnackenburg's comments on Tradition and Redaction, 59–74, to his discussion of Theological and Topical Interests, and the corresponding sections in Brown (xxxix–xxxiv and lxvii–lxxix) offer an equally illuminating exercise.

8 Scarcely needed in the circle of Festival participants, but probably helpful in a wider context is S. Schulz's reminder.

> The point of all history of religions work – not only on the Fourth Gospel – is not to rob the works in question (here the Johannine discourses) of their uniqueness, but to exhibit this. (n. to K. Kittel, *Spätjudentum*. 19). For every history of religions comparison showed how taking an idea over always involved editing it, i.e. it was criticized, modified, re-centred. And what is theologically decisive and significant lies in this process of editing and interpreting anew. *Komposition und Herkunft der johanneischen Reden* (Stuttgart, 1960) 140.

9 See now Meeks' review of Käsemann (1968) in *USQR*, 24 (1969) 414–20. On the whole Meeks' own monograph has apparently not received the thorough treatment in written reviews which it deserves. An exception is the review by R. Schnackenburg in *BZ*, 13 (1969) 136–8, where the book is given a serious and responsible critique.

10 Note particularly his paper read at the meeting of SBL in Berkeley, December 20, 1968: "Source and Redaction in the Fourth Gospel's Portrayal of Jesus' Signs" ("S and R") [and the article of the same title in *JBL* 89 (1970) 151–66].

11 I have sketched these possibilities on the basis of suggestions offered in such works as the commentaries by Schackenburg and Brown and the mono-

graphs by Käsemann and Meeks. They are not intended to comprise an exhaustive list.

12 The theological implications of such patterns of thought have been several times voiced by Käsemann (1969) 138–67, etc.

13 Meeks (1967).

14 Käsemann (1968) 9 and *passim* citing Baur, Wetter, and Hirsch. I doubt that the reader of Käsemann's *Testament* will fully understand it until he makes some careful comparisons with F. C. Baur's work on the Fourth Gospel, a task to which Käsemann's footnotes invite him. See also note 29 below.

15 A. S. van der Woude, *Die messianische Vorstellungen der Gemeinde von Qumran* (1957); F. Hahn, *The Titles of Jesus in Christology* (1969); G. P. Wetter; *Der Sohn Gottes* (1916). See also Meeks, 22ff.

16 H. Conzelmann, *An Outline of the Theology of the New Testament* (1968) 335.

17 See e.g., R. Travers Herford, *Christianity in Talmud and Midrash* (1903) 255ff.; 291ff.; G. F. Moore, *Judaism* (1927) i, 364ff.

18 Cf. E. Haenchen, "Johanneische Probleme", *ZTK*, 56 (1959) 19–54; "Der Vater, der mich gesandt hat", *NTS* 9 (1962–3) 208–16; Fortna, "S and R"; Paul Meyer, "Seeing, Signs and Sources in the Fourth Gospel", a paper read at AAR in Dallas, November, 1968. I do not cite all of these studies as support for the statement in the text, but rather as relevant to the question whether or not John and SG had distinguishable attitudes toward the signs. Haenchen, Fortna, and Meyer are not of a common mind on this question.

19 Fortna, "S and R", 9.

20 Martyn (1968) 112ff.

21 Fortna, "S and R", 10ff.

22 P. Borgen (1965) 74.

23 See note 12.

24 Martyn (1968) *passim*.

25 I paraphrase 3:13 according to the results of Meeks' exegesis, 297–301.

26 Points to be developed in a forthcoming study in which Käsemann's structural analysis is accepted as correct.

27 "If the formulae of his commission through the Father and his unity with the Father are isolated from each other, the result will be subordinationism or ditheism. Both formulae are correlative and complementary, because only together do they describe the truth that Jesus is nothing but the revealer and, on the other hand, that Jesus is the only revealer of God and therefore belongs totally on the side of God while he is on earth" (Käsemann [1968] 11).

28 E. Haenchen, "Johanneische Probleme", *ZTK*, 56 (1959) 50. Doesn't John thereby diminish the initiative of Jesus (contra Fortna, "S and R")? I think so. I quite agree with Käsemann that Jesus' obedience "is the form and concretion of Jesus' glory during the period of his incarnation" (*Testament*, 10f.). Nevertheless, compared with SG's portrait, that of John emphasizes at points Jesus' subordination to the Father, and, I think, for the reasons suggested above.

29 Essentially, therefore, I find myself standing with Käsemann as regards "unreflektierter Doketismus" (contra Bornkamm). To believe that John *intended* 1:14 to guard against docetism one would have to hold, it seems to me, that he was asleep when he wrote the words "and dwelt among us". But even that would be scarcely possible, since these words carefully point forward to "the paradoxical

'A little while' of the farewell discourses in 14:19ff; 16:16ff; as already in 7:33; 12:35; 13:33" (*Testament*, 10 n. 10).

30   That this resounding "No" should come from the "orthodox" Jewish authorities in John's setting, rather than from thinkers in his own messianic community tells us something of the distance between John's world and that of Paul. It has frequently been pointed out that Torah as the way of salvation is not the problem for John that it is for Paul (e.g., Bultmann [1955], 8). But to make this observation in the correct context, to make it with precision, and only then to explicate it theologically are tasks not yet fully accomplished.

31   Here a good bit turns, of course, on the literary analysis of John 9. Bultmann allotted the drama of that chapter to the Semeia-Quelle: see Moody Smith (1965) 42f. But he regarded 9:22 as a remark which the Evangelist inserted in SQ: Comm 335 n. 5: "The Evangelist's style is apparent". For Bultmann the three *aposynagōgos* references point to a period which stretches approximately from Paul to Justin (428). Ray Brown gives 9:22 to stage 5, the final redaction by someone other than the evangelist, because – if I read him correctly – (a) it is inconceivable in stage 1, and (b) it is literarily parenthetical. I feel the force of both reasons, but in light of 12:42 and especially 16:2, and noting the harmony between 9:22 and 9:34, I am afraid I do not see ample justification for bringing in the final redactor at this point. Haenchen allots most of John 9 to the source, much as did Bultmann, and he does not find himself convinced by such exegetes as Hirsch and Windisch who refer to the Evangelist as a gifted dramatist on the basis of that chapter. Whether it is truly consistent to give the post-miracle scenes in chapter 5 to the Evangelist and to deny him what appear to be corresponding scenes in chapter 9 is a question I must ponder. There seem to me to be at least three grounds for crediting the Evangelist with the drama of chapter 9: (1) the apparent relationship of 9:4a to 14:12; (2) the structural similarity as regards scene presentation of the trial before Pilate (Paul Meyer in Meeks 1967, 293). I quite agree with Haenchen (1984, 88) that for the Evangelist "the real meaning of the story lay not in the legitimising miracle but in the allusion in 9:5 'I am the light of the world'". But that does not tell me that John cannot be responsible for the drama. Quite the opposite. It supports such an interpretation if one perceives that John is interested not only in the *that* of this *hint* but also in the *how*, namely the two-level drama.

32   *History and Theology*, 45–77.

33   See note 20 above.

34   (1970) 242.

35   Fortna, "S and R" 5.

36   Ibid., 13.

37   *Testament*, 7: "Apart from a few remarks that point ahead to it, the passion comes to view in John only at the very end."

38   Bornkamm is fully justified, of course, in taking exception to the statement of Käsemann quoted in my preceding note: in this volume, p. 89.

39   Which law is this? I suppose the reference – as in the case of 5:18 – is to Deuteronomy 13:5, 9, as this law was interpreted and developed in Rabbinic tradition.

40   Meeks (1967) 60f. Dodd reaches a similar conclusion by a somewhat different route (1963, 95), as Meeks notes.

41   Bornkamm (1968): in this volume, pp. 88f.

42   Meeks' review is mentioned in note 9 above. See particularly 419.

43   (1955) 53.

44 *Testament*, 17ff.

45 Ibid.

46 *Testament*, 9.

47 See Meeks (1967) 297–301.

48 See e.g. H. Odeberg (1929) 73; R. Schackenburg (1968) 551; also Schackenburg, *Present and Future* (1966) 176f.

49 Meeks (1967) 297.

50 Haenchen, in a letter to J. M. Robinson, Spring, 1966.

51 It would be intriguing to see what would be shown by putting Fortna and Meeks together regarding the portraits of Moses and of Jesus as Kings. For example, Fortna gives 6:14 to SG and 6:15 to the Evangelist. Is the tradition of Moses as King unknown or unimportant to the author of SG? I have had insufficient time to explore this question and others which might similarly arise.

52 This is one of Odeberg's careful statements which would now have to be changed.

53 H. Odeberg (1929) 214ff.

54 See Moody Smith (1965) 37f., and Bultmann (1971) 108 n. 6, and 113 n. 2. On the basis of *Yoma* 29a (St.-B. II 409f.) Bultmann ponders whether already in Judaism the OT miracles had been numbered and placed in a series.

55 Again, one should be warned, of course, that much turns on the precise contours of SG.

56 Fortna, 234.

57 Brown, lxxiv.

58 I do not mean to suggest that John's own church is Ebionite in any proper sense of that term, but I am still struck with the natural way in which Johannine references crop up so often in H. J. Schoeps' *Theologie und Geschichte des Juden-christentums* (1949). There is surely *something* to it.

7

The Johannine Church and History*

NILS ALSTRUP DAHL

The Problem

In his *Theology of the New Testament* Rudolf Bultmann presented the theology of the Fourth Gospel without dealing with the attitude to the OT and the history of salvation in the old covenant.[1] This does not mean that Bultmann considers all quotations and allusions to the OT to be secondary – only a minority of them are attributed to the ecclesiastical editor[2] – but he thinks that they are of no serious theological importance. Eduard Schweizer, who has recently written on "The Concept of the Church in the Gospel and Epistle of St. John",[3] takes more seriously the OT background of Johannine concepts. According to Schweizer, John has solved the difficult problem of how the Church here and now can live by what happened in Jesus of Nazareth at another time and another place: "There is no longer any problem about bridging over the distance in time and space between the events of salvation and the contemporary Church. For the Church is not a people based on an act of God in history.... It is the Church only in so far as it lives 'in' the Son and he in it. The Son is present in the Church today just as he was then, through the message...." "Here Church is placed in the present time and is proof against all forms of historicism and of millenarianism." But Schweizer sees one danger, "that the Church may become detached from history".[4]

Bultmann would, possibly, rather see an advantage where Schweizer sees a danger. The first question to be asked is, however, whether the Church, as conceived by John, is really detached from history or more closely bound to it than both Bultmann and Schweizer suppose.

* First published in *Current Issues in New Testament Interpretation*, ed. W. Klassen and G. F. Snyder (1962) 124–42.

Obviously, their point of view is not without some basis. The usual ecclesiological terminology of the NT is not found in the Fourth Gospel; words like *hē ekklēsia, hoi hagioi, ho laos tou theou* are lacking, and so is the opposite term *ta ethnē*. The Church is conceived as the community of the believers, in contrast to the world, rather than as the people of God in contrast to the Gentile nations. We do not find any specific command of Gentile missions (cf. 20:21);[5] from the beginning it is made clear that the mission of Jesus is a mission to the world (1:9–10; 3:16–17); the existence of the disciples in the world is in itself a mission to the world (17:18). Schweizer himself points to the OT background of the imagery of the true vine (15:1ff., cf. esp. Ps. 80:14–16) and of the good shepherd and his flock (10, cf. Ezek. 34). But such images are no longer employed in order to depict the way of God's dealing with his people in the course of history; they represent the actual relation between Christ and those who belong to him.

Not even Bultmann would, however, pretend that Johannine theology is completely detached from history. The word became flesh; the concrete, historical man Jesus from Nazareth is proclaimed as the revelation of God. Schweizer stresses the fact that John, after all, wrote a Gospel and not a dogmatic treatise. Further, the allusions to persons and events of the OT do not look merely like traditional features. The significance of Christ is, certainly, in the Fourth Gospel more often than in the rest of the NT, expressed by means of nouns or by sentences in the present tense. But this does not mean that the past and the future have simply been absorbed by the present. The Evangelist makes use of a number of temporal nouns and adverbs; he distinguishes between the tenses, and between "now" and "afterward" (13:7, 36), "hitherto" (16:24) and "henceforth" (14:7), "not yet" (2:4; 7:6; 8:20) and "now" (12:23, 27; 17:1), "before" and "when" (14:29).

Some features of the Gospel seem to favor an "existential" interpretation; others seem more easily to lend themselves to an interpretation in terms of *"Heilsgeschichte"*. This fact may be taken to indicate that this alternative to the modern approach of biblical theology does not do justice to the originality and complexity of the Fourth Gospel and its conception of Church and history.

The Time of the Church and the Time of Jesus

In his testimony (*martyria*) to the earthly ministry of Jesus, John at the same time bears witness to his presence in the Church. Jesus of Nazareth, as John sees him, is "the Christ of faith"; to that extent

Schweizer is right: there is no distance in time and space to be bridged. Yet that is not the whole truth. The Evangelist is fully aware of a distinction between the time of Jesus and the situation of the post-resurrection Church. The Johannine Christ is looking forward – not so much to an eschatological consummation on the last day as to the day of his glorification and of his renewed presence among the disciples. Before his glorification the Spirit was not yet given (7:39); not until after his departure could the Paraclete be sent (16:7). Until "that day" the disciples were not praying in his name (16:26; cf. 16:23). "That day", the post-resurrection time, brings a deeper understanding (14:20; cf. 2:22; 12:16; 13:7) and greater deeds (5:20; 14:12). Then the disciples shall follow Jesus as they were not able to do at the time of his life on earth (13:36; cf. 12:26; 14:4–6).

The difference of time has also a spatial aspect. The early ministry of Jesus was restricted to Israel. This fact is not so strongly emphasized in the Fourth Gospel as in the first one; but John does not make Jesus move outside the Holy Land, nor does he report that he had contacts with individual Gentiles. The miracle of 4:46–53 might be an exception, but it is – in contrast to Matt. 8:5–13 and Luke 7:1–10 – not directly said that the "official" was not a Jew. This cannot simply mean that the question of nationality was not relevant any more; other texts prove that John does reflect upon the position of the Greeks with regard to Jesus. We hear that the Jews misunderstand the saying of Jesus concerning his departure (7:33–6). They supposed that he intended to go to the dispersion among the Greeks and teach the Greeks. As often in the Fourth Gospel, the misunderstanding conveys the truth: Jesus was, indeed, going to the Father, and thus also going to the Greeks – through the word of his missionary witnesses (cf. 10:16 and 11:52).[6]

The coming of Greeks, who wish to see Jesus, is the sign "that the hour has come for the Son of man to be glorified" (12:20ff.). His earthly ministry in Israel has come to an end; the universal mission is to be inaugurated by the death of Jesus: The grain of wheat has to die in order to bear much fruit (12:24). Lifted up from the earth, Jesus will draw all men to himself (12:32). The Greeks are to see him – as the glorified one. The great missionary text in John 12:20–33 shows why John does not need to report any specific commandment of Gentile missions given by the risen Christ. The historical and geographical limitations of the ministry of Jesus are dissolved by the very fact of his death, which in its unity with the resurrection is also his ascension to the Father. This finds its symbolical expression in the inscription which Pilate put on the cross, "Jesus of Nazareth, the King of the Jews". It was written in Hebrew, in Latin, and in Greek *handwritten: end of gospel = post J. death.*

(19:19–22). The kingship of Jesus is not of this world. Bearing witness to the truth, he already exercised it during his ministry among the Jews (18:36–7); but not until he was crucified as "the king of the Jews" was he proclaimed even to Greeks and Romans, and his voice heard by "every one who is of the truth".

As there is a clear distinction between the time before the departure of Jesus and the time after his ascension, so there are in the Fourth Gospel also two stages within the earthly ministry of Jesus, the time before his "hour" had come. By and large, these two stages correspond to the two main literary sections of the Gospel, chapters 1—12, dealing with the public ministry of Jesus, and chapters 13—20 (21), dealing with the departure of the ascending Saviour.[7] The coming of the Greeks, the missionary outlook, and final verdict on the unbelieving Jews in 12:20–50 mark the gap and the bridge at the point of transition. The farewell discourses center around the departure of Christ and its consequences for the disciples in the time to come, whereas the conflict with the Jews is a main theme in chapters 1—12. Even in the first part, however, many sayings point forward to that which is to come (e.g., 3:11–15; 6:61–2). The situation of the post-resurrection Church is prefigured and anticipated during the earthly ministry of Jesus in Israel.

The visit of Jesus to Samaria may here be taken as an important and illustrative example (4:1–42). The account of the dialogue between Jesus and the Samaritan woman allows the Evangelist to show that the contrast between Jews and non-Jews is transcended by the coming of Christ – without letting the historical Jesus move outside the Holy Land and the sphere of the OT revelation. The Samaritan woman rightly recognizes Jesus to be a Jew (4:9) – salvation is from the Jews (4:22); but in the end he is hailed, not only as the Christ (4:25–6, 29), but as the Saviour of the world (4:42). Jesus is greater than the father Jacob, as much as the "water" given by him is of a higher quality than that of Jacob's well (4:12–15). The coming of the Samaritans illustrates the missionary situation: "The fields are already white for harvest" (4:30–8). After two days, however, Jesus departed to Galilee; that means the work in Samaria had the character of an anticipation, the earthly ministry of Jesus being characterized by the saying about the prophet who has no honor in his own country (4:43–4).

Within this context we find the Johannine formula "the hour comes and is now" (4:23). It is a formula of eschatological anticipation (5:25), but the coming day of fulfillment is that which is inaugurated by the ascension of Jesus, the "hour" in which the Church is living. The "hour", when the Father shall be worshiped neither on Gerizim nor in Jerusalem, but in spirit and truth, is identical with "that day", in which the disciples will pray in the name of Jesus (16:26), and when the Spirit of truth has been sent by the Father. This coming hour is already present, as Jesus during his earthly ministry is already the Saviour of the world. But the point of the formula is not simply to state the eschatological character of the present hour; it serves, rather, to visualize the relation between the "time" of the earthly ministry and the "time" of the Church; in spite of the temporal distance, there is an essential identity. What is present in the time after the ascension was anticipated in the life of Jesus, and the witness borne to his historical ministry is, therefore, at the same time a testimony to his presence here and now. It would be as false to stress only the identity of the qualified time and dehistoricize the Gospel as it would be to stress only the diversity of the chronological time and give a historicizing, biographical interpretation of the Gospel.

The Jews and the Messiah

The relation between the Church and the Jews is of fundamental importance for the NT understanding of the Church and of the history of salvation. In the Fourth Gospel the Jews appear as a rather homogeneous mass, hostile to Christ; this hostility often seems to be implied in the term *hoi Ioudaioi* itself. This way of speaking must date from a time when the cleavage between Jews and Christians had become definite; John carries the cleavage back to the days of Jesus himself (9:22; 12:42). The Johannine attitude should, of course, not be confounded with any form of modern anti-Semitism. It differs also from the anti-Judaism of the "Epistle to Barnabas", to name but one extreme example from the ancient Church. The Jews of the Fourth Gospel are representatives of the world in its hostility to God. That has been well established by Bultmann.[8] It is, however, equally important that *the Jews* are those who represent the world.

John does not make use of the traditional distinction between the people of God (*ho laos*) and the Gentile nations (*ta ethnē*). But his point of view is based upon the Jewish idea, that Israel is the center of the world.[9] This conception is, however, interpreted in a new and revolutionary way in the Fourth Gospel. Positively, it implies that the mission of Jesus in Israel is a mission to the world and that he fulfilled his ministry to the world within Israel. Negatively, it means that the world's enmity and opposition to God gets its concentrated expression through the Jews.

In the Fourth Gospel, discussions concerning matters of the law and Sabbath observances (5:9–18; 7:21–4; 9:13–16) are but the starting point for debates on the real issue, the question of the authority of

Jesus. In the Synoptics, this question is latent in the background; in the Fourth Gospel it has become the manifest center of all discussions. Chapter 5 is especially instructive: Jesus defends his Sabbath healing by pointing to the activity of the Father, who is still working after the completion of the six days' work of creation – even on the Sabbath (5:17). What makes the opposition of the Jews so violent is this answer, by which Jesus makes himself equal with God. The basic conflict is throughout a christological one, not in the sense that matters of christological dogmatics are debated, but in the sense that the opposition is caused by the witness which Jesus bears to himself.

The Johannine Christ is much more than the "Messiah" in the Jewish sense of this word. But it is a remarkable fact, often overlooked, that the title *Christos* in the Fourth Gospel has not been made obsolete by predicates like "Logos", "Son of God", "Saviour of the world".[10] John alone in the NT brings the title in its original form, the Messiah (1:41; 4:25). He is also aware of its meaning as a synonym to "king of Israel" (1:50). Moreover, John is familiar with the vagueness of Jewish messianic expectations, in which the Messiah was but one of several figures, like Elijah and "the prophet" (1:20–1) – a fact which has only recently been clearly observed by scholars.

To the Evangelist, Jesus is the Messiah in the sense that of him "Moses in the law and also the prophets wrote" (1:45). He also brings in a number of formula quotations and allusions in order to show that the prophecies are fulfilled in Jesus. But at the same time in a most remarkable way he makes it clear that the term "Christ" means something very different in the Christian confession to Jesus (9:22; 20:31) and in the mouth of the Jew, who discusses whether he could possibly be the Christ or not (7:26–7, 41–2; 10:24; 12:34). To the Jews, the Messiah is a political king (6:15; 11:48; 19:12). Jesus is king, but in quite another sense (18:33–7). When the Jews find a lack of conformity between the appearance of Jesus and messianic dogmatics, they are at fault because they understand everything in a this-worldly manner. The origin of Christ is hidden to men, as they say, but so it is, because he comes from above (7:26–9). Christ is to remain forever – as the ascended one (12:34).

John does not try explicitly to refute Jewish doubts as to the messiahship of Jesus; obviously, he has no hope that they would be convinced by exegetical arguments. That would rather be the opinion of Luke (e.g. Acts 17:2–3) and later on of Justin, who try to prove (1) that the messianic prophecies are to be interpreted in a way which makes them conform to the portrait of Jesus and (2) that, therefore, Jesus is the Christ.[11] As John sees it, a teacher of Israel is not in need of exegetical explanations, but of a new birth (3:1ff.). What matters is the witness which the Scriptures in their totality are bearing to Christ (5:39, 46), and this testimony cannot be understood by men who judge according to the flesh (cf. 8:15). The Scriptures, as understood by John, bear witness to Christ in the present, rather than to a history of salvation in the past, with an importance of its own. And yet, it is not ignored that there was a history even before Christ.

Witnesses Before Christ

Like the earlier evangelists and the tradition before them, John makes the Gospel story begin with John the Baptist. But in the Fourth Gospel the point is not that a new epoch within a continuous history of salvation begins. The Baptist is nothing but the voice of one crying in the wilderness; he is misunderstood if he is taken to have any greatness of his own (1:19–27; 3:25–30). His only function is to bear witness to Christ (1:6–8, etc.). In the Fourth Gospel a witness is conceived as one who tells what he has seen and heard (e.g., 3:11, 32; 19:35). This pattern is applied also to John the Baptist; what happened at the baptism of Jesus is understood as a revelation given to the Baptist, who can, therefore, say: "I have seen and have borne witness that this is the Son of God" (1:32–4). John came before Jesus, but his priority in time is only a this-worldly one: "He who came after me ranks before me, for he was before me" (1:15, 30).

The OT history is interpreted in a similar way. The historical persons and events are not spiritualized by means of an allegorical interpretation in the way of Philo. The Evangelist rather insists upon their inner-worldly nature; in themselves, isolated from Christ, they are of no redemptive value. Whoever drinks of the well, which Jacob gave to his descendants, shall thirst again (4:10–14). Moses did not give the true bread from heaven; the fathers ate manna in the wilderness, and they died (6:32, 49). Abraham died too, and so did the prophets (8:52). Like John the Baptist, the OT fathers and prophets are, in the Fourth Gospel, witnesses to Christ, and that is their only true greatness.

As a witness, Isaiah "saw his glory and spoke about him" (12:41). The vision of Isaiah 6 is, thus, interpreted as a vision of Christ; the Lord, sitting upon a throne, is identified with the Lord Jesus. A christological interpretation of the *kyrios* of the Septuagint is frequently found in the NT, and the OT theophanies are in the ancient Church understood as revelations of the pre-existent Christ. According to Philo it was the divine Logos who revealed himself. But the Johannine interpretation of Isaiah 6 does not seem to be derived from a Logos doctrine of the Philonic type. The wording of John 12:41

comes very close to that of the Targum of Isaiah, which speaks of "the glory of YHWH" (6:1) and "the glory of the Shekinah of YHWH" (6:5). Within Jewish "Merkabah mysticism" the vision of the prophet must have been thought to imply a visionary ascent to heaven.[12] Traditions of this type are taken over by the Christian apocryphon *"The Ascension of Isaiah"*; here are added specific Christian elements: in his heavenly vision Isaiah also saw the hidden descent and the triumphant ascent of the Saviour. In the Fourth Gospel there is no mythological imagery of this type, but the basic idea in 12:41 is akin to that of *"The Ascension of Isaiah"*; the prophet is supposed to have seen, not simply the glory of the pre-existent *Logos asarkos*, but the glory of Christ incarnate and crucified. In the context of John 12 there can be no doubt that this is the meaning.

The reference to Isaiah's vision is preceded by two quotations from the prophet (12:37–40). The first is taken from Isa. 53:1, the first verse in the chapter on the suffering servant, identified with Christ, the report of whom was not believed, and through whom the arm of the Lord was not revealed – in spite of the many signs which he had done. The second quotation is based upon the Hebrew text of Isa. 6:9–10. The verbs *hšmn* and *šʿ*, normally understood as imperatives, are read as perfects (*hišmin* and *hešaʿ*). Christ, the object of Isaiah's vision, is also the speaking subject in the words reported by the prophet; he could not heal the Jews, because God had blinded their eyes and hardened their hearts. The meaning is clear; Isaiah could report on Christ's saying concerning the predestined unbelief of the Jews because he had in his vision seen the glory of the crucified Son of God.

This interpretation is confirmed by the correspondence between 12:41, "He saw his glory", and 1:14, "We saw his glory". That this correspondence is intentional is confirmed by the observation that the latter part of the Prologue alludes to another OT theophany, the vision of Moses (Exod. 33:17—34:9).[13] Moses was not allowed to see the face of God, whom no one has ever seen (Exod. 33:20, John 1:18). And yet, God in another way made him see his glory and revealed himself as a God merciful, "abounding in steadfast love and faithfulness' (*rab ḥesed w'emēth*, Exod. 33:18, 22; 34:5–6). The disciples saw the glory of the Logos incarnate, who was "full of grace and truth" (*plērēs charitos kai alētheias*). The Evangelist, I should think, assumes that Moses too, like Isaiah, saw *his* glory. In any case, Moses is conceived as a witness of Christ, who wrote about him (5:46). In its Johannine context, the statement in 1:17 can hardly be taken to imply the Pauline contrast between the law and the grace and between works and faith. The Johannine contrast is that between the law, given through Moses, which is a testimony, and the reality to which Moses bore witness, the true grace and gracious truth, which came through Jesus Christ. The Jews are at fault when they appeal to Moses in order to oppose Christ (9:28). They search the Scriptures because they think to have eternal life in them; but the Scriptures bear witness to Christ – and to believe this testimony is the only way to have life through them (5:39). Because the Jews do not see that, Moses, who is a witness to Christ, will become their accuser – and not their advocate and defender as he was supposed to be (5:45).[14]

The witness which the Father is bearing to the Son (5:37a) must be identical with the witness of the Scriptures. This becomes evident as soon as it is seen that 5:37b alludes to the revelation at Sinai. There the Israelites heard the voice of God, and – in spite of Deut. 4:12 – according to some texts and traditions they also saw his "form" (shape, image, or glory).[15] Midrash *Mekilta* comments on Exod. 19:11 thus: "This teaches that at that moment they saw what Isaiah and Ezekiel never saw." The saying in John 5:37–8, "His voice you have never heard and his form you have never seen; and you do not have his word abiding in you", must be understood against this background. The meaning is that the Jews, refusing to believe in Jesus, prove that they have no share in the revelation given to Israel at Mount Sinai.[16]

A further reference to the giving of the law, as understood in the Haggadah, is found in Jesus' answer to the accusation for blasphemy, John 10:34–6: "Is it not written in your law, 'I said you are gods'? If he called them gods to whom the word of God came (and scripture cannot be broken), do you say of him whom the Father consecrated and sent into the world, 'You are blaspheming', because I said, 'I am the Son of God'?" The quotation here is taken from Psalm 82; in rabbinic interpretation it was applied to the restitution of the original, glorious state of mankind by the giving of the law. Receiving it, the Israelites became like angels, "gods". And yet, they had to die like men (Ps. 82:6), because of their sin with the golden calf.[17] Those "to whom the word of God came" are, thus, the Israelites at Sinai. They are called "gods"; should not then Christ, whom the Father sent into the world, and to whom the word of God, revealed at Sinai, bears witness, have a right to the name "Son of God"?

The reasons for the Jewish opposition of Jesus are most clearly stated in 8:30–59. The Jews will not let the Son make them free because they claim already to be free, being descendants of Abraham and having God as their Father. Jesus gives the answer: "If you were Abraham's children, you would do what Abraham did, but now you seek to kill me . . .; this is not what Abraham did." To do what

Abraham did would have meant to believe in Jesus (8:45). This is also made clear at the end of the discussion: "Your father Abraham rejoiced that he was to see my day; he saw it and was glad" (8:56). As it is Christ who is contemporaneous with Abraham, and not vice versa (8:57–8), the reference here must be to an experience of Abraham during his life on earth. According to Jewish lore, mainly based upon Gen. 15:7–21 (the text following immediately after the words about Abraham's faith, Gen. 15:6), Abraham – like other fathers and prophets – had a vision of heaven and hell, and of the time to come and the end of the world.[18] In the Fourth Gospel this vision is taken to have been a vision of Christ's day, in analogy to Isaiah's vision of his glory. The joy of Abraham may be compared to that of John the Baptist (3:29). The Jews, who were not glad, but tried to kill Jesus, thereby proved that they were not Abraham's children, and that not God but the devil was their father (8:41–7). Claiming that the Father is their God, they do not know him (8:55).

The Jews, according to the Fourth Gospel, take the law and Moses, the Scriptures and the fathers, even God himself, as a religious possession of their own. Thinking that they do already have life and freedom, they use their religious possessions as means of self-defense when they are confronted with the true God, revealed in Christ. That is what makes the contrast so radical. John does not think that Jews and Christians are standing on a common ground, faith in God and reverence for the Scriptures, diverging only on the question of the messiahship of Jesus. That would rather be the opinion of Luke and of Justin. To John, "no one who denies the Son has the Father" (1 John 2:23); "he who does not honor the Son does not honor [= dishonors] the Father who sent him" (John 5:23). Man's relation to the Father and his revelation in the OT depends upon the attitude which he takes to the Son. By their opposition to Christ and their appeal to Abraham, Moses, the Scriptures, and God himself, the Jews prove that they are not children of Abraham, that the word of God, revealed at Sinai, does not abide in them and that God is not their Father.

In all this, the Jews do represent the world in its opposition to God. The essential nature of this world is the self-assertion over against God, the vanity to assume that life and liberty are man's own possession, so that he does not need the gift of God in Christ. When the world's opposition against God gets its concentrated expression through the Jews, it is because to them alone God has been revealed. They alone can use the name and the word of God as means of their own religious self-assertion and, thus, as means of the world's opposition to God. Only those who knew God and the law could find it blasphemous that Jesus pretended to be the Son of God; the Jews alone could demand that Jesus should be crucified.

There is an element of irony in the Johannine account of the Jewish opposition to Jesus; the climax of it appears in the proceedings which led to his crucifixion.[19] The reason, alleged by the high priest in his political opportunism, proved to be prophetic, "Jesus should die for the nation – and not for the nation only . . ." (11:47–53). In their blind zeal for God and the law, the Jews conclude by saying, "We have no king but Caesar" (19:15). Thus, they end up representing the world even in putting Caesar at the place of God, whereas they deny the fundamentals of their own faith and forfeit the history of Israel.

The Fourth Gospel sees the importance of the Scriptures in the witness they bear to Christ. What matters in the history of Israel is the existence of witnesses to Christ before the coming of Christ. When Jesus in 4:36–8 speaks about "others" who have labored and sown, and into whose labor the disciples have entered, this is, after all, probably to be understood as a reference to these witnesses of Christ before Christ. In any case, the fathers, the prophets, and the Scriptures point to something beyond themselves; whoever heard the word of God in their testimony would be open to hear and see, to believe and rejoice, when he met the revelation of God in Christ, full of grace and truth.

The True Israelites

The continuity between Israel and the Church is not only to be seen in the facts that Jesus was a Jew and that the Scriptures were taken over by the Church. In Israel Jesus also finds his first, prototypical disciples, those who come, see, and confess, "We have found the Messiah", "him of whom Moses and the prophets wrote". In a special way, Nathanael is the type of those within Israel whom the Father gives to the Son (cf. 6:37; 17:2–3); already his name indicates it. As "an Israelite indeed, in whom, there is no guile", Nathanael recognizes Jesus as the Son of God, the king of Israel (1:47–9).

To Nathanael and his fellow-disciples is given the promise, "You will see heaven opened, and the angels of God ascending and descending upon the son of man" (1:51). This is another example of Johannine allusions to OT visionary experiences, in this case to the dream of Jacob at Bethel. The true Israelite is to see what his ancestor saw. The angels are said to ascend and descend "upon the Son of man"; this does not mean that Jesus is identified with the ladder. The Johannine version has, rather, its analogy in rabbinic traditions, where "on it" (*bô*) can be taken to mean "upon him", that is, "over Jacob".

Further, in the Haggadah, Gen. 28:12, like other visionary texts, is often combined with Dan. 7 and Ezek. 1; the ascending and descending angels can be taken to refer to the worldly empires and to Israel.[20] In this context appears also the notion of the heavenly image (or model) of Jacob, an idea which must have had its scriptural base in the "human form" seated above the throne (Ezek. 1:26).[21] Possibly, the Johannine idea of the Son of Man is also connected with this notion; this could explain the longer text in 3:13: "the Son of man who is in heaven" (cf. also 1:18b). Whatever connections there may be found here, the main point of the Johannine text seems to be clear. Nathanael is to see "greater things"; in analogy with 5:20 and 14:12 this promise will refer to the ascension of Jesus. Even the ascending and descending angels must in some way represent his glory, or his glorification (cf. Mark 8:38; 13:26–7!).[22] The main meaning of the promise given to Nathanael and his fellows is that they shall see the glory of the Son of Man; they shall see the Son of Man glorified.

The true Israelites, of whom Nathanael is the type, are the "sheep" who belong to "this fold", the fold of Israel, in chapter 10. They know the voice of the shepherd and follow him. The "Jews" do not believe, because they do not belong to the sheep of Jesus (10:26); but there are some in Israel who do believe. Jesus has also "other sheep, that are not of this fold" (10:16). In order to "bring them also", Jesus as the good shepherd has to lay down his life (10:15, 17). These "other sheep" are identical with the "children of God who are scattered abroad"; Jesus had to die, in order to gather them into one (11:52). In other words, they are those outside Israel who are "of the truth", who hear – or heed – the voice of Jesus (18:37). That they are drawn to Jesus (12:32) and, thus, gathered into one implies that they are united with those within Israel who are "of the truth". "So there shall be one flock, one shepherd." In its Johannine context this saying neither states a program for ecumenical action nor refers to a purely "eschatological" unity of an invisible church; it looks forward to the unity which is to be realized after the ascension of Jesus, the unity of the "children of God scattered abroad" with those within the Jewish nation who hear the voice of Jesus and follow him.

In some respects this Johannine conception comes rather close to the Pauline one (Rom. 11:16–22; Eph. 2:11–22): the kernel of the Church is those Israelites who believe in Christ. To John, the most important point in this connection will be that the disciples in Israel are the primary witnesses to Jesus (17:20–1). Only in communion with them can the believers outside Israel see what they saw: the glory of Christ incarnate. Continuity within the history of the Church is the continuity of the witness borne to Christ (cf. 1 John 1:1–4; and also John 1:14; 19:35; and 21:24).

A Christocentric and Forensic Conception of History

The Fourth Gospel distinguishes between two classes of men, those who are of the world (from below, of the devil) and those who are of the truth, belong to the Father and are "sheep" of Christ (8:23, 44, 47; 10:26–7; 17:6, 9, 14; 18:37). As the origin betrays itself in the deeds, the distinction is at the same time one between those who "do evil" and those who "do the truth" (3:20–1; cf. 5:29). I need not discuss here how far the idea is that of a divine predestination or, rather, that of a human predisposition for faith and for unbelief. We should certainly not think that John would say that people of high moral standards are more inclined to believe than others, nor that he holds to the doctrine of a fixed number of the predestined. Only when a man is confronted with Christ does it appear what kind of man he is and to which category he belongs. He can come to Christ only through a decision of faith; if he comes, this fact proves that he is one of those who are drawn by the Father and given to the Son (6:37, 39, 44, 65).

In accordance with this view, John does not speak about a "change of peoples" by which the Jews are rejected and a new covenant people created.[23] The Jews who do not believe because they are "of the world" have never been true children of Abraham; those who do believe have already been potential members of the Church, whether they be true Israelites or "dispersed children of God". Before the coming of Christ both categories have been mixed, within the Jewish nation and also outside it. The cause has been suspended – if that word be allowed. The word of Christ is the judgment by which the sentence is passed and the two groups are separated. Those who do evil prefer to remain in darkness; those who do the truth come to the light of Christ and receive the gift of life from him (3:19–21; 5:21–4).

The two categories are not distinguished by metaphysical qualities, as in Gnosticism. What John sees is already latent in pre-Christian mankind, is, simply, the duality which appears in the attitude taken to Christ. The whole outlook of the Fourth Gospel is characterized by its consistent Christocentricity. The sin of the world is its self-assertion against the Word in which it was created, the Word who was in the beginning with God and who became flesh and dwelt among us. The conflict between light and darkness, between Christ and the world, is the one essential theme of history. The incarnation of Christ made the conflict an open one; by his revelation of the

Father, and of himself as the revealer, the darkness of the world became manifest too, as did the distinction between those who were of the world and those who were of the truth. The Church, as understood in the Fourth Gospel, can be said to be the totality of those who are of the truth – insofar as they have already heard the voice of Jesus.[24]

John is a witness to Christ; he is not concerned with a philosophy of history. But the Johannine concepts of "witness" and "testimony" have juridical connotations; thus, they are linked up with something which might be called a Johannine conception of history, because the conflict between God and the world is also conceived in forensic terms.[25] In this cosmic lawsuit Christ is the representative of God, and the Jews are representatives of the world. In their pleading, the Jews base their arguments upon the law, and Jesus appeals to the witness borne to him by John the Baptist, by his own works, and by the Scriptures, and refers also to precedents in OT history. In the proceedings before Pilate the lawsuit reaches its climax. By his apparent defeat, Jesus won the case. By his ascension he was vindicated and proved right in his claim to be the Son of God, with authority to act and speak as the delegate of the Father and to give eternal life to those who believe in him. This vindication of Jesus implies legal defeat of the world and of the Jews as its representatives. The prince of this world has been cast out from the heavenly court, so that he can no longer plead the cause of the world and oppose those who belong to Jesus (12:31; cf. Rev. 12:9–12). The claims of the world and of the Jews have been proved untrue; vindicated through his ascension, Jesus will draw all men to himself (12:32). The ministry of Jesus in Israel, his voluntary death as "king of the Jews", and his glorification by God are, thus, the historical and juridical basis for the life of the Church and for the witness which it brings to all men.

In the time of the Church, the world is still opposing God, but as a world already legally defeated; in their tribulations the disciples shall know that Christ has overcome the world (16:33). After the departure of Jesus, the Paraclete is pleading his case, assisting the disciples and convincing the world of sin (its lack of faith), of righteousness (the vindication of Jesus by his ascension), and of judgment (the sentence passed upon the prince of this world, 16:7–11). As the fathers and the prophets were witnesses to Christ before his coming, so the disciples have to bear testimony to him after his departure, and thus to play their role in the lawsuit of history. By their word the decision which fell when Jesus was glorified is applied to the individuals: those who believe receive the gift of eternal life; those who do not are already judged and remain in darkness. This, however, does not mean that the believers within the Church are already safe. Even the Jews to whom Jesus is speaking in John 8 are said to have believed; only those who remain in the word of Jesus are true disciples (8:31). Judas was one of the Twelve; in the fourth Gospel he is the type of those who belong to the Church but who are not of the truth and do not remain in Jesus (6:64–5, 70–1; 13:10–11; cf. 15:6; 1 John 2:19). Thus the members of the Church are constantly on trial, whether they really are of the truth or not.

The coming of a last day is presupposed, but it is not thought to bring a new and independent act of judgment. It will, rather, reveal the final outcome of the lawsuit which has been going on. Even on the last day the word of Jesus will be the judge of those who did not believe (12:46–50; cf. 5:25–9).

John is not a historian telling about the past and trying to find causes and effects. Neither is he a theologian of *Heilsgeschichte*, seeing a series of redemptive acts of God in history. His attitude to history is more like that of an advocate, who appeals to witnesses which have been rendered and to precedents and judicial decisions of the past. The situation of the Church, as it is conceived in the Fourth Gospel, is hardly to be compared to the military situation between "D-Day" and "V-Day". We should rather use forensic similes: The high court has already spoken its verdict, but its decision has still to be applied to individual cases. Trials are still going on; those who do not fulfill the conditions for acquittal are already judged by the sentence passed. Before local courts, who do not recognize the supremacy of the high court, the cause must still be pleaded, but the final outcome is only the consequence of the legal victory already won.

The historical and "legal" base for the existence of the Church is, thus, the glorification of Jesus through death and resurrection. The consistent Christocentricity of the Fourth Gospel does not exclude a sense of historical continuity, going backwards from the Church Universal to the first disciples and eyewitnesses of Jesus in Israel and farther back to those who believed and bore witness to him before his incarnation. In this sense, even John is aware of a "history of salvation" and sees the Church as the "true Israel" to which the "children of God scattered abroad" have been added. The Church has also a historical task in the present, through its existence and through its preaching to bear testimony to Christ in a world which is still hostile to him, even if it has already been legally defeated.

It is obvious that John's conceptions of the past are rather different from those of modern historical criticism. The problem of the relation between the "Johannine Christ" and the "Jesus of history" is not the only one; we could also ask how the figures of Abraham, Moses,

Isaiah, and John the Baptist in the Fourth Gospel are related to the historical persons with the same names. But that would be an anachronistic way of putting the question. With regard to the OT history, the Evangelist uses not only exegetical methods of his own time but also haggadic traditions, taken over from Judaism. With much of the freedom of the Haggadah, John may have used also the Gospel traditions at his disposal, traditions which are mostly independent of the Synoptics.[26] All his material the author interprets in order to make it serve his one purpose, to bear witness to Christ.

As the Gnostics often made use of the OT and of Gospel traditions to illustrate the one theme of the saving knowledge, the OT background of the Fourth Gospel does not disprove its affinity to gnosticism. One example of this affinity may be seen in the conception of the Church as the community of those who are of the truth and have heard the voice of the Saviour. But it is not necessary to assume that the Gospel presupposes any fully developed gnostic system; pre-gnostic trends within Judaism and early Christianity are more likely to have been part of the environment of the Evangelist. The Qumran idea of the more or less predestined "children of light" who are gathered into a community of the true Israel in some respects comes rather close to the Johannine conception of the Church. And very remarkable indeed is the attention which the Gospel pays to texts of importance for the Jewish Merkabah mysticism.[27] But John stresses that no one has ever seen God, and no one has ascended into heaven (1:18; 3:13; 6:46). The christological interpretation of OT visions and theophanies, therefore, seems to have a polemical note directed against a type of piety which made the patriarchs and prophets heroes of mystical visions of the heavenly world. Even a Docetic Christology may have been supported by allegorical interpretations of the OT.[28] Over against such tendencies, John bears witness to the true humanity of Jesus and to the reality of his death (6:41–2, 61; 19:35). Facing the danger that the Church might become detached from history, he counters it at the essential point and insists that those who see Jesus see the Father (14:9), and that God is to be seen in no other way. The question may remain as to whether the OT is not, factually, deprived of a historical meaning of its own when Moses and the prophets are simply made supporters of John's own testimony to Christ. But basically, John shares the OT faith in God, the Creator, who acts in history and is, accordingly, not an unknown God to be reached by a mystical escape from history. The continuity between Israel and the Church is understood in a peculiar way, but it is not dissolved.[29]

NOTES

1 The "Jewish religion" is merely discussed as an illustration of the perverted state of the world, in Section 44 (1955) 26–32.

2 In Bultmann (1971) only the quotations in 1:22–3; 7:38; and 10:34 are attributed to the "ecclesiastical editor". Those in 2:17; 6:31, 45; 12:39–40; 13:18; 15:25 are supposed to be contributions of the Evangelist, 12:38 to be derived from the "Semeia-source", and 12:15; 19:24, 28–9, 36–7 to be taken from a tradition akin to that of the Synoptics. Only the "speeches of revelation" do not bring any quotations.

3 In *New Testament Essays*, Studies in Memory of T. W. Manson (Manchester, 1959) 230–45.

4 Ibid., 240–1. The German text (*Studia Evangelica* [TU 1959] speaks about "the danger that history may simply be dissolved".

5 Cf. my "Kristus, jödene og verden etter Johannesevangeliet", *NTT* 60 (1959) 189–203, an article which deals with much of the same material as the present essay but pays special attention to the conception of missions.

6 J. A. T. Robinson, "Destination and Purpose of St. John's Gospel", in *Twelve NT Studies* (1962) 126–38, would take "the Greeks" of the Fourth Gospel to be Diaspora Jews. I have not been convinced. That the Greeks of 12:20 are said to have gone up to worship at the feast could possibly mean that the Jewish Diaspora has had a preparatory mission, as part of the means by which men are drawn by the Father to the Son (cf. 4:38; 6:45). Time and space do not allow for a fuller discussion.

7 The interrelation between the farewell discourses and the earlier parts of the Gospel is a special problem, the importance of which has been pointed out in articles by Alv Kragerud, "Kjaerlighetsbudet i Johannesevangeliet" and "Jesu äpenbaring av de jordiske og de himmelske ting", *NTT* 57 (1956) 137–49; and 58 (1957) 17–53.

8 (1971) 86 etc.

9 Cf. A. Fridrichen, "La pensée missionaire dans le quatrième Évangile", *Arb. u. Mitt. aus d. ntl. Seminar zu Uppsala*, 6 (1937) 39–45.

10 Cf. B. Noack, "Johannesevangeliets messiasbillede og dets kristologi", *Dansk teol. tidsskr.*, 19 (1956) 129–85; and W. C. van Unnik, "The Purpose of St. John's Gospel", *Studia Evangelica*, TU 73, 382–411.

11 Cf. van Unnik, op. cit., 395f. To me the distance between John and Justin appears greater than what van Unnik allows.

12 This may be inferred from the central importance of Isa. 6:3 (often combined with Dan. 7:10) in accounts of mystical ascensions; cf. G. Scholem, *Major Trends in Jewish Mysticism* (London, 1955) 40–79. Only scanty references to Isaiah's vision are found in Jewish sources known to me, but cf. Sir. 48:22–5; bab. Talmud *Hagigah* 13b (*Raba*) and *Yebamoth* 49b (id.), the Hebrew apocalypse translated by M. Gaster, *Studies and Texts* (London, 1925) I, 156–8. Cf. also F. W. Young, "A Study of the Relation of Isaiah to the Fourth Gospel", *ZNW*, 44 (1955) 215–32.

13 Cf., e.g., M.-E. Boismard, *Le prologue de saint Jean* (Paris, 1953). On the vision(s), and the ascent of Moses, cf. Sir. 45:2–5; *Jubilees* 1; Ps-Philo, *Ant.bibl.* 12:1; 4 Ezra 14:5; Syr. Baruch 59. In rabbinic traditions Ps. 68:19 and Ps. 8 are applied to Moses ascent to God, bab. Talmud *Shabbath* 88b–89a etc.; cf. Str-B III, 596–8;

M. Abraham, *Légendes juives apocryphes sur la Vie de Moïse* (Paris, 1925). Further literature in TDNT, IV, 848.

14 On Moses as the advocate of Israel, cf. N. Johansson, *Parakletoi* (Lund, 1940) 67, 124–5, and 162–6; J. Jeremias in *TDNT*, IV, 852–64.

15 According to Exod. 20:18 the Israelites "saw" the voice; cf. further Exod. 24:10–11, 17; Deut. 5:24; 18:16; Sir. 17:6. Some of the rabbinic material is referred to by J. Jervell, *Imago Dei* (Göttingen, 1960) 115. For combinations of Exod. 19 (and 24) with Ezek. 1, see also G. Kretschmar, "Himmelfahrt und Pfingsten", *Zeitschrift für Kirchengeschichte*, 66 (1954–5) 209–53.

16 Cf. J. Giblet, "Le Témoignage du Père (Jn 5:31–47)", *Bible et vie chrétienne*, 12 (1955) 49–59. This article is known to me only from *NT Abstracts*, 1 (1956) 16.

17 Cf. C. K. Barrett (1955) 319–20; Str-B II, 543.

18 Ezra 3:14; Syr. Baruch 4:4; *Apocalypse of Abraham* 9–32 (!); *Mekilta Ex* 20:18; Palestinian Targums and *Genesis Rabbah* on Gen. 15:7–13; Targum *Isaiah* 43:12; cf. Str-B III, 525–6. Most interesting allusions to Gen. 15:7ff. are also to be found in the Apostolic Constitutions VII.33 and Ps.-Clem. *Recognitions* I.32.

19 Cf. H. Clavier, "L'ironie dans le quatrième Evangile", *Studia Evangelica* (TU 73) 261–76.

20 *Genesis Rabbah* 68–9, especially 68:12; 69:3; *Leviticus Rabbah* 29:2; *Tanhuma Wayyese* 38a; cf. Str-B III, 49–50; H. Odeberg (1929) 32–42. An eschatological, or mystical, interpretation of Gen. 28:12 is presupposed already in Wis. 10:10: "She (Wisdom) showed him God's kingdom".

21 *Genesis Rabbah* 68:12; Palestinian Targums on Gen. 28:12; *Pirqe de Rabbi Eliezer* 35, 82a; cf. Str-B I, 976–7. According to *Hekaloth Rabbathi* 9, *Beth ha-Midrasch,* ed. Jellinek, III, 90, God embraces the image of Jacob whenever the Israelites say the "Holy". In "normative Judaism" the image is identified with the human face of the four "living creatures", Ezek. 1:10. But as Jervell, op. cit., 117, has seen, the original reference must have been to Ezek. 1:26. This seems to be confirmed by one of the Gnostic texts from Nag Hammadi (No. 40), in which themes from Jewish Merkabah mysticism have been incorporated; cf. J. Doresse, *Les livres secrets des gnostiques d'Égypte* (Paris, 1958) 189: "Alongside Sabaoth is found a first-born called Israel: the man who sees God". Possibly, the heavenly "image" has originally not been conceived as a statue but been identical with the archangel "Israel", a version of the divine vice-regent elsewhere called Yaoel, Metatron, the "lesser YHWH", with whom also the Philonic Logos has some connections; cf. *De conf. ling.* 146. For further material and hypothetical reconstructions cf. J. Daniélou, *The Theology of Jewish Christianity* (London, 1964) 132–4 ("The angel Israel"); P. Winter, *"MONOGENES PARA PATROS"*, *Zeitschr. f. Religions- u. Geistesgeschichte*, 5 (1953) 335–65, and "Zum Verständnis des Johannes-Evangeliums", *TLZ*, 80 (1955) 142–50; G. Quispel, "Het Johannese-vangelie en de Gnosis", *Nederlands Theologisch Tijdschrift* 11 (1957) 173–203.

22 On John 1:51 cf., further, E. Eidem, "Natanaels kallelse", *Till ärkebiskop Söderbloms sextioårsdag* (Stockholm, 1926) 131–40; H. Windisch, "Angelophanien um den Menschensohn auf Erden", and "Joh. 1, 51 und die Auferstehung Jesu", *ZNW* 30 (1931) 215–33; and 31 (1932) 199–204; G. Quispel, "Nathanael und der Menschensohn", *ZNW* 47 (1956) 281–3; S. Schulz (1957) 97–103.

23 The term "change of people" is coined by A. V. Ström, *Vetekornet* (Stockholm, 1944) 269, etc. Ström finds this idea also in the Fourth Gospel, especially in 12:34 (394–403), but cf. my critical review in *Svensk Exegetisk Årsbok* 11 (1946) 120–35.

24 Cf. Bultmann (1955) 92.

25 Th. Preiss (1954) 9–31.

26 Cf. especially B. Noack, *Zur Johanneischen Tradition* (Köbenhaven, 1954). K. Stendahl, *The School of St. Matthew* (Lund-Copenhagen, 1954) 31 and 163, assumes the existence of a "school of St John", and I think that my observations give new support to his thesis. A. Kragerud, *Der Lieblingsjünger im Johannese-vangelium* (Oslo, 1959), would rather think of the Johannine circle as a collective body of wandering prophets, symbolized by the beloved disciple; even if this hypothesis hardly carries conviction, it draws attention to the inspired nature of John's handling of texts and traditions. Cf. as an analogy 1QpHab 2:5–10.

27 The standard texts of the Merkabah mysticism (Exod. 19, Isa. 6, Ezek. 1, Dan. 7, etc.), which in Jewish tradition were combined with one another and also with Gen. 15:7–13, 28:12, etc., in a remarkable way reappear in the Revelation of St John. The vision of John, Rev. 4—5, may help us to understand how the OT witnesses' visions of Christ were visualized by the author of the Fourth Gospel.

28 The heretics combated by John (cf. also John 2:18–27; 4:1–6; 5:5–8; 2 John 7) seem to have been of much the same type as those of the Ignatian letters – cf. E. Molland, "The Heretics Combated by Ignatius of Antioch", *Journal of Ecclesiastical History*, 5 (1954) 1–6. E. Schweizer also recognizes an anti-Docetic tendency in the Fourth Gospel: cf. "Das Johanneische Zeugnis vom Herrenmahl", *EvT* 12 (1952–3) 341–63. I do not suggest that the antiheretic purpose should be taken to be the major one; the aim is, certainly, also missionary, apologetic, and devotional. We should, I think, not even expect any precise answer to the question whether the Gospel is intended for Christian, Jewish, or Gentile readers. According to the Johannine concept, the answers which might be given are aspects of the one purpose of the Gospel, to bear witness to Christ in the "lawsuit" between God and the world.

29 I have not taken account of questions of literary criticism in this essay, not because I do not think a complicated history of tradition preceded the present literary form of the Gospel, but because I am inclined to think that the Evangelist was himself the "ecclesiastical editor" of the traditions of the Johannine "school".

8

The Man from Heaven
*in Johannine Sectarianism**

WAYNE A. MEEKS

The uniqueness of the Fourth Gospel in early Christian literature consists above all in the special patterns of language which it uses to describe Jesus Christ. Fundamental among these patterns is the description of Jesus as the one who has descended from heaven and, at the end of his mission which constitutes a *krisis* for the whole world, reascends to the Father. Not the least of Rudolf Bultmann's enduring contributions to Johannine studies was his recognition and insistence that any attempt to solve the "Johannine puzzle" must begin with this picture of the descending/ascending redeemer. Moreover, he saw that it is not simply a question of explaining the *concept* "pre-existence", but rather of perceiving the origin and function of a *myth*. The solution could not be found, therefore, by comparisons with philosophical developments in the hellenistic schools, such as the long-favored *logos spermatikos* of the Stoics, or its adaptation by middle Platonists or Alexandrian Jews. Myths have a logic of their own, which is not identical with the logic of the philosophers.[1]

Nevertheless, Bultmann's own proposed solution has not commanded general assent. To be sure, his observation that the closest extant analogies to the Johannine myth are to be found in the literature of gnostic movements stands firm and has been reinforced by more recent discoveries. The problem comes in assessing the very important differences between the typical gnostic myths and that of John, and therefore the direction of the relationship between the two patterns. Perhaps the most important difference, which Bultmann did not fail to notice, is the fact that in gnostic myths most comparable with the Johannine pattern the redeemer's descent and ascent parallel the fate and hope of the human essence (soul, pneuma, seed, or the like), while in the Fourth Gospel there is no such *analogia entis* between

---

* First published in *JBL* 91 (1972) 44–72.

redeemer and redeemed. Bultmann's hypothesis is that the typical gnostic myth was deliberately modified by the fourth evangelist, effectively "demythologizing" it. This hypothesis, plausible as it is, ran into difficulties of two sorts: (1) It required the support of very complex additional hypotheses about the literary sources of John, about the relationship between the Johannine Christians and the disciples of John the Baptist, and about the latter's role in the origins of the Mandean sect. None of these hypotheses has received support from further specialized investigations.[2] (2) The *typical* gnostic myth with which Bultmann compared the Johannine pattern is an abstraction, obscuring the variety of actual gnostic myths in extant texts.[3] Furthermore, Bultmann's synthetic myth is heavily dependent on the terminology of the Fourth Gospel; there is hardly any single document other than John in which all the elements of the "gnostic redeemer myth" listed by Bultmann in his 1925 article are integrally displayed.[4]

A number of scholars have proposed to stand Bultmann's hypothesis on its head: Johannine Christology was not an adaptation of gnostic myth, they would say, but a step *towards* gnosticism. Older forms of this proposal, supported only by pointing to the lateness of the Mandean and Manichean sources used by Bultmann, are not adequate. While no extant document of definite pre-Christian date may present a descending/ascending redeemer of the gnostic type, sufficiently strong inferences may be derived from later sources to make an argument from silence highly precarious.[5] More weighty are studies which use the logic and literary form of the Johannine christological discourses to suggest a historical location somewhere between primitive Christianity and emerging gnosticism. For example, Siegfried Schulz's study of the Son of Man passages in John, despite the occasional artificiality of his "themageschichtliche Analyse", is able to show frequently that the reinterpretation of a basic substratum of *apocalyptic* motifs serves as the center for "Crystallizations of gnostic hellenistic elements".[6] Helmut Koester locates the Johannine farewell discourses at "a crucial place in the development of the genre 'Revelation'" which would lead to such theophany-type revelations as the Apocryphon of John.[7] M. Jack Suggs has very plausibly argued that the identification of Christ with Sophia by Matthew, in contrast to Q, and by Paul, in contrast to his opponents in Corinth (so also Koester, against Wilckens), created a peculiar symbolic dialectic that paved the way for the developed gnostic Sophia-myths.[8] What he says could be applied *mutatis mutandis* to John.

It is now commonly agreed that the Jewish Wisdom myth in some form lies behind both the Johannine Christology and the gnostic soul and savior myths.[9] The question is whether both the Johannine and the gnostic myths are independent variants of the Jewish, or whether one has influenced the other. The present essay will not attempt a direct answer to that question by re-examining the possible antecedents of John's symbolism, but will only explore the function of the mythical pattern within the Johannine literature. Such a study may have its own contribution to make to the question of inter-group influence.

The problem has been treated too one-sidedly as a problem in the history of ideas. Mythical language tends to be reduced to theological categories, and *historical* judgments are then made on the basis of the presumed *logical* priority of one or other of these categories. Where this has occurred, Bultmann's insight, that the language of myth has a special logic, has been ignored. The Bultmann–Jonas theory of myth as the objectivation of the religious person's sense of his relationship to self and world was a significant step towards a more appropriate hermeneutic for mythical language. Yet, as Jonas later observed, the categories of existential philosophy that seemed to fit the *gnostic* myths so well are by no means a universal key.[10] And even Bultmann tends to reduce the function of myth in John to theological categories; that is shown by his obsessive attempt to discover a *rational* sequence in the Johannine discourses and narratives by the incredibly complex rearrangement–hypotheses in his commentary. We have not yet learned to let the symbolic language of Johannine literature speak in its own way. It is symptomatic of the impasse in NT hermeneutics that we have as yet no adequate monograph on the Johannine symbolism as such.[11]

Bultmann's starting point was the observation that the symbolic picture of Jesus as the man who descended and ascended constituted a *puzzle* within the Fourth Gospel. It seemed to identify Jesus as a revealer come from the heavenly world, and therefore able to communicate what he had "seen and heard" in that world – but his promise to do so was never fulfilled in the Gospel. He revealed only *that* he is the revealer.[12] Bultmann's solution involves the argument that this pattern ordinarily, in the gnostic milieu posited for the Johannine group, depicted a "revealer". The pattern as such therefore did not have to make sense within the literary structure of the Gospel; it made sense in the extrinsic historical setting. The only thing necessary for John was to show that Jesus *was* the one and only one to whom the well-known pattern ought to be applied. If we are not satisfied with Bultmann's reconstruction of the historical situation in which the puzzle could be explained, then we are forced to ask his initial question all over again: In what situation does a literary puzzle provide an appropriate means of communication?

The problem may be best approached by complicating it: this pattern is not the only puzzling thing about the Fourth Gospel. The major literary problem of John is its combination of remarkable stylistic unity and thematic coherence with glaringly bad transitions between episodes at many points. The countless displacement, source, and redaction theories that litter the graveyards of Johannine research are voluble testimony to this difficulty. Many of the elements of the unitary style are probably not specific to a single author, but belong to the Johannine "school", for they are frequently found distributed between portions of the Gospel which, on other grounds, we would attribute to "source", "evangelist", and "redactor". On the other hand, not all the *aporiae* in the present form of the Gospel can be attributed to clumsy redaction; most of them evidently were acceptable to the evangelist, despite his ability to produce large, impressively unified literary compositions (the trial and crucifixion scenario, as the most notable example). There are a number of examples not only of double entendre which are progressively clarified by repetition and modification, but also of self-contradiction that are manifestly deliberate ("I do not judge ... yet if I do judge ...", 8:15). Above all there are parallel, slightly varying formulations of similar thematic complexes, ranging from double Amen-sayings side by side within one didactic dialogue ("Unless one is born *anōthen* ["anew, from above"] he cannot *see* the Kingdom of God"//"Unless one is born of *water and spirit* he cannot *enter* the kingdom of God", 3:3, 5)[13] to whole compositions that seem to be alternate interpretations of the same group of themes belonging to different stages of the history of redaction of the Gospel (chap. 14//chaps. 15—16).[14]

We may find a clue to the proper understanding of these peculiar relationships in the attempt of some contemporary anthropologists to get at the function of myths in the societies that create them by means of close analysis of their *structure*. For example, the distinguished English scholar Edmund Leach proposes that the way in which myths work may be understood by analogies drawn from the study of electronic communications. If a message is to be conveyed in the face of pervasive distractions – "noise", or, in the case of myth, the overwhelming complexity of the total social matrix – then the communicator must resort to "redundance". He must repeat the signal as many times as possible, in *different* ways. From the repeated impact of varying signals, the basic *structure* which they have in common gets through. It is, therefore, only by paying attention to the underlying structure of the components in a system of myths that an interpreter can "hear" what the myths are "saying", or, to put it another way, can discover the function which the myths have within the group in which they are at home.[15]

It is astonishing that attempts to solve the Johannine puzzle have almost totally ignored the question of what *social* function the myths may have had.[16] No one, of course, is in a position to write an empirical sociology of Johannine Christianity. Nevertheless, it has become abundantly clear that the Johannine literature is the product not of a lone genius but of a community or group of communities that evidently persisted with some consistent identity over a considerable span of time. We know at least a few things about its history – all from direct allusions in the documents themselves. The group had to distinguish itself over against the sect of John the Baptist and even more passionately over against a rather strong Jewish community, with which highly ambivalent relationships had existed. It suffered defections, conflicts of leadership, and schisms. I shall argue that one function of the "symbolic universe" communicated in this remarkable body of literature was to make sense of all these aspects of the group's history. More precisely, there must have been a continuing dialectic between the group's historical experience and the symbolic world which served both to explain that experience and to motivate and form the reaction of group members to the experience.

In the following pages an attempt is made to discern the function which the motif "ascent and descent" serves, first, within the literary structure of the Fourth Gospel, then, by analogy, within the structure of the Johannine community and its relationships to its environment.

I

At the outset it may be as important to indicate what is *not* said about the descent and ascent of Jesus as what is said. For example, the descent from heaven is not described in John, but everywhere presupposed as a *fait accompli*. The prologue offers no real exception, for it is not really a "prologue in heaven" though the standpoint of the poem's narrator is, in a sense, *sub specie aeternitatis*. The story of Jesus in the Gospel is all played out on earth, despite the frequent indicators that he really belongs elsewhere. Consequently, those stories which describe the commissioning of an envoy, his arming for the journey, and the dangers of the descent itself are not parallels, for the center of attention in them is different. In this general category could be included not only many of the Mandean myths of the descent of the messengers of light, but also the more ancient myths of the descent of gods or heroes into the underworld: Inanu, Demeter,

Heracles, Orpheus, etc. The references to descent and ascent are introduced into the middle of things in John, as explanations of something else. *The motif belongs exclusively to discourse, not to narrative.* A description of a descent or ascent, in narrative form, can identify the actor as a hero, by describing the dangers he overcomes. Or it can serve the quite different function of an occasion for a cosmography: the geography of Hades, for example. In John, neither use of the motif is present. It is used exclusively to identify Jesus – but not as a hero. It depicts him rather, as a detailed analysis of specific passages will show, as the Stranger *par excellence*.

The pair of verbs *anabainein/katabainein*, "ascend/descend", appears in John for the first time[17] in the perplexing promise made to Nathanael in 1:51: "Amen, amen I say to you, you will see heaven opened and the angels of God ascending and descending upon the Son of Man." This traditional logion[18] depends on a midrash on Gen. 28:12,[19] from which the participles, in just this peculiar order, are drawn.[20] As Eduard Schwarz noticed in his famous article on the "aporiae" in the Fourth Gospel, the saying has the form of a solemn prophecy which, because of its place at the beginning of the book, demands some fulfillment in the subsequent narrative.[21] This is all the more so if, as Schulz argues, the logion's purpose is to use the Bethel midrash to "correct" the traditional prophecy of the parousia which is found in similar form in the Synoptics (Mark 14:62 par.; cf. 13:26; Luke 17:22; Mark 16:7 par.) in the direction of a "realized eschatology".[22] Yet there is certainly no explicit fulfillment in John; as Windisch notes, there are no angelophanies in the Fourth Gospel.[23] Nevertheless, to suppose that the evangelist has merely extracted the prophecy from a source in which there *were* angelophanies (Windisch) is a solution of embarrassment, while the more common explanation, that the "ascending and descending" angels are merely a "symbol" of the union of the celestial and terrestrial worlds,[24] evades the exegete's responsibility to deal with the specific way in which the author handles symbols. This larger question is one which can only be approached after we have gathered more information about the over-all structure of our theme. At the moment it is enough to notice that the prophecy in its present context does two things: (1) It introduces the title "Son of Man", thus completing the series of titles whose announcement is evidently one of the major functions of the whole section vv. 29–41.[25] (2) It introduces the *pattern* of ascending and descending. If angels play no further role in John, perhaps it is precisely this *pattern* which is to be remembered from the saying. In any case, it is a mistake to focus upon the question, what are the angels supposed to be doing for the Son of Man?[26] It may not be entirely accidental that the next time the Son of Man title appears in the Gospel is also the next time the verb-pair "ascend/descend" appears, 3:13, where we are told that ascending and descending are the exclusive properties of the Son of Man. There is a curiously close connection throughout the Gospel between this title and the descent/ascent language.[27] Moreover, while the promise of the vision of "greater things" is made in 1:51 to Nathanael, "the real Israelite",[28] it is "the teacher of *Israel*", Nicodemus, who in 3:11–13 is told that he cannot or will not see certain superior things.[29]

In the dialogue with Nicodemus the evangelist has brought together a number of disparate traditional motifs[30] which have to be understood in terms of their place in the rather loose structure of the dialogue as a whole.[31] In vv. 11–14, the third Amen-saying of the section is followed by three statements that are merely juxtaposed without any clear connecting links. Within this small collection the descent/ascent of Jesus seems to serve as the warrant for the esoteric revelation which he brings. Only he can tell about "heavenly things", because only he has descended from heaven – and no one else has ascended. As Odeberg showed, the *exclusivity* of the revelation by the Son of Man must be construed as a polemic, not against claims of other gnostic revealers (since they, too, would claim to have "descended"), but against the claim of prophets or seers to have received revelations by means of "heavenly journeys", as for example in apocalyptic or in the *merkābāh* speculation, or in the traditions of the theophanies to Moses and the Patriarchs.[32] Note that this statement clarifies the ambiguous meaning of the previous two Amen-sayings, for the unusual formulation "to see the kingdom of God" in v. 3 can only refer to "heavenly-journey" tradition.[33] The more traditional-sounding saying of v. 5, asserting that only one born of water and spirit can *enter* the kingdom, is thus re-interpreted to refer to an *ascent to heaven*,[34] while v. 13 shows that *anōthen* has to mean "from above" and that "the one born from above/from the spirit" can only be the Son of Man, Jesus. This interpretation is confirmed by vv. 31–6, which provide a reprise of the themes of the dialogue, for there "he that comes from above" is "he that comes from heaven", as the one "above all" – even above John the Baptist – is obviously Jesus alone. Whether the general formulations in vv. 3, 5, and especially 8, leave room for reference *secondarily* to the community of believers is a very important question which must be discussed in another context below. Initially, v. 13 provides a fair summary of the whole dialogue: Jesus alone has access to heavenly secrets. On the surface, then, the descent/ascent motif serves here as a warrant for the truth of those secrets. Careful analysis of the form of the dialogue, however, will show that the revelation-warrant language is here being used for a special purpose.

Nicodemus plays a well-known role: that of the rather stupid disciple whose maladroit questions provide the occasion (a) for the reader to feel superior and (b) for the sage who is questioned to deliver a discourse. The genre is widespread in the Greco-Roman world,[35] though perhaps the closest parallels to the present dialogue are to be found in the dialogues between the seer and the interpreting angel in apocalypses and in the gnostic revelations such as the Apocryphon of John or the Pistis Sophia. In such contexts, one frequently meets the cliché, "You do not understand earthly things, and you seek to know heavenly ones?" This may serve to mock a student who seeks to know something beyond his powers,[36] or to rebuke an attempt to ascend to heaven.[37] Only the use of the Johannine term *pisteuein* ("believe") distinguishes v. 12 from this commonplace. Precisely because the riposte is a cliché, whose function is always to administer a more-or-less serious warning or rebuke – that is, to put the would-be learner in his place – the difficulty in deciding just what are the "earthly things" which Jesus has told Nicodemus is not so important as most commentators have believed. The point of v. 12 is not at all the contrast between earthly and heavenly information, but the contrast between the questioner and the one who possesses the information.

The first and primary message of the dialogue is thus simply that Jesus is incomprehensible to Nicodemus. They belong to two different worlds, and, despite Nicodemus' initial good intentions (v. 2), Jesus' world seems quite opaque to him. It becomes important then to discover just what or whom Nicodemus represents, that his obtuseness should be depicted so paradigmatically by the evangelist. Of course, the specific designations "ruler of the Jews" (v. 2; 7:50) and "the teacher of Israel" (3:10) provide a solid starting point. His two subsequent appearances in the Gospel are as fraught with ambiguity as this one; this ambiguity is doubtless an important and deliberate part of the portrait of this obscure figure. Nevertheless, there is a consistent analogy between the narratives about Nicodemus and certain statements about the Jews in John which gives us important clues about his function in the Gospel and also about the extraordinarily subtle way in which certain themes are elaborated in this Gospel.

First, he comes to Jesus "by night", a detail hardly necessary to the story, but also not merely a random bit of color, for the evangelist takes pains to remind his readers of it later on, in a note which in fact *characterizes* Nicodemus as "the one who came to him previously [or, 'at first'] by night" (19:39). This casts a certain suspicion over him, because of what is said in the dialogue itself about the division between people who come to the light and those who remain in darkness (3:19–21). Nicodemus does *come* to the light, but he is depicted as one who does not perceive that light very clearly, and who is hesitant and unable to make the decisive step from darkness to light.

Nicodemus' opening statement to Jesus is, in effect, a declaration of faith. He believes that Jesus has "come from God", and the basis for that belief is the *signs* which Jesus has performed. Nicodemus' case is, therefore, rather closely parallel to that of the blind man healed by Jesus in chap. 9, who on the same grounds, viz., Jesus' signs (especially, of course, the one performed to his own benefit; but also in general, "such signs", 9:16), declares that Jesus is "a prophet", not a sinner, but "from God" (9:16–17, 30–3). Like that man, Nicodemus confesses a faith in Jesus which, if imperfect, at least corresponds to an acceptable first stage of faith as viewed by the Johannine community.[38] Also like the "enlightened" blind man, Nicodemus will defend Jesus before the authorities (7:50f.). But unlike him, Nicodemus will not go so far as to master the "fear of the Pharisees" [or, "of the Jews"] and risk being expelled from the synagogue (9:22, 34; 12:42). And unlike him, he is unable to comprehend the identity of the Son of Man (9:35f.; 3:13ff.). When he appears for the third and last time – in a distinctly Johannine addition to the Joseph of Arimathea tradition (19:39) – it is to bury Jesus. His ludicrous "one hundred pounds" of embalming spices indicate clearly enough that he has not understood the "lifting up" of the Son of Man.[39]

Nicodemus thus becomes the representative of those Jews mentioned in 2:23f., who "believed in [Jesus'] name because they saw the signs which he did", but to whom Jesus would not "entrust himself" because of his suprahuman knowledge of their hearts. The theme of Jews who have begun to believe in Jesus but whose faith is not to be trusted is further developed in 8:30–59, a dialogue that depicts them in such dark tones – potential Christ-killers and sons of Cain or the Devil – that the shabby treatment of Nicodemus in chap. 3 seems mild by comparison. More attention must be given to chap. 8 below, for in that context occurs the most sharply dualistic statement of the above/below theme in the Fourth Gospel. It is already apparent, however, that the theme is closely connected with the trauma of the Johannine Christians' separation from the synagogue.[40]

The final portion of chap. 3 (vv. 31–6) is so closely related to the themes of the Nicodemus dialogue that many commentators have proposed that in some original form of the Gospel these verses stood immediately after v. 21. Such rearrangement hypotheses result from failure to perceive one of the most striking characteristics of the evangelist's literary procedure: the elucidation of themes by progressive repetition.[41] In part this procedure was probably forced upon the author by the nature of the traditional material he was using, which had evidently produced, within the Johannine community, a number of stylized didactic units, in the form of the "revelation discourse", on overlapping themes. Alternative formulations produced by the community did not always perfectly coincide. The variant formulations could be simply juxtaposed, and that in fact is most frequently the case in the collective literature of sects which make use of the revelation discourse form, whether apocalyptic or gnostic.[42] That can happen also in the Fourth Gospel, but characteristically the variants are interspersed with narrative episodes or other kinds of material, with connectives and restatements by the evangelist. The result is not only a dramatic effect produced by the connection between discourse and narrative, but also a certain distance for the reader from the ambiguous and paradoxical statements, so that the internal tensions of the material begin to work in a progressive, didactic spiral.[43] John 3:31–6 is a splendid example. As the composition of the evangelist, it brings together in his own language the principal themes of the Nicodemus dialogue, which was composed in part from pre-Johannine material. A number of ambiguities from the dialogue are here cleared up. For example, as we noticed above, *anōthen* in v. 31 can only mean "from above". Moreover, implications which, in our analysis above, were suggested by the *structure* of the dialogue are here stated explicitly. Thus, while the traditional style of the dialogue suggested that the one "from above" would communicate supraterrestrial *knowledge*, the net effect of the dialogue was only and purely to indicate *his own* superiority to the questioner – and to any "earthly" person. That is precisely what is now said in v. 31: "He who comes from above *is* above all." Verse 32 is exactly parallel with v. 11, but in the third person singular rather than the communal, confessional first plural. The empty "revelation form" persists: "what he has seen and heard, this he testifies", but the subsequent verses (33–6) make it even plainer than do vv. 11–21 that the question is not whether one is able to receive the special information which the heavenly messenger brings, but whether one will accept the messenger himself. The evangelist will later develop this further, in a classic example of his deliberate and didactic use of self-contradiction. In 5:31–41 Jesus is made to insist that he does not testify to himself; in 8:12–20 he takes up the same theme, in response to a "Jewish" accusation, with the remarkable concession:

> Even if I testify about myself, my testimony is true ...
> I do not judge anyone,
> but even if I judge, my judgment is true. ...

The total "testimony" of Jesus in the Fourth Gospel, the sole object of his mission in "the world" (18:37), is in fact about himself, and the presentation of that self-testimony is depicted as the *krisis* of the world. But the Johannine "self-contradiction" forces the reader to think of Jesus' self-testimony in distinction from a false kind of self-testimony (that identified with the arrogance of the false prophet in Deut. 18:33, the seeking of *doxa* from men: 5:44).[44] Because this *krisis* of faith or unfaith is the major point of the dialogue, both the dialogue (vv. 16–21) and the evangelist's summary (vv. 35–6) conclude with a statement about it in connection with the sending of the "beloved" son.

But why should the summary be separated from the dialogue it summarizes by an apparently irrelevant discussion of the relationship of Jesus to John the Baptist? The transition from v. 30 to v. 31 makes the reason rather plain. Because Jesus, being "from above", is "above all", John "must diminish" in comparison with him. There is no escaping the conclusion that, for the evangelist, John and his movement belong among those who are "of the earth" (v. 31). By placing his summary immediately after this self-testimony of John, therefore, the evangelist makes a statement which is functionally the equivalent of the "Q" saying, "among those born of women none is greater than John; yet he who is least in the kingdom of God is greater than he" (Luke 7:28//Matt. 11:11).

Thus the dialogue with Nicodemus and its postscript connected with John the Baptist constitute a virtual *parody* of a revelation discourse. What is "revealed" is that Jesus is *incomprehensible*, even to "the teacher of Israel" who holds an initially positive belief in him – within the context of Jewish piety – and even to the Baptist who has been his primary human witness (5:32–5). The forms of speech which would ordinarily provide warrants for a particular body of information or instruction here are used in such a way that they serve solely to emphasize Jesus' strangeness.

Yet it is not quite accurate to say with Bultmann that Jesus reveals only that he is the revealer. He reveals rather that he is an enigma. But he also reveals some positive content of the Johannine Christology; i.e., the dialogue is the vehicle for introducing into John's literary schema several significant christological themes: (1) the ironic "exaltation" (= crucifixion) pun,[45] (2) the mystery of the origin and destiny of the spirit-born ("whence he comes and whither he goes", v. 8),[46] and (3) the explicit identification of the Son of Man with "he who descended" (v. 13).[47] As we have seen, these themes become clear only as their progressive development is traced through the Gospel. The form of the dialogue itself is such that the reader without special prior information would be as puzzled as Nicodemus. Only a reader who is thoroughly familiar with the whole Fourth Gospel or else acquainted by some non-literary means with its symbolism and developing themes (perhaps because he belongs to a community in which such language is constantly used) can possibly understand its double entendre and its abrupt transitions. For the outsider – even for an interested inquirer (like Nicodemus) – the dialogue is opaque.

II

Space does not permit an analysis of the other occurrences in John of the ascent/descent motif in the same detail that we have devoted to the Nicodemus dialogue. It can readily be seen, however, that wherever the motif occurs, it is in a context where the primary point of the story is the inability of the men of "this world", pre-eminently "the Jews", to understand and accept Jesus.

This is quite clear in the "midrash" in chap. 6 on the "bread from heaven".[48] This discourse is linked to the traditional feeding and sea-crossing stories by a question from the crowd to which Jesus responds, as he responded to Nicodemus, with an Amen-saying totally unrelated to the question. If Nicodemus came to Jesus because he saw signs, the crowd comes, Jesus tells them, because they *failed* to see signs – a failure that is confirmed, in typical Johannine fashion, by their own words in v. 30. The irony in vv. 30–1 is very heavy, for precisely the "sign" which they request – one analogous to the manna which Moses gave – has already been provided, for the "men who saw" (v. 14).[49] The crowd which crosses the lake – though the evangelist does not distinguish it from "those who saw" in v. 14 – does not see and cannot believe (vv. 36, 40). The irony is now carried yet farther by the identification of the "bread from heaven" not with the bread of the miracle but with "the Son of Man". The theme is announced by the positive half of Jesus' Amen-saying (v. 27), which introduces the motifs that, by a complex series of interweavings with the biblical texts cited in vv. 31 and 45, provide organization of the entire discourse, reaching its summation in v. 58.[50] That organization, insofar as it relates to our theme, can be made plain by a simple outline of the discourse's progression: (1) "Work for the food that remains for eternal life, which the Son of Man gives" (vv. 27, 58). (2) "Work" means "believe" in the one whom God has sent (v. 29, cf. 36–40, 45–7). (3) The "food" that the Son of Man gives is "bread which descends from heaven" (vv. 31–3), which God, not Moses, gives. (4) That bread is identical with the Son of Man himself, for he *is* "he who descended from heaven" – as we learned in chap. 3 (vv. 35, 38, 48–51).[51] (5) The "murmurings" of the Jews produce an even more pointed statement: the bread of life is the very flesh of the Son of Man (vv. 51b–58).[52]

The descent of Jesus from heaven is of course unacceptable to "the Jews", for they say: "Is this not Jesus, the son of Joseph, whose father and mother we know? How then does he say, 'I have descended from heaven'?" (v. 42). Quite analogously, in the following dialogue with those disciples who are disturbed by the notion of "eating the flesh of the Son of Man", the ascent of the Son of Man "where he was before" offers "a still greater offense".[53] In the chapter as a whole, the movement is from a concept familiar to Jews (something which comes down from heaven is given by the hand of a prophet), but doubted in the specific instance of Jesus, to their total alienation by his outrageous claim to be *himself* that which comes down from heaven – and returns thither. We may perhaps compare the movement we observed earlier, from the promise to Nathanael of something like Jacob's Bethel vision ("angels ascending and descending upon the Son of Man") to the statement to Nicodemus that only the Son of Man (not angels, and not *merkābāh* visionaries) ascends and descends.

In one sense what is happening in the Johannine dialogues is the combination of familiar patterns from Jewish tradition – above all the picture of the apostolic prophet, that of the heavenly Wisdom that seeks a home among men only to be rejected, and, perhaps, that of the angel who bears Yahweh's name[54] – in such a way that the basic relationships are exaggerated to the point of virtual absurdity. Thus while the tradition of the apostolic prophet includes the performance of signs to authenticate his commission,[55] the signs in John place their observers in a situation where more and more is demanded of them until they are forced to accept or to reject an unlimited claim, as is the case with Nicodemus and the witnesses of the bread miracle. Basic to the common definition of the apostolic prophet was the understanding that he did not speak his own words but the words of him who commissioned him, and that is a prominent motif in the Fourth Gospel.[56] This notion could be underlined by the mythical picture of the apostle's assumption to heaven to receive the secret message,[57] and that was doubtless a point of contact for the development of the Johannine picture of Jesus' descent and ascent, in connection with the Wisdom myths. But as we have already seen, the secret message which Jesus brings is virtually reduced to the statement of the descent and ascent, and of the relationship to God which that pattern implies. The content of his prophetic *martyria* is progressively more clearly identified with his knowledge of his own origin and destiny, which demonstrates his unique relationship to the Father.

The pattern, descent and ascent, becomes the cipher for Jesus' unique self-knowledge as well as for his foreignness to the men of this world. His testimony is true *because* he alone knows "where I came from and where I am going" (8:14). The evangelist has carefully laid the groundwork for this statement. In 3:8 he introduced the motif, with the statement to Nicodemus that of both the Spirit and of the one born of the spirit (= "from above") "you do not know where he comes from and where he goes". The Jerusalemites at the feast of Tabernacles think they know where Jesus is from: his Galilean origin precludes his being the Prophet or the Christ (7:37–52).[58] Moreover, simply the fact that, as they think, "We know where he is from", means he cannot be the Christ, for "the Christ – when he comes, no one knows where he is from" (7:27). This is a choice example of the evangelist's irony, for not only does the dialogue itself tell the reader that the Jews do not really know where Jesus is from (7:28–9: he is from God), but in a later dialogue he has them precisely reverse the basis for their rejection, in the process admitting that they do not know where he is from: "We know that God spoke to Moses, but this man – we do not know where he is from" (9:29). Pilate also asks Jesus, "Where are you from?" (19:9) and receives no answer. The descent and ascent of the Son of Man thus becomes not only the key to his identity and identification, but the primary content of his esoteric knowledge which *distinguishes* him from the men who belong to "this world".

In this manner the descent, as a "coming into the world", is clearly identified as the judgment of the world (9:39, but adumbrated already in 3:14–21). With that an element of the prologue becomes clear. It is commonly recognized that 1:10 and 11 are parallel and that the Wisdom myth, particularly in the form seen most clearly in 1 Enoch 42, provides the essential background. Commentators are divided on the question whether *hoi idioi* ("his own") in v. 11 are the Jews or mankind.[59] From the dialogues which we have analysed it should be apparent that the Jews are meant – precisely as the representatives of the disbelieving world. Only recognition of this essential part of the Johannine symbolism reveals the full pathos of the prologue. Verse 10 expresses the central theme of the common Jewish version of the Wisdom myth: Wisdom sought a home among men, in the world which was made through her, but found no acceptance – except, most Jewish versions would add, finally in Israel, through the revelation at Sinai. It is precisely that exception that is rejected by v. 11: those who accepted – and there were some who accepted

(v. 12)[60] – are *not* "his own", the Jews, but some yet-to-be-defined group whose extraordinary status, belonging neither to "the world" nor to "his own", is miraculous (v. 13).

If the "descent" of the Son of Man, his "coming into the world", is construed in the early dialogues of John as the *krisis* of the world, the dramatic structure of the second half of the book identifies the judgment rather with his *ascent*, his "being lifted up". The remarkable sentence in 13:1–5, the elegant periodic structure of which contrasts with the usual Johannine style[61] and which formally divides the Gospel in half, speaks in two solemn clauses of Jesus' descent and ascent. The turning-point has come because Jesus knows:

> "that his hour had come to depart out of this world to the Father",

and

> "that he had come from God and was going to God".

Naturally more and more emphasis is placed on the ascent as the book progresses, and it becomes apparent that descent and ascent are not treated in precisely symmetrical fashion. The ascent is more complex, for more independent motifs have been bound together in the Johannine picture of Jesus' leaving the world than in the picture of his coming into it.

One constituent of the ascent bundle of metaphors is the pun on "being lifted up" which was introduced in 3:14. A great deal of confusion has surrounded the linguistic nature of the double entendre, and from the supposed Aramaic original impossible conclusions have been reached about the provenance of the Fourth Gospel.[62] These problems are of no concern here, for the pun was evidently a common one, in Greek as well as in Semitic languages, and it could be expressed with a variety of verbs.[63] What is of interest is the way in which the fourth evangelist introduces this jarring bit of gallows-humor and progressively unfolds its implications. For as Kittel noted, the merging of assumption with hanging produces a deliberately jarring, incongruous metaphor, and the literary development clearly indicates that it is intended to call attention to itself, not merely to make use of a common idiom.[64] Characteristically, the first statement of the motif 3:14) leaves it unexplained. Whether the brief typological statement, comparing the Son of Man's "elevation" with the elevation of the bronze serpent by Moses, is created by the evangelist or, more likely, a pre-formed bit of tradition, he inserts it here to interpret his own very important christological rule, "No one has ascended into heaven except he who descended, the Son of Man" (v. 13). That ascension is *not* like the heavenly journey of the *merkābāh* mystics or of Moses, but is like the exposure of the bronze snake. But what does that mean precisely? The reader is not told explicitly that *hypsōthēnai* ("to be lifted up") means crucifixion until 12:32 so that some commentators can insist that 3:14 does not even have crucifixion in mind.[65] But 3:14 is only the first statement of the thrice-repeated saying of Jesus which "signified what sort of death he was to die" (12:33) and which was "fulfilled" when the Jews demanded a Roman execution (18:32). Once the reader is aware of this further explication, he finds sufficient hints already in chap. 3 that the death of the Son of Man is his exaltation. There is a formal parallelism, not often noticed, between vv. 14–15 and v. 16, a parallelism created by clauses which, assuming v. 14 to be traditional, are clearly the work of the evangelist:

> so must the Son of Man be lifted up,
> > that whoever believes in him may have eternal life.
> For God so loved the world
> > that he gave his only Son,
> > that whoever believes in him should not perish but have eternal life.

The "giving" of the Son that believers in him may have life is equivalent to his "being lifted up" for the same end. If, on one hand, one recognizes the allusion in v. 16 to the binding of Isaac (Genesis 22)[66] – and it would be easy to pass over it – or, on the other hand, if one is aware already of the "lifted up"/"crucified" pun – and one needs to be acquainted with the whole Johannine language of symbols to be certain of it – then this equivalence is immediately plain. Thus again we meet in John language that has many more nuances for an initiated reader than for an outsider.

The second occurrence of the *hypsōthēnai* ("to be lifted up") language (8:28) adds an important new motif: the *identity* of the Son of Man (*egō eimi*, "I am") will be revealed by the elevation, and until then the direct question of the Jews, "Who are you?" (v. 25) must remain unanswered. How, concretely, this promise is fulfilled is not absolutely certain, though the extraordinary emphasis placed upon the trilingual placard on the cross in John 19:17–22 suggests that it may be taken as one aspect of the evangelist's dramatization of this final self-revelation.[67] Be that as it may, the identity of Jesus here, as in the other examples of the ascent/descent motif which we have examined, is bound up with the pattern of his coming from heaven and going back there.

The final occurrence of the *hypsōthēnai* theme, which finally makes the double entendre explicit for the dull reader (12:33), also adds a new dimension: Jesus' elevation will result in his drawing all men (*pantas*) to himself (v. 32). The disbelieving response evoked by this statement (vv. 34–6) warns us against too hasty a conclusion that with this *pantas* the sharp division of mankind and narrowing of the circle of believers that has characterized the function of the ascent/ descent motif everywhere else in the Gospel is here replaced by a universalism. Rather, the saying is to be understood in the light of 12:23–6: in death the "grain" ceases to be "alone". "This means that Jesus' death has been understood in its significance as creating the community of the Church."[68] Those he draws to himself are those who believe, the exceptional ones who "receive" him (1:12; 3:33), who accept his unearthly strangeness and are thus drawn into becoming an unearthly community with him.

The ascension theme in John is thus fraught with opportunity for misunderstanding. Remarkably, the evangelist makes this possibility into an occasion for advancing his didactic purpose, by introducing into the fictional narrative transparent misunderstandings by Jesus' dialogue partners, both opponents and disciples. Thus in 7:33–6, when Jesus tells "the Jews" that he will be with them only "a little time" more before going to the one who sent him, where they can neither find him nor follow him, they say, "Where is he about to go that we shall not find him? He is not about to go to the diaspora of the Greeks and teach the Greeks, is he?" Later the reader will learn that the appearance of "Greeks" from the diaspora is indeed the signal for Jesus that "the hour has come for the Son of Man to be glorified", i.e., "lifted up", to "draw all men" to himself (12:20–36). Meanwhile, the prediction to "the Jews" has been made a second time (8:21), and this time their "misunderstanding" recognizes that Jesus' "departure" means his death: "He will not kill himself, will he?" (8:22). There is a certain truth in their sarcasm, for this is a pejorative way of saying what the evangelist puts positively in Jesus' words, "No one takes [my life] from me, but I lay it down of my own accord" (10:18). The Jews' statement represents the view of the voluntary death "from below"; Jesus' statement, the view "from above" (8:23).

Not only "the Jews" misunderstand, but also the disciples. The farewell discourses begin with a statement of the glorification/ ascension theme, followed by precisely the same prediction which offended the Jews, even though he addresses this group as "children": "You will seek me and, *just as I said to the Jews*, 'Where I am going you cannot come', now I tell you also" (13:33). However, Peter's response (v. 36)[69] is not a third-person aside like that of the Jews (7:35; 8:22), but a direct question, "Lord, where are you going?" Jesus' reply now replaces the neutral *elthein* ("to come") by *akolouthēsai* "follow", "be a disciple", and adds the all-important qualification, "not ... now, but ... afterward" (v. 36). Peter's further question and affirmation make it clear that it is now understood that "to go/follow" means "to lay down one's life". Note that the evangelist has constructed this whole dialogue in order to provide a new setting for the traditional logion predicting Peter's denial (v. 38), so that the denial is now reinterpreted in the light of the descent/ascent motif that separates Jesus from all earthly men, even the disciples. On the other hand, the descent/ascent motif has received a further nuance, for the *future* ascent of *the disciples* is promised.

The following dialogue (14:1–5) takes up another side of the same theme, with a new interlocutor, Thomas. Now the purpose of Jesus' departure *for* the disciples is adumbrated: He goes to prepare "dwellings" (*monai*), "a place" for the disciples.[70] Thomas' "ignorant" question then permits a reply that shifts the terms of the metaphor to a more abstract level: "I am the way" (v. 6). "Following Jesus" does not mean, as the reply to Peter had suggested immediately before, merely imitating him or accepting a similar fate; it is to go *by means of him*. Stylistically, this shift recalls the "illogic" of chap. 10, in which Jesus himself is both the good shepherd who comes by means of the door and the door by means of which the sheep go in and out.

The "yet a little while" saying is repeated yet once more, but with significant variations, in 14:19: "the world" replaces "the Jews" as those who will not be able to see Jesus, and now a distinction is made, in contrast with 13:33, between the world that will *not* be able to see and the disciples who *will* see him. The "I shall come" of v. 18 is hardly a reference to the parousia in the conventional sense, as vv. 22–3 make plain: Jesus and the Father (being one) will make their *mone* with the believers, unseen by the world. Note that this conception of the mutual "dwelling" "corrects" the commonplace notion of an ascent to heaven after death which was suggested by vv. 2–3, though of course the two are not mutually exclusive.[71]

These themes are repeated in chap. 16 with minor variations. The statement of 16:5b, "None of you asks me, 'Where are you going?'" which flatly contradicts 13:36; 14:5, is surprising and lends support to the hypothesis that chaps. 15—16 are an independent formulation of the "farewell discourse" parallel to 13:31—14:31. That would also explain the curious statement in vv. 29–30, appropriate at the end of a discourse comprising chaps. 15—16, but mystifying after the rather clear statements of chap. 14. Variants of the theme "you will not see me; you will see me" are found in vv. 10, 16. The principal new motif, in comparison with chap. 14, is the close connection between Jesus' departure and the coming of the Paraclete (vv. 7–15).

One of the primary purposes of both versions of the farewell discourse is reflection on the purpose of Jesus' departure from the world *as it affects the chosen community*. These chapters provide a poignant expression of the group's negative identity, their fear of being *orphanoi* ("desolate") in the world (14:18). They no longer belong to this world (17:14–15), yet they are "not yet" permitted to "follow" Jesus on his ascent. Hence the farewell discourses assemble their reflections on the purpose of the separation: "a place" is being prepared with the Father; Jesus and the Father will come and make their "dwelling" with them; the Paraclete, whose functions parallel those of the descending/ascending Son of Man, will come to them; the Paraclete's work, through them, constitutes a certain continuing mission in the world (cf. chap. 17).

Chapter 17 as a whole is only intelligible within the descent/ascent framework, for it is the summary "de-briefing" of the messenger who, like the prince in the Hymn of the Pearl (v. 100), has accomplished his work in the lower regions and is returning: "I have glorified you on the earth; I have completed the work which you gave me to do" (v. 4); "I am no longer in the world, ... but I am coming to you" (v. 11). The trial and crucifixion narratives are remarkably empty of this motif, save for Pilate's unanswered question, "Where are you from?" (19:9) and the ambiguous *anōthen* in 19:11. It is rather the drama of these scenes, totally reconstructed by the evangelist,[72] which as a whole completes the theme, while on the other hand the development of the "elevation" and "glorification" themes by the evangelist places the traditional passion narratives in quite a new interpretive context. More difficult to explain is the final definite reference to the ascension: "Do not touch me, for I have not yet ascended to the father ... I am ascending to my father and your father, my God and your God" (20:17). We can only observe that, since the fourth evangelist's dramatic compression of exaltation and crucifixion motifs into one has left the traditional Easter appearances in a kind of limbo, this strange statement imparts to that limbo a sacred liminality.[73] Jesus is no longer in the world, but not yet ascended; he belongs to the intermediate zone that violates these categories and renders him untouchable. Yet even here the promise of further intimacy with the disciples is promised in the words "my father and your father, my God and your God", which is fulfilled in the subsequent appearance to the disciples (20:19–23) and especially in the invitation to Thomas to touch the wounds (20:27). Perhaps by this time it should not surprise us that the evangelist's final use of the theme is in the form of an enigma, and that it paves the way to the concluding statements of the Gospel, first about the disciples' faith and task, then about those who are to believe and obtain life *by means of this book* (20:30–1).

III

Many well-known commentaries, particularly those in English, treat the descent/ascent motif in John, if they discuss it at all, as a symbol of unity. It is supposed to represent the union of heaven and earth, the spiritual and the physical, eternity and history, God and man.[74] Our analysis of the function of this motif and its related components within the literary structure of the Gospel suggests an interpretation diametrically opposed: in every instance the motif points to contrast, foreignness, division, judgment. Only within that dominant structure of estrangement and difference is developed the counterpoint of unity – between God and Christ, between God, Christ, and the small group of the faithful.

The dualistic tendency of the motif in John can be seen most sharply in the elliptical use of the adverbs "above" and "below" in 8:23:

> You are from below,
> I am from above;
> You are of this world,
> I am not of this world.

The Jews who have just been told by Jesus that they will die in their sins, and who have just "misunderstood" Jesus' saying about going away, are now told that they *cannot* believe or understand, *because* they are "from the lower world". This sounds like a typical expression of gnostic self-consciousness, in which the separation between those who can understand and those who cannot is an ontological one, explained by a myth of their origin, as in the *Hypostasis of the Archons*:

> for the psychics (*psychikos*) will not be able
> to reach the pneumatic (*pneumatikos*),
> because they are from below,
> but he is from above.[75]

That mythical picture is reinforced by the following dialogue, for even those Jews who respond to Jesus' speech with belief (8:30) are quickly provoked by his further pronouncements into hostility, because they are not "children of God", but children of the devil (via their father Cain, the devil's son).[76] "He who is *ek tou theou* ('from God') hears the words of God; for this reason you do not hear, because you are not *ek tou theou*."

Yet the Fourth Gospel never provides us with the myth which

160

explains how some men could be from below and others from above. Indeed, since being "from above" is in John the exclusive property of "the Son of Man" (3:13!), it is difficult to see how *any* man could respond to his words with the kind of faith required here. The most significant difference between the Johannine use of the descent/ascent motif and the use in gnostic literature is precisely the fact that the disciples of Jesus, those who do "hear" his words, are *not* ever identified as those *pneumatikoi* who, like himself, have "come down from heaven". They *are* identified as those who are "not of this world" (*ouk ek tou kosmou toutou*) (15:19; 17:14ff.). As those who are *ek tou theou*, they can be contrasted with the "false spirits" (false prophets) who are *ek tou kosmou* (1 John 4:1–6). But this status is a *conferred* one, not an ontological one: "I chose you out of the world" (15:19); "I manifested your [God's] name to the men whom you gave me out of the world" (17:6); "they are not of the world, *as I am not* of the world" (17:14). Thus we have in the Johannine literature a thoroughly dualistic picture: a small group of believers isolated over against "the world" that belongs intrinsically to "the things below", i.e., to darkness and the devil. Yet that picture is never rationalized by a comprehensive myth, as in gnosticism, or by a theory of predestination, as later in the Western Catholic tradition.

So long as we approach the Johannine literature as a chapter in the history of *ideas*, it will defy our understanding. Its metaphors are irrational, disorganized, and incomplete. But if we pose our questions in the form, What functions did this particular system of metaphors have for the group that developed it? then even its self-contradictions and its disjunctures may be seen to be *means of communication*.

This point can be illustrated by our attempt to understand the function of the ascent/descent motif within the Fourth Gospel. The unbiased reader feels quite sympathetic with poor Nicodemus and the "believing" Jews with whom, it seems, Jesus is playing some kind of language-game whose rules neither they nor we could possibly know. What we are up against is the self-referring quality of the whole Gospel, the closed system of metaphors, which confronts the reader in a fashion somewhat like the way a Semitist once explained to me how to learn Aramaic: "Once you know *all* the Semitic languages," he said, "learning any one of them is easy." The reader cannot understand any part of the Fourth Gospel until he understands the whole. Thus the reader has an experience rather like that of the dialogue partners of Jesus: either he will find the whole business so convoluted, obscure, and maddeningly arrogant that he will reject it in anger, or he will find it so fascinating that he will stick with it until the progressive reiteration of themes brings, on some level of consciousness at least, a degree of clarity. While an appeal to the reader's subjective experience may appear highly unscientific, I have tried to show that such an experience is grounded in the stylistic structure of the whole document. This is the way its language, composed of an enormous variety of materials, from the standpoint of the history of traditions, has been organized, partly by design, i.e., by the actual composition by the evangelist, and partly by pre-redactional colloca-tion of the different ways of talking in the life of the community. *The book functions for its readers in precisely the same way that the epiphany of its hero functions within its narratives and dialogues.*

While this function of the book is undoubtedly the hallmark of some one author's genius, it is unthinkable apart from a particular kind of religious community, in the same way (though not perhaps to the same extent) that the *pesher* on Habakkuk is unthinkable without the Qumran sect, and the convoluted and overlapping myths of the Mandean *Ginza* unaccountable without the perduring Nazoreans. Unfortunately we have no independent information about the organization of the Johannine group, and even the Johannine literature gives little description of the community and hardly any statements that are directly "ecclesiological". Nevertheless, the struc-tural characteristics of the literature permit certain deductions.

The observation that the book functions in the same way that its Jesus functions can be elaborated. As we have seen, the depiction of Jesus as the man "who comes down from heaven" marks him as the alien from all men of the world. Though the Jews are "his own", when he comes to them they reject him, thus revealing themselves as not his own after all but his enemies; not from God, but from the devil, from "below", from "this world". The story describes the progressive alienation of Jesus from the Jews. But something else is happening, for there are some few who do respond to Jesus' signs and words, and these, while they also frequently "misunderstand", are progressively enlightened and drawn into intense intimacy with Jesus, until they, like him, are not "of this world". Now their becoming detached from the world is, in the Gospel, identical with their being detached from Judaism. Those figures who want to "believe" in Jesus but to remain within the Jewish community and the Jewish piety are damned with the most devastatingly dualistic epithets. There can be no question, as Louis Martyn has shown, that the actual trauma of the Johannine community's separation from the synagogue and its continuing hostile relationships with the synagogue come clearly to expression here.[77] But something more is to be seen: coming to faith in Jesus is for the Johannine group a change in social location. Mere belief without joining the Johannine community, without making the decisive break with "the world", particularly the world of Judaism, is a diabolic "lie". Thus, despite the absence of "ecclesiology" from the Fourth Gospel, this book could be called an etiology of the Johannine group. In telling the story of the Son of Man who came down from heaven and then re-ascended after choosing a few of his own out of the world, the book defines and vindicates the existence of the community that evidently sees itself as unique, alien from its world, under attack, misunderstood, but living in unity with Christ and through him with God. It could hardly be regarded as a missionary tract,[78] for we may imagine that only a very rare outsider would get past the barrier of its closed metaphorical system. It is a book for insiders, for if one already belonged to the Johannine community, then we may presume that the manifold bits of tradition that have taken distinctive form in the Johannine circle would be familiar, the "cross-references" in the book – so frequently anachronistic within the fictional sequence of events – would be immediately recognizable, the double entendre which produces mystified and stupid questions from the fictional dialogue partners (and from many modern commentators) would be acknowledged by a knowing and superior smile. One of the primary functions of the book, therefore, must have been to provide a reinforcement for the community's social identity, which appears to have been largely negative. It provided a symbolic universe which gave religious legitimacy, a theodicy, to the group's actual isolation from the larger society.

The sociology of religion has not yet developed theoretical categories adequate for describing the formation of a "sect" of the sort we are discovering in the Johannine group,[79] but the discipline of the "sociology of knowledge", particularly in the form proposed by Peter Berger and Thomas Luckmann,[80] provides categories which help us to understand how a figure like the Johannine Jesus, through the medium of a book like the Johannine Gospel, could bring about a change of world. For one's "world" in the sociology of knowledge is understood as the symbolic universe within which one functions, which has "objectivity" because it is constantly reinforced by the structures of the society to which it is specific. Faith in Jesus, in the Fourth Gospel, means a removal from "the world", because it means transfer to a community which has totalistic and exclusive claims. The Fourth Gospel not only describes, in etiological fashion, the birth of that community; it also provides reinforcement of the community's isolation. The language patterns we have been describing have the effect, for the insider who accepts them, of demolishing the logic of the world, particularly the world of Judaism, and progressively emphasizing the sectarian consciousness. If one "believes" what is said in this book, he is quite literally taken out of the ordinary world of social reality. Contrariwise, this can hardly happen unless one stands already within the counter-cultural group or at least in some ambivalent relationship between it and the larger society.

I do not mean to say that the symbolic universe suggested by the Johannine literature is *only* the reflex or projection of the group's social situation. On the contrary, the Johannine dialogues suggest quite clearly that the order of development must have been dialectical: the christological claims of the Johannine Christians resulted in their becoming alienated, and finally expelled, from the synagogue; that alienation in turn is "explained" by a further development of the christological motifs (i.e., the fate of the community projected onto the story of Jesus); these developed christological motifs in turn drive the group into further isolation. It is a case of continual, harmonic reinforcement between social experience and ideology.[81]

The dialectic we have suggested would surely continue, producing a more and more isolated and estranged group until some disruption occurred. The Johannine letters show a progression of that sort: tighter internal discipline, more hostility towards "the world" and everything "in the world", schism occasioned by a docetic group, whose denial that Jesus could have "come in the flesh" would seem a fairly logical deduction from the symbols we have analyzed.

The analysis undertaken here does not answer the question of the relation between the Johannine Christology and gnostic myths, but it provides clues which may be helpful in pursuing that problem. The Fourth Gospel is content to leave unanswered the question how there could exist in "this world" some persons who, by some pre-established harmony, could respond to the Stranger from the world above and thus become, like him, men "not of this world". But that enigma cries out for some master myth to explain it. Both pressures from outsiders and internal questioning would assure that the cry did not long remain unheeded; the legitimation of the sect's counter-cultural stance would lead to the projection of some myth explaining that members of the group had an origin different from that of ordinary men. In gnosticism it was the Sophia myth that provided the basic images for that projection – the same Sophia myth which provided important elements of the descent and ascent of the Son of Man in John. As the archetype of the soul-to-be-redeemed, Sophia recovers her normal feminine guise, making possible the elaborate sexual imagery that in the gnostic myths describes the relations between Christ or Logos and Sophia or the soul. In the Fourth Gospel there is no trace of the usual feminine Sophia; she has become entirely the masculine Logos, the Son of Man. But the Fourth Gospel does introduce the motif of Christ's union with the believers, which comes at times quite close to sexual metaphor.[82] Thus once the Fourth Gospel had identified Christ-Wisdom with the masculine Logos, and once the social dynamics of the anti-worldly sect were in motion, all the forces were present for the production of a myth of the Valentinan type. We cannot say that it happened that way, or that the Johannine literature was the only place where ingredients were brought into the necessary creative association.[83] But these conjectures suggest that it is at least as plausible that the Johannine Christology helped to create some gnostic myths as that gnostic myths helped create the Johannine Christology. A satisfactory answer may be achieved only when studies of gnosticism also begin to ask not only about ideational structure and antecedents, but also about social functions.[84]

NOTES

1. See R. Bultmann (1925) and especially his criticism of Ernst Percy in "Johanneische Schriften und Gnosis", *OLZ* 43 (1940) 150–75 (*Exegetica*, 230–54) and C. H. Dodd in *NTS* 1 (1954–55) 77–91 (ET: *Harvard Divinity Bulletin* 27 [1963] 9–22). Dodd's focus upon "the logos-doctrine" as the *tertium comparationis* between John and the Hermetica and Philo was particularly vulnerable to this objection.

2. For example, K. Rudolph's careful investigation of the Mandean materials convinced him that "John the Baptist and his disciples had, on the evidence of the available sources, no connection with the Mandeans" (*Die Mandäer*, Vol. I: *Prolegomena* [Göttingen, 1960] 80). Both E. Käsemann (1969) and E. Haenchen ("Probleme des johanneischen 'Prologs'", *ZTK* 60 [1963] 305–34 [reprinted in *Gott und Mensch* (Tübingen, 1965) 114–43]) reject the hypothesis of a *Redenquelle* ("discourse source"). See also D. M. Smith, Jr. (1965).

3. Cf. C. Colpe, *Die religionsgeschichtliche Schule* (Göttingen, 1961) especially 186–208. See also A. D. Nock, "Gnosticism", *HTR* 57 (1964) 255–79.

4. This is even clearer in his article "Johannesevangelium", *RGG*[8] 3. 840–50.

5. E. Haenchen has established a high probability that the essential gnostic features of Simon Magus were developed in the Simonian sect prior to any Christian influence ("Gab es eine vorchristliche Gnosis?", *ZTK* 49 [1952] 316–49; reprinted in *Gott und Mensch* 265–98). The question of the date and interpretation of the *Hymn of the Pearl* is more difficult; see most recently C. Colpe, "Die Thomaspsalmen als chronologischer Fixpunkt in der Geschichte der orientalischen Gnosis", *Jahrbuch für Antike und Christentum* 7 (1964) 77–93; and the survey by K. Rudolph, "Gnosis und Gnostizismus, ein Forschungsbericht", *TRu* 34 (1969) 214–21. The Nag Hammadi documents prove that Christian Gnostics did borrow and adapt mythical elements from non-Christian Gnostics – and vice versa – at a later period. While these sources cannot directly prove anything about first century gnosis, careful analysis of them is providing cumulative evidence that myths of descending/ascending revealers flourished without any Christian influence. See, e.g., G. W. MacRae, "The Coptic Gnostic Apocalypse of Adam", *HeyJ* 6 (1965) 27–35, and F. Wisse, "The Redeemer Figure in the Paraphrase of Shem", *NT* 12 (1970) 130–40. Finally, it is impossible to dismiss the question

whether the NT itself may not provide the earliest documentation of pre-Christian gnosticism, depending upon one's evaluation, for example, of the opponents of Paul in Galatia, Corinth, and Colossae, and of the sources of mythical elements found in liturgical traditions that are quoted in Pauline and deutero-Pauline letters. There remain, however, many vexed questions in this area.

6   (1957) 179.

7   "One Jesus and Four Primitive Gospels", *HTR* 61 (1968) 240; reprinted in *Trajectories through Early Christianity*, ed. J. M. Robinson and H. Koester, (Philadelphia, 1971) 197.

8   *Wisdom, Christology, and Law in Matthew's Gospel* (Cambridge, Mass., 1970) 10 n. 14; 42 n. 18; 53 n. 41; and especially 58 n. 49.

9   G. W. MacRae ("The Jewish Background of the Gnostic Sophia Myth", *NT* 12 [1970] 86–101) seems to me correct against U. Wilckens (*Weisheit und Torheit* [Tübingen, 1959]) that it was precisely the *Jewish* form of the Wisdom myth that was used by the gnostics – at least those that may be usefully compared with the Fourth Gospel. On the other hand, I doubt the propriety of speaking of a *single* Jewish Wisdom myth or one single Wisdom movement. "Wisdom" as the ideology of a royal bureaucracy was obviously different from the "Wisdom" cultivated in an apocalyptic conventicle, for example.

10   *The Gnostic Religion* (rev. edn; Boston, 1963) 320–1. The Bultmann–Jonas concept of "objectivation" is significantly parallel to the notion of "projection", particularly as the latter has been redefined by C. G. Jung. The reaction of Bultmann and other kerygmatic theologians to the "psychologism" of earlier theological Liberalism has blocked off what might have been a fruitful area of interaction, particularly in view of the Jung school's profound interest in gnosticism. However, Jung's discussion of the motif of descent and ascent as it occurs in medieval alchemy (*Mysterium Coniunctionis* [2nd edn; Princeton, 1970] 217–24) offers little that is directly useful for our present discussion.

11   The analysis by E. Schweizer in his early work *Ego Eimi* (Göttingen, 1939, Part IV) is abstruse and rather artificial. The perennial attempts to discover OT typologies in John have usually demonstrated more the ingenuity of eisegesis than the grammar of Johannine symbols. E. Stemberger's recent *La symbolique du bien et du mal selon saint Jean* (Paris, 1970), violating the impressive canons in his own introduction, reduces the symbols to a puzzle picture where the categories of moral theology are to be discovered.

12   (1925) 102.

13   On this form, see K. Berger, *Die Amen-Worte Jesu* (Berlin, 1970) 95–117.

14   See J. Becker, "Die Abschiedsreden Jesu im Johannesevangelium", *ZNW* 61 (1970) 215–52.

15   "Genesis as Myth", *Discovery* (London) n.s. 23 (1962) 30–5; reprinted in *Myth and Cosmos*, ed. John Middleton (Garden City, N.Y., 1967) 1–13. This "structural" approach is now associated especially with the theories of the French social anthropologist Claude Lévi-Strauss (see, e.g., the latter's *Structural Anthropology* [New York, 1963], especially chaps 2 and 11), but Leach has brought *structuralisme* into connection with the functionalist and empirical traditions of English and American social anthropology. See his fascinating appreciation and critique in *Claude Lévi-Strauss* ("Modern Masters", ed. F. Kermode [New York, 1970]). Among other recent examples of the social-structural analysis of myth-systems which I have found suggestive for developing my own method are: V. W.

Turner, "Colour Classification of Ndembu Ritual", *Anthropological Approaches to the Study of Religion*, ed. M. Banton (New York, 1966) 47–84; J. Z. Smith, "Birth Upside Down or Right Side Up?", *History of Religions* 9 (1969–70) 281–303; W. D. O'Flaherty, "Asceticism and Sexuality in the Mythology of Siva", ibid. 8 (1968–9) 300–37; 9 (1969–70) 1–41.

16 Two partial exceptions are A. Kragerud's proposals to see certain of the symbols, particularly the "beloved disciple", as a covert self-justification of a charismatic sect of Christianity (*Der Lieblingsjünger im Johannesevangelium* [Oslo, 1959]) and E. Käsemann's attempts to explicate the argument between Diotrephes and the Elder ("Ketzer und Zeuge", *ZTK* 48 [1951] 292–311; reprinted in *Exegetische Versuche und Besinnungen*, 1, 168–87) and the "naive docetism" of the Gospel (1968) within "conventicle piety" in conflict with "early catholicism". Kragerud's thesis, however, is undercut by highly arbitrary exegesis at points; Käsemann's by the imposition of categories from post-Reformation church history on the first-century phenomena (see my review in *USQR* 24 [1968] 414–20). More important, J. L. Martyn has made a major contribution towards locating the kind of milieu in which the anti-Jewish polemic of one stratum of the Johannine materials was formed (1969). His position is reinforced by the investigation, from quite a different perspective, of H. Leroy, *Rätsel und Missverständnis* (Bonn, 1968). I became acquainted with Leroy's careful and provocative monograph only after I had completed the present essay; hence I shall forgo the detailed *Auseinandersetzung* with him which would be appropriate at points where our analyses run parallel. While our methods are different (but not, I believe, incompatible) and the passages and motifs he examines only partially overlap those treated here, I am delighted to find a remarkable convergence of my results with his. On the basis of a wide-ranging survey of the *riddle* in folklore and literature (13–45), Leroy describes the form of the Johannine dialogue-with-misunderstanding as a "hidden riddle", which presupposes a tight-knit community with a *Sondersprache* ("special language") unintelligible to outsiders. In order to "know the truth", one must join this community – probably a cluster of small congregations – hear its preaching, be instructed in its catechesis, and participate in its ritual.

17 The descending (*katabainon*) of the spirit (1:32–3) is from the traditional baptism pericope which the evangelist has deliberately omitted, substituting only a report by John of the Spirit's descent.

18 R. E. Brown (1966) 88–91; Schulz (1957) 98; K. Berger, *Amen-Worte*, 113. Whether *all* double-Amen sayings in John are traditional logia or rephrasing of such, as Berger claims, is open to question.

19 C. F. Burney, *The Aramaic Origin of the Fourth Gospel* (Oxford) 115–16; H. Odeberg (1929) 33–42; C. H. Dodd (1953) 244–5; B. W. Bacon, *The Gospel of the Hellenists* (New York, 1933) 158–9; G. Quispel, "Nathanael und der Menschensohn (John 1:51)", *ZNW* 47 (1956) 281–3; N. A. Dahl, *Das Volk Gottes* (2nd edn; Darmstadt, 1963) 170; "The Johannine Church and History", in this volume, pp. 122–40; Schulz (1957) 96–103.

20 From the Heb. text or its equivalent, as Burney points out. The LXX has finite verbs and, of course, removes the ambiguity of the *bô*, "on him"/"on it", which is the starting point of the midrash. (The latter point is ignored by the interpretations of Quispel [see previous note] and J. Jeremias, "Die Berufung des Nathanael [Jo 1, 45–51]", *Angelos* 3 [1930] 2–5).

21 "Aporien im vierten Evangelium", *Nachrichten der Göttingischen Gelehrten Gesellschaft der Wissenschaften* (1908) 517.

22 (1957) 99–013.

23 "Angelophanien um den Menschensohn auf Erden", *ZNW* 30 (1931) 215–22, esp. 226–7.

24 W. Bauer (1925) 42; Odeberg (1929) 37; Bacon, *Gospel of the Hellenists*, 158–9.

25 Windisch, "Angelophanien", 215–19.

26 As Jeremias does, "Berufung des Nathanael".

27 Cf. Bacon, *Gospel of the Hellenists*, 325; E. M. Sidebottom, "The Ascent and Descent of the Son of Man in the Gospel of St. John", *ATR* 2 (1957) 115–22.

28 R. Kieffer is certainly correct in his observation that *alēthōs* ("truly"), as usual in John, modifies the predicate (cf. R. Bultmann [1971] 104 n. 4), but his translation "here is a man who is truly 'a seer of God'", which appeals, I assume, to Philo's allegory of the name Israel, is an overinterpretation (*Au delà des recensions?* [Lund, 1968] 153).

29 The sacral name Israel is extremely rare in John, elsewhere only 1:31 (where it is rather clearly an introduction to the manifestation of Jesus to the "real Israelite" in 1:48–51) and in 12:13 (which like 1:50 is a confession of Jesus as King of Israel). Cf. W. Meeks (1967) 82–3.

30 Cf. Schulz's analysis (1957) 104–9.

31 The attempt to reconstruct a written source from which the evangelist may have drawn here (Bultmann (1971) 130–67; H. Becker, *Die Reden des Johannesevangeliums und der Stil der gnostischen Offenbarungsrede* [Göttingen, 1956] 94–6) produces more difficulties than it solves.

32 Odeberg (1929) 72, 89; Bultmann (1971) 150 n.1; Meeks (1967) *passim*; *contra* Sidebottom ("Ascent and Descent", 119–22), who sees no polemic at all here.

33 Cf. Wis. 10:10, where we are told that Sophia "showed him [sc. Jacob] the kingdom of God and gave him knowledge of holy things". This passage proves that, at this significantly early date, Jacob's vision at Bethel was understood as a vision of the *merkābāh* (see Dahl, "Johannine Church" above, pp. 132f. and n. 20). On the significance of the fact that the typical form of early Jewish mysticism was associated with *royal* imagery ("basileomorphism": Graetz), see G. Scholem, *Major Trends in Jewish Mysticism* (New York, 1961) 54–7.

34 Cf. K. Berger, *Amen-Worte* 103.

35 Cf. the observations by H. A. Fischel, "Greco-Roman Rhetoric and the Study of Midrash", a paper read to the Biblical Literature Section, American Academy of Religion, October 25, 1970, as yet unpublished.

36 Formally, the closest parallel is 4 Ezra: 1–11, 20–21. Compare the story of Thales, who fell into a pit while looking at the stars. To his plea for help an old woman retorted: "Do you suppose, Thales, that you will be able to understand what is in the sky when you cannot see what is at your feet?" (Diogenes Laert. I. 34). Similarly, Alexander the Great, giving a moral blow to Nectanebus while the latter was trying to teach him astrology, said: "You enquire about what is in the sky without knowing what is on earth" (Ps.-Callisthenes, *Life of Alexander*, 1.14). Cf. Wis. 9:16 and Ign. *Trall.* 5:1–2, as well as Cicero, *De Rep.*, 1.30: "No one looks at what is in front of his feet; they study the reaches of the sky."

37 So Alexander's attempt to ascend to heaven is rebuked: "Without knowing mundane matters, Alexander, do you seek to grasp heavenly ones? So turn back to earth with all haste" (Ps.-Callisthenes, 2.41; mss Leiden and Paris Supp. 113; not in the oldest recension). And in Seneca's satire of Claudius' would-be apotheosis (*Apocolocyntosis*, 8.3), one of the gods says to Hercules: "He does not

know what he is doing in his own bedroom; and he is already studying the reaches of the sky!" (So O. Weinreich, *Senecas Apocolocyntosis* [1923] 140; Waltz's text reads *nescio* ("I do not know") for *nescit* ("he does not know"), but that would spoil the point of the quip. "Caeli scrutatur plagas" is an oft-quoted line from Ennius, *Iphigenia*; see the Cicero quotation in n. 36).

38 This is not the place to raise again the vexed question of "sign faith" in the *Redaktionsgeschichte* of John. I believe that the difference between the viewpoint of the "signs source" and that of the evangelist is not so great as Bultmann (1971, *passim*) and Haenchen ("Johanneische Probleme", *ZTK* 56 [1959] 19–54; reprinted in *Gott und Mensch*, 78–113) and others have maintained. See the paper by P. Meyer, "Seeing, Signs, and Sources in the Fourth Gospel" (read to the Gospels Section, American Academy of Religion, October 18, 1968, unfortunately unpublished), for a different view. R. Fortna's source analysis (1970) has moved the discussion towards a solid footing, though at times the assumption of divergent theologies seems to enter his *Quellenscheidung* ("distinguishing sources") decisions as an *a priori*. His summary evaluation is a model of clarity and precision ("Source and Redaction in the Fourth Gospel's Portrayal of Jesus' Signs", *JBL* 89 [1970] 151–66). For a survey of recent literature on the subject and a defense of Haenchen's position, see J. M. Robinson (1971) 238–56.

39 Suggested by P. Meyer, in private communication.

40 In this respect I am in full accord with Martyn (1968), though I doubt whether the separation can be identified specifically with the *Birkat ham-Minim* promulgated at Yavneh, and whether that decree itself can be dated so precisely. Cf. the criticism by Stemberger, *Symbolique* 106, n. 3.

41 E. Hoskyns (1940) 7, who speaks of the Fourth Gospel's "self-contained allusiveness", has seen this more clearly than any other commentator I know.

42 D. M. Smith, Jr. (1965) 178 makes this point effectively against Bultmann's rearrangement hypotheses.

43 I am grateful for suggestions made by Jan Wojcik, a graduate student in comparative literature at Yale, who has compared the Johannine style with the didactic dramaturgy of Berthold Brecht.

44 See Meeks (1967) 47–57, 303–4.

45 See above, pp. 155–7.

46 See above, pp. 153–5.

47 Presupposed in the midrashic dialogue of chap. 6: above, pp. 155f.

48 P. Borgen (1965) has demonstrated the midrashic character of the discourse and has shown that a number of motifs incorporated in it were already familiar in Alexandrian Judaism and attested somewhat later in haggadah from Palestinian sources. A number of details of his reconstruction are unconvincing, but his work is fundamental for the understanding of this passage.

49 Fortna guesses that v. 14 is the evangelist's rewriting of the source's conclusion to the feeding miracle, which already contained the acclamation of Jesus as a prophet (1970, 61). If so, it is "not impossible", as he puts it with due caution, that the identification of the feeding with the manna tradition was also pre-Johannine.

50 Verses 27 and 58 form an inclusion; my chief criticism of Borgen's analysis is that he fails to see this because of his fixation on the scripture text so loosely cited in v. 31. Consequently his work seemed vulnerable to G. Richter's ingenious attempt to show that vv. 51–8, by Borgen's own method, ought to be regarded as a later

addition ("Zur Formgeschichte und literarischen Einheit von Joh 6:31–58", *ZNW* 60 [1969] 21–55). The literary unity of vv. 27–58 seems to me assured, whatever theological self-contradictions it may contain. Though it is a saying of Jesus rather than a scripture text that provides the starting point of the "midrash" (and we should therefore recognize that the form of explication may have had a wider application in rhetoric than only the exposition of sacred texts), that saying already has the manna tradition in mind, for the manna's propensity to "perish" was a part of the biblical story (Exod. 16:19–21), as was the death of the wilderness generation that fed on it.

51   If G. Vermes' ingenious reading of Targum *Neofiti* on Exod. 16:15, "He [viz., Moses] is the bread which the Lord has given you to eat", is correct, then we have a striking parallel in the Moses haggadah. See "He is the Bread", *Neotestamentica et semitica*, ed. E. E. Ellis and M. Wilcox (Edinburgh, 1969) 256–63. However, I am inclined to believe with Prof. Schreiber (ibid. 258 n. 7) that the antecedent *mšh* is a simple scribal error for *mšhw*, "what it was".

52   The fact that both the "murmuring" and the giving of "flesh" are motifs found in the biblical manna story (note especially Exod. 16:8 and compare John 6:51b with Num. 11:18 "the Lord will give you meat to eat") reinforce my conviction that vv. 51b–58 are an integral part of the midrashic discourse that begins with v. 27, but further analysis of the connection would lead us too far from the present topic. Even more difficult is the question whether vv. 60–71 belong to the same stage of redaction as vv. 27–59. Logically, of course, the "offense" occasioned by the notion of eating the *flesh*, which here upsets "some of the disciples", comes later in the development of the tradition than the notion of descending from heaven, which offends "the Jews". But historically both offenses would have been repeated many times, so we can draw no necessary conclusions about the stages of redaction. In any case, vv. 60–71 are closely connected with the preceding discourse in their present form. At whatever stage they were added to the bread dialogue, they clearly presuppose it and are built upon it.

53   Schulz (1957) 117 n. 5.

54   It appears to me more and more likely that the combination of these figures, perhaps also the connection with the title Son of Man, had been prepared for by *merkābāh*-exegesis in mystical Jewish sources. The "angel of the face", the image of Israel in heaven (*Gen. R.* 68:12), the "human face" on the beasts of the *merkābāh* (Ezekiel 1 and 10), and the "one like a son of man" of Dan. 7:13 could readily be identified. However, the problem cannot be pursued here.

55   A fundamental element in the Moses haggadah, beginning in the biblical accounts; see my *Prophet-King* 162–4, 302–3.

56   7:16, 18; 8:26; 12:49; 14:24; cf. 4:34; 5:19, 30; 6:38–9; 9:4; 10:37–8; 17:4; see my *Prophet – King* 301–11.

57   See W. Meeks, "Moses as God and King", *Religions in Antiquity*, ed. J. Neusner (Leiden, 1967) 354–71. Recently C. Colpe has suggested that the *Himmelsreise* tradition flourishes only in religions that include the figure of the "shaman" ("Die 'Himmelsreise der Seele' ausserhalb und innerhalb der Gnosis", *Le origini dello gnosticismo*, ed. U. Bianchi [Leiden, 1967] 429–47).

58   W. Meeks, "Galilee and Judea in the Fourth Gospel", *JBL* 85 (1966) 159–69.

59   Bultmann, following Merx, insists (1971) 56 n.1, that "the sentence, 'He came into his own ...' may mean what it will; but one thing it cannot mean, namely: He came to the Jews ..." Brown, however, says, "The reference is clearly to the people of Israel" (1966) 10. Dodd, despite his platonizing interpretation of the

prologue as a whole, recognizes the specific referent here as "the Jews" (1953) 402; R. H. Lightfoot (1956) 83 does not. Barrett and McGregor in their commentaries adopt mediating positions.

60 Haenchen's argument that vv. 12–13 are the work of a later redactor who has not fully understood v. 11 (*ZTK* 60 [1963] 329; *Gott und Mensch*, 138–9) is unconvincing. His view that v. 12b describes, in "becoming children of God", a "higher status" than mere faith, a notion found in the Johannine epistles, but not in the Gospel, is an overinterpretation. The paradox of vv. 11–12 is one of the fundamental themes of the Gospel as a whole.

61 Cf. F. Blass and A. Debrunner, *A Greek Grammar of the New Testament*, tr. R. W. Funk (Chicago, 1961) §464.

62 A. Schlatter's observation that Syr *zqp*, "raise", "set up", came to be used in the sense of "impale" or "crucify" was used by E. Hirsch to argue that the Johannine *Grundschrift* was written in Antioch. G. Kittel ("*zdqp* = *hypsōthēnai* = gekreuzigt werden: Zur angeblichen antiochenischen Herkunft des Vierten Evangeliums", *ZNW* 35 [1926] 282–5) exposed the fallacies in that argument, while showing that the pun was *possible* in any Aramaic dialect. It was perhaps least likely in Syr, where, as Joseph A. Fitzmyer kindly informs me, *zqp* could hardly be found with the meaning "elevate". In Mandean it could be used in the sense of "ascend (to the Abiding Dwelling'" (GL 83:10; see E. S. Drower and R. Macuch, *A Mandaic Dictionary* [Oxford, 1963] 169–70). However, the pun is equally possible in Greek.

63 Although I know no example in a source antedating John, the fact that Artemidorus, in his late second-century collection of dream interpretations, mentions various omens of a dream of crucifixion that depend upon such a pun assures us that it must have belonged to the folklore of the eastern Mediterranean for some time. A crucifixion dream is a good omen for a poor man, "for the crucified is exalted (*hypsēlos*)"; for a slave it portends freedom, "for those crucified are not subordinate (*anhypotaktoi*)"; and a dream of crucifixion in the city "signifies a government position (*archē*) corresponding to the place where the cross stood" (*Oneirokritikon*, 2.53). The somewhat later Alexander novel by Ps.-Callisthenes tells how Alexander traps the assassins of Darius by his oath to "make them exalted above all men (*periphanestatous ... pasin anthrōpois*)", which he does – by crucifying them (*Life of Alexander*, 2.21). A haggadic midrash on Exod. 30:12 explains Moses' intercession for Israel by a parable in which a king is persuaded by an advisor to change his impetuous condemnation of his only son to beheading (*s'ô 't r'šô*) ("lift up his head") to a command to promote him (*yrômmô 't r'šô*) (*Pesikta Rabbati*, 10).

64 Kittel, *'zdqp*, 285.

65 Odeberg (1929) 111; Schulz (1957) 106, thinks the pre-Johannine logion was an unambiguous reference to exaltation.

66 C. K. Barrett (1955) 180; Brown (1966) 147; N. A. Dahl, "The Atonement – An Adequate Reward for the Akedah? (Ro. 8:32)", *Neotestamentica et Semitica* 15–29 esp. 28 n. 64. Reprinted in *The Crucified Messiah* (Minneapolis, 1974) 146–60.

67 See *Prophet-King*, 78–80.

68 E. Schweizer, *Lordship and Discipleship* (London, 1960) 86.

69 With good reason, many commentators regard vv. 34–5 as an interpolation. See J. Becker, "Abschiedsreden" 220, and the references there.

70 The striking resemblance of this saying to the speech of Hibil-Ziwa to the children

of Adam in the Mandean *GL* (ed. Lidzbarski, 442, ll. 28–30, and 443, ll. 5–6) has often been noted. The Mandean *šᵉkīnātā* is the equivalent of *monai*.

71 See the very suggestive discussion of this point by Martyn (1968) 138–40.

72 See *Prophet-King* 61–78.

73 On the notion of the liminal, neither one thing nor the other, neither here nor there, as a category of the sacred, see J. Z. Smith, "Birth Upside Down", and "A Place on Which to Stand: Symbols and Social Change", *Worship* 44 (1970) 457–74.

74 Though not many in this century would put it in such Hegelian language as J. N. Sanders, "To accomplish the Father's loving purpose, the Logos became man, so uniting flesh and spirit, and making possible the gift of holy spirit [*sic*] to men" (1969) 19.

75 CG II, 4: 87[135], 17–20; tr. R. A. Bullard, *The Hypostasis of the Archons* (Berlin, 1970) 21. Cf. the statement of Norea to the Great Archon, 92 [140] 25–6: "I am not from you, [but] I came from above."

76 See N. A. Dahl, "Der Erstgeborene Satans und der Vater des Teufels (Polyk. 7:1 und Joh 8:44)", *Apophoreta*, BZNW 30 (1964) 70–84. For an exploration of the background of the "children of Abraham" motif in this chapter and an ingenious attempt to reconstruct a conflict between the Johannine community and a more conservative Jewish–Christian group, see the 1971 AAR student Prize Essay by my student Bruce Schein, "'The Seed of Abraham' John 8:31–59", AAR/SBL Annual Meeting, October 31, 1971.

77 *History and Theology*, *passim*.

78 Against a large number of scholars, including K. Bornhäuser, D. Oehler, J. A. T. Robinson, W. C. van Unnik, and C. H. Dodd, I thus find myself in agreement with R. E. Brown that John's distinctive emphases "are directed to crises within the believing Church rather than to the conversion of non-believers" (1966) lxxviii.

79 I am using "sect" here in a somewhat different sense from the classic definitions by Weber, Troeltsch, and Niebuhr. On the special problems of an adequate definition, see P. Berger, "The Sociological Study of Sectarianism", *Social Research* 21 (1954) 467–85; also his *The Sacred Canopy* (Garden City, N.Y., 1967) 196 n. 22. Eventually the work of social psychologists on the formation and functioning of counter-cultural groups may provide useful models for the historian; see the survey by T. F. Pettigrew, "Social Evaluation Theory: Convergences and Applications", *Nebraska Symposium on Motivation 1967*, ed. D. Levine, 241–311.

80 *The Social Construction of Reality* (Garden City, N.Y., 1966); cf. P. Berger, *The Sacred Canopy*, chaps. 1, 2. Also extremely helpful is the definition proposed by C. Geertz, "Religion as a Cultural System", *Anthropological Approaches to the Study of Religion* (New York, 1966) 1–66. Reprinted in *The Interpretation of Cultures* (New York, 1973).

81 This is something like the interaction between scripture text, group organization, and historical experience in the development of apocalyptic ideology proposed by N. A. Dahl in the very important essay, "Eschatology and History in the light of the Qumran Texts", *The Future of our Religious Past*, ed. J. M. Robinson (New York, 1971) 9–28. Reprinted in *The Crucified Messiah* (Minneapolis, 1974) 129–45.

89 This was first pointed out to me by one of my students, the Rev. James Ameling. Note how Paul explicitly uses Gen. 2:4 to express the same notion in 1 Cor. 6:16–17.

83 Philo's peculiar dialectic between Logos and Sophia, and the successive characterization of the wise man's soul as feminine and masculine at different stages of progress, show that such speculations were not unknown to hellenistic Judaism

prior to the birth of Christianity. R. A. Baer, Jr., *Philo's Use of the Categories Male and Female* (Leiden, 1970) collects and analyzes the most important passages, but offers little help in discerning the pre-Philonic forms of the myths.

84 Lately there have been a few preliminary signs of a recognition of this need: E. M. Mendelson, "Some Notes on a Sociological Approach to Gnosticism", *Le origini dello gnosticismo*, 668–75; the two essays by J. Z. Smith mentioned above (notes 15, 73); H. G. Kippenberg, "Versuch einer soziologischen Verortung des antiken Gnostizismus", *Numen* 17 (1970) 211–31 (marred by tendentious over-generalizations, coupled with a Feuerbachian "explanation" of religion); and S. Laeuchli, "The Sociology of Gnosticism", a paper read to the Biblical Literature Section of the American Academy of Religion, October 30, 1971.

Bibliography

The bibliography that follows is divided into four sections: (1) Surveys, in several languages, of recent literature; (2) Commentaries in English; (3) Foreign books and articles referred to in the introduction; (4) A selective list of articles and monographs in English. If these lists seem more perfunctory than usual, this is because the huge array of bibliographical aids relating to John's Gospel discourages competition. All recent monographs include lists of books and articles relating to individual topics; furthermore, most of the longer commentaries have extensive bibliographies of their own. Of these the most useful are those of Brown and Haenchen, the latter thoroughly up-dated by his German editor, Ulrich Busse. By breaking down the secondary literature into manageable chunks and attaching these to successive sections of their commentaries they reduce the student's sense of helpless disarray and greatly facilitate the task of selection.

1 *Surveys of work on the Fourth Gospel*

For the period up to 1960 see R. E. Brown (1966) xxiiff. Subsequently:

(ENGLISH) R. Kysar, *The Fourth Evangelist and His Gospel* (Minneapolis, 1975); "The Fourth Gospel. A report on Recent Research", *Aufstieg und Niedergang der römischen Welt*, ed. H. Temporini and W. Haase, vol. II, 25.3 (Berlin/New York, 1985) 2391–480.

(GERMAN) H. Thyen in *TRu* 39 (1974) 1–69; 222–52; 289–330; 42 (1977) 211–70; 43 (1978) 328–59; 44 (1979) 97–135; J. Becker in *TRu* 47 (1982) 279–301; 305–47; 51 (1986) 1–78; R. Schnackenburg, *BZ* 18 (1974) 272–87; 27 (1983) 281–7.

(FRENCH) J. Dubois, in *Etudes Théologiques et Religieuses* 51 (1976) 373–81; X. Léon-Dufour in *RSR* 68 (1980) 271–316.

(SPANISH) J. O. Tuñi in *Actualidad Bibliográfica de filosofía y teología* 11 (1974) 243–89; 14 (1977) 92–110; 21 (1984) 36–81.

2 *A selection of commentaries composed in or translated into English*

B. F. Westcott (1882); J. H. Bernard, 2 vols. (1928); G. H. C. MacGregor (1928); H. Odeberg (1929); E. C. Hoskyns (1940); R. H. Strachan ³(1941); C. K. Barrett (1955; ²1978); R. H. Lightfoot (1956); A. Richardson (1959); A. M. Hunter (1965); R. E. Brown, 2 vols. (1966, 1970); J. Marsh (1968); J. N. Sanders and B. A. Mastin (1968); R. Schnackenburg, 3 vols. (1968, 1980, 1982); J. Fenton (1970); L. Morris (1970); R. Bultmann (1971); R. V. G. Tasker (1971); B. Lindars (1972); R. Kysar (1976); D. M. Smith

(1976); G. W. MacRae (1978); S. Smalley (1978); J. McPolin (1979); E. Haenchen, 2 vols. (1984, 1985).

3 *Foreign books and articles referred to in the Introduction*
Bauer, W., *Das Johannesevangelium*² (Tübingen, 1925).

Boismard, M.-E., "L'Évolution du thème eschatologique dans les traditions johanniques", *RB* 68 (1961) 507–24.

Bühner, J. A., *Der Gesandte und sein Weg im vierten Evangelium* (Tübingen, 1977).

Bultmann, R., "Die Bedeutung der neuerschlossenen mandäischen und manichäischen Quellen für das Verständnis des Johannesevangeliums", *ZNW* 24 (1925) 100–46 = *Exegetica* (Tübingen, 1967) 55–104.

Faure, A., "Die alttestestamentliche Zitate im vierten Evangelium und die Quellenscheidungshypothese", *ZNW* 21 (1922) 99–121.

Hartingsveld, L. van, *Die Eschatologie des Johannesevangeliums* (Assen, 1962).

Käsemann, E., *Jesu letzter Wille nach Johannes 17*³ (Tübingen, 1971).

Langbrandtner, W., *Weltferner Gott oder Gott der Liebe* (Frankfurt, 1977).

La Potterie, I. de, *La vérité dans Saint Jean* (Rome, 1977).

— "La structure du Prologue de Jean", *NTS* 30 (1984) 188–216.

Pétrement, S., *Le Dieu séparé: les origines du gnosticisme* (Paris, 1984).

Richter, G., "Präsentische und futurische Eschatologie im 4. Evangelium", *Studien zum Johannesevangelium* (Regensburg, 1977) 346–82.

Saussure, F. de, *Cours de linguistique générale* (Paris, 1922).

Schlatter, A., *Die Sprache und Heimat des vierten Evangeliums* (Gütersloh, 1902).

— *Der Evangelist Johannes* (Stuttgart, 1920).

Schottroff, L., *Der Glaubende und die feindliche Welt* (Neukirchen-Vluyn, 1970).

Schulz, S., *Untersuchungen zur Menschensohn-Christologie im Johannesevangelium: zugliech ein Beitrag zur Methodengeschichte der Auslegung des 4. Evangeliums* (Göttingen, 1957).

Serra, A. M., "Le tradizioni della teofania sinaitica nel Targum dello Pseudo-Jonathan Es. 19, 24 e in Giov. 1,19—2,12", *Marianum* 33 (1971) 1–39.

Tröger, K.-W., "Ja oder Nein zur Welt: War der Evangelist Johannes Christ oder Gnostiker?", *Theologische Versuche* 7 (Berlin, 1976) 61–77.

Wellhausen, J., *Das Evangelium Johannis* (Berlin, 1908).

4 *A selection of books and articles in English*
Ashton, J., "The Transformation of Wisdom: a Study of the Prologue of John's Gospel", *NTS* 32 (1986) 161–86.

Aune, D. E., *The Cultic Setting of Realized Eschatology in Early Christianity* (Leiden, 1972).

Barrett, C. K. "Unresolved New Testament Problems – the Place of Eschatology in the Fourth Gospel", *ExpTim* 59 (1947/8) 302–5.

— "The Dialectical Theology of St. John", *New Testament Essays* (London, 1972) 49–69.

— *Essays on John* (London, 1982).

Beasley-Murray, G. R., "The Eschatology of the Fourth Gospel", *EvQ* 17 (1946) 97–108.

Borgen, P., *Bread from Heaven* (Leiden, 1965).

— "Some Jewish Exegetical Traditions as Background for Son of Man Sayings in John's Gospel (Jn 3, 13–14 and context)", *L'Évangile de Jean*, ed. M. de Jonge (Leuven, 1977) 243–58 [= Borgen 1983, 133–48].

— "The use of Tradition in John 12, 44–50", *NTS* 26 (1980) 18–35 [= Borgen 1983, 49–66].

— *Logos was the True Light – and other essays on the Gospel of John* (Trondheim, 1983).

Box, G. A., "The Jewish Environment of Early Christianity", *The Expositor* 12 (1916) 1–25.

Brown, R., "The Kerygma of the Gospel according to John", *New Testament Issues* (London, 1970) 210–25.

— "Johannine Ecclesiology – The Community's Origins", *Int* 31 (1977) 379–93.

— "Other Sheep not of This Fold: The Johannine Perspective on Christian Diversity in the Late First Century", *JBL* 97 (1978) 5–22.

— "The Relationship to the Fourth Gospel Shared by the Author of 1 John and by His Opponents", *Studies in the New Testament presented to Matthew Black* (Cambridge, 1979) 57–68.

— *The Community of the Beloved Disciple* (London, 1979).

Bultmann, R., "The Eschatology of the Gospel of John", *Faith and Understanding* (London, 1969) 165–83. German 1928.

— *Theology of the New Testament*, vol. 2 (London and New York, 1955). German 1953.

Culpepper, R. A., *The Johannine School* (Missoula, 1975).

— "The Pivot of John's Prologue", *NTS* 27 (1981) 1–31.

— *The Anatomy of the Fourth Gospel* (Philadelphia, 1983).

de Jonge, M., *Stranger from Heaven and Son of God* (Missoula, 1977).

— ed., *L'Évangile de Jean: Sources, redaction, théologie* (Leuven, 1977). (Fourteen of the essays are in English.)

Dodd, C. H., *The Interpretation of the Fourth Gospel* (Cambridge, 1953).

— *Historical Tradition in the Fourth Gospel* (Cambridge, 1963).

Duke, P. D., *Irony in the Fourth Gospel* (Atlanta, 1985).

Dunn, J. D. G., "Let John be John – A Gospel for its Time", *Das Evangelium und die Evangelien*, ed. P. Stuhlmacher (Tübingen, 1983) 309–40.

Fortna, R. T., *The Gospel of Signs* (Cambridge, 1970).

Harvey, A. E., *Jesus on Trial* (London, 1976).

Horbury, W., "The Benediction of the *Minim* and Early Jewish–Christian Controversy", *JTS* 33 (1982) 19–61.

John and Qumran, ed. J. H. Charlesworth (London, 1972).

Johnston, G., *The Spirit-Paraclete in the Gospel of John* (Cambridge, 1970).

Käsemann, E., "The Structure and Purpose of the Prologue to John's Gospel", *New Testament Questions of Today* (London, 1969) 138–67.

— *The Testament of Jesus* (London, 1968).

Léon-Dufour, X., "Towards a Symbolic Reading of the Fourth Gospel", *NTS* 27 (1981) 439–56.

Lindars, B., *Behind the Fourth Gospel* (London, 1971).

— "Discourse and Tradition: The Use of Sayings of Jesus in the Discourses of the Fourth Gospel", *JSNT* 15 (1981) 83–101.

— "John and the Synoptic Gospel: A Test case", *NTS* 27 (1981) 287–94.

— "The persecution of Christians in John 15:18—16:4a", *Suffering and Martyrdom in the New Testament: Studies presented to G. M. Styler*, ed. W. Horbury and B. McNeil (Cambridge, 1981) 48–69.

— *Jesus Son of Man* (London, 1983).

Loader, W. R. G., "The Central Structure of Johannine Christology", *NTS* 30 (1984) 188–216.

Martyn, J. L., *History and Theology in the Fourth Gospel* [1](New York, 1968) [2](1979).

— *The Gospel of John in Christian History* (New York, 1979).

Meeks, W. A., *The Prophet-King: Moses Traditions and the Johannine Christology* (Leiden, 1967).

— "'Am I a Jew?' Johannine Christianity and Judaism", *Christianity, Judaism and Other Greco-Roman Cults. Studies for Morton Smith*, ed. J. Neusner (Leiden, 1975) 163–86.

— "The Divine Agent and his Counterfeit in Philo and the Fourth Gospel", *Aspects of Religious Propaganda in Judaism and Early Christianity*, ed. E. S. Fiorenza (Notre Dame, 1976) 43–67.

Minear, P. S., "The Original Function of John 21", *JBL* 102 (1983) 85–98.

Moloney, F. J., *The Johannine Son of Man* [2] (Rome, 1978).

Morton, A. Q. and McLenan, I., *The Genesis of John* (Edinburgh, 1980).

Mussner, F., *The Historical Jesus in the Gospel of St John* (London, 1967).

Olsson, B., *Structure and Meaning in the Fourth Gospel* (Lund, 1974).

Painter, J., *John: Witness and Theologian* (London, 1975).

Preiss, T., *Life in Christ* (London, 1954).

Robinson, J. A. T., *Twelve New Testament Studies* (London, 1962).

Robinson, J. M., "The Johannine Trajectory", *Trajectories through Early Christianity*, by J. M. Robinson and H. Koester (Philadelphia, 1971) 232–68.

Rowland, C., "John 1.51, Jewish Apocalyptic and Targumic Tradition", *NTS* 30 (1984) 498–507.

Schnackenburg, R., "On the Origin of the Fourth Gospel", *Jesus and man's hope* I, ed. D. G. Buttrick (Pittsburgh, 1970) 223–46.

Segal, A. F., *Two Powers in Heaven* (Leiden, 1977).

— "Ruler of This World: Attitudes about Mediator Figures and the Importance of Sociology for Self-Definition", *Jewish and Christian Self-Definition* II, ed. E. P. Sanders (London, 1981) 245–68.

Sidebottom, E. M., *The Christ of the Fourth Gospel* (London, 1961).

Smith, D. M., *The Composition and Order of the Fourth Gospel* (New Haven, 1965).

— *Johannine Christianity* (Columbia, 1985).

Talbert, C. H., "The Myth of a Descending–Ascending Redeemer in Mediterranean Antiquity", *NTS* 22 (1976) 418–39.

Wilson, R. McL., "Nag Hammadi and the New Testament", *NTS* 28 (1982) 289–302.

Index of Johannine References